Bible Nurture and Reader Series

From a child thou hast known
the HOLY SCRIPTURES
which are able to make
thee wise unto salvation.

Bible Nurture and Reader Series

Stories About God's People

Reading Teacher's Manual

Grade 2

Rod and Staff Publishers, Inc.
Crockett, Kentucky 41413
Telephone (606) 522-4348

BIBLE NURTURE AND READER SERIES

"If you train your children carefully until they are seven years old, they are already three-quarters educated." This quote recognizes the importance of the critical early years in molding a child's life. The influences of childhood become powerful, lasting impressions.

The type of schoolbooks used certainly affects the developing appetites of our children for reading material. We will not instill in them appreciation for godly values by feeding them frivolous nonsense. We hold the Bible to be the highest guide for life and the best source of training for our children. The Bible reveals God and His will. Proverbs 9:10 says, "The fear of the LORD is the beginning of wisdom: and the knowledge of the holy is understanding." It is important that our children are exposed to truth from the beginning of their learning experience.

For the student to be exposed to the truth of God's Word only in textbooks is not sufficient to give him the very best. It is necessary for the tutor, be he parent or other teacher, to be firmly rooted in the Word of God and have the power of God's presence in his life. The Bible must be treasured as God's message to mankind. On that conviction this series is built, with the Scriptures as its very substance.

This book is designed as part of a series and will be most effective if so used. The grade two material includes the following books.

Pupil's Reader Units 1-3
Pupil's Reader Units 4, 5

Reading Workbook Unit 1
Reading Workbook Unit 2
Reading Workbook Unit 3
Reading Workbook Unit 4
Reading Workbook Unit 5

Phonics Workbook Unit 1
Phonics Workbook Units 2, 3
Phonics Workbook Units 4, 5

Reading Teacher's Manual
Phonics Teacher's Manual

Copyright, 1987
First edition, copyright 1964; revisions 1970, 1986
By
Rod and Staff Publishers, Inc.
Crockett, Kentucky 41413

Printed in U.S.A.

ISBN 978-07399-0382-7
Catalog no. 11291.3

13   14   15   16   17   —   21   20   19   18   17   16   15   14   13   12

Table of Contents

A Word of Appreciation

It is with thanksgiving to God that we present these textbooks to those who are concerned about the spiritual welfare of their children. We believe that children are a heritage of the Lord and a sacred trust and that we dare not fail them in any area of their lives.

The *Bible Nurture and Reader Series* is possible only because of the work and leading of God in the lives of many faithful servants of His. We think first of all of our parents, ministers, and teachers who had a concern for us and faithfully taught and nurtured us in the Word of God. We appreciate those who have had a vision of the need for textbooks based on the Bible and have given their encouragement and help in the writing and publishing of these books.

We appreciate the work of the author, Sister Lela Birky, who has a deep burden for Bible-based school texts to nurture children in the fear of God.

We want to give recognition to the fact that we have used ideas from many textbooks, workbooks, reference books, and other sources. Sister Amy Herr was the writer for the present revision of the workbooks and teacher's manuals. Acknowledgment is also given to Sisters Marla Martin and Pauline Witmer and many other teachers who have developed and shared helps for teaching this series. Much effort was again devoted to artwork for the new books.

The Lord has provided strength in weakness, grace in trials, wisdom because we have none, joy in service, victory in opposition, financial help and faithful laborers in this work. May His Name receive honor and praise, and may we rejoice that we can be laborers together with Him.

Phonetic Symbols

/a/ as in *hat*   /ā/ as in *pay*
/e/ as in *yes*   /ē/ as in *see*
/i/ as in *sit*   /ī/ as in *by*
/o/ as in *top*   /ō/ as in *go*
/u/ as in *bug*   /ū/ as in *cube*
                          /ōō/ as in *food*

/ä/ as in *swap*
     same as /o/   /är/ as in *park*
/ô/ as in *saw*   /ėr/ as in *her, fir, bur,*
/oo/ as in *foot*   *earn,* and *worm*
                          /ôr/ as in *corn*
/ou/ as in *out*   (allowing /ōr/)
/oi/ as in *boy*   /âr/ as in *square* and *chair*
                               (allowing /er/ or /ar/)
                          /ēr/ as in *dear* and *deer*
/sh/ as in *she*   (allowing /ir/)
/ch/ as in *chop*   /ə/ the indefinite vowel sound
/wh/ as in *when*   heard in an unaccented syl-
/th/ as in *thin*   lable, representing any of
/th/ as in *that*   the five vowels as in a*lone,*
/ng/ as in *sing*   *listen, flexible, consider,*
/zh/ as in *measure*   *suppose*

Until the schwa symbol is learned, unaccented syllables are given with short vowel sounds rather than the schwa. The apostrophe is used to represent the indefinite vowel sound in *le* syllables. Example: table (tā•b'l)

Unit 1

UNIT 1
General Plan

Reader

Unit 1 reviews the stories from Genesis covered in grade one, the first lesson being a poem on creation that was used in first grade.

New words are listed at the end of the reader as well as with each workbook lesson.

Workbook

Remove and file the unit test from the back of each workbook before you give them to the children.

The reading workbook lessons are divided into two sections—*Before You Read the Story* and *After You Read the Story*. They are designed to be used just that way, having the children read the lesson in the reader between doing the two workbook sections.

Teacher's Manual

Daily lesson plans are presented in sections titled *Before You Read the Story*, *Reader*, and *After You Read the Story*. Sometimes a fourth section suggesting an extra activity is given. Each of these sections is listed below with a general explanation.

I. Before You Read the Story

A. Vocabulary

The new words for each lesson as well as some review words from grade one are listed in this part of the workbook lesson. The children are to do this part to become acquainted with the words and prepare them for reading the lesson. Directions are given in the manual for introducing this activity to the class, but after they are accustomed to the work, the children should do all of this section on their own without help from the teacher.

B. Oral Vocabulary Drill

Some children will need oral drill and more practice with the words beyond the exercises given in the workbook. You may choose to have a class session to introduce and drill the words as a regular part of the reading lesson. The teacher's manual includes some oral exercises to be used at your discretion. Regularly print the new words on the board. Use that list for oral drill and leave it there for a visual reminder to the children. Printing the words in a different order from the way they appear in the workbook enhances word recognition rather than rote memorization of the list.

C. Reading Incentive

The manual includes some discussion to motivate the children with a purpose for reading the story.

II. Reader

Always have the children read the lesson silently after they have done the first exercises in the workbook. Require a second or third reading to develop better expression and understanding, especially at the beginning of the year.

Oral reading procedures may vary greatly according to the size of your class, but insist that each child pays attention and follows the words as another one reads. The larger the class, the more difficult this will be, but the more necessary, because the less opportunity each child has to read aloud, the more he needs the practice of silent reading as another reads aloud.

Oral Reading Class Pointers

1. A change in position fosters attention and concentration. Have the class file to a set of chairs or stand in a line for oral reading class.
2. Teach a high standard for posture and handling of the book. Have the children use two hands on the book, one under the binding and the other on the pages to hold a marker under the line of print being read or just to hold the book from taking flight.
3. Teach the children to turn pages by laying a finger on the upper corner of a page and pulling it toward themselves.
4. Oral reading class may be held before or after the discussion suggested under the Reader section in the daily lesson plans. You may want to vary the procedure.

III. After You Read the Story

This section of the daily lesson plan includes the answer key. Check the first part of the workbook lesson by going over the questions and letting the children say what they wrote for the answers. Have them correct any wrong answers with colored pencil or pen to distinguish from their original work for your grading evaluation.

Discuss the directions for the rest of the exercises and assign the work. The children may soon be able to proceed with this part and follow the directions without any help from the teacher.

Practice daily recitation of the Bible memory verse. Printing the verse helps secure it in the memory but that should not be the sole means of teaching as the child can too easily turn a few pages to prompt his pencil.

Grading

If your schedule permits, check the lesson with the class, discussing corrections as an aid to growth in comprehension skills. Class discussion and correction can keep you well informed of the children's ability and progress, and may suffice for much of your grading evaluation. Occasional lessons are indicated in the answer key as suitable ones for objective records. They are marked with the word *Gradebook* and the number of points graded.

Reading Lessons   Unit 1

LESSON 1
The First Week

In order to give thorough instruction in all of the new activities of school, it may be advisable to allow two days for the first lesson. Do *Before You Read the Poem* one day and *After You Read the Poem* the next day. It would be well to have the lesson read orally both days.

I. Before You Read the Poem

Let the children browse through the readers and comment on what they find. Direct attention to the table of contents. Point out the unit divisions, lesson numbers, titles, and page numbers. Find the page of Bible verses and Lesson 1. Give each child a marker to place in his book at Lesson 1.

Then have the children open their workbooks to Lesson 1. "Look for the title *Before You Read the Poem.* You may circle that title with your pencil. Now turn the pages until you see the title *After You Read the Poem.* Circle that title with your pencil too. There are two parts to each workbook lesson, one to do before we read the story in the reader and one to do after we have read. Let us see what to do in the first part."

Discuss the directions and give time for the children to silently consider the lists of words, marking any that they do not know. Let the children tell how many they marked with X. "Now look at the next title on the page. We will do these questions and see if they help you to learn the words you did not know." Let someone read number 1. Find the correct word for the answer and tell the children to print a little *1* beside the word *shone* in the list. Tell them to wait until later to print the answer in the blank.

Discuss number 2, and as you find the answers have the children mark the words in the list with *2a*, *2b*, etc.

Continue through the exercise with the children, helping them to unlock any words they did not know in the lists. Printing words on the board with syllable divisions may aid pronunciation. Have the word lists read orally several times until the children can read them well.

Discuss the directions for the phrase practice and let the children read them orally until they can read them well. Then let the children on their own to start at the beginning and redo what you have done in class, printing the words in the blanks, and practicing the words and phrases silently.

Oral Vocabulary Drill

These exercises may be used for additional drill or review if the same lesson is used the second day. Print the words on the board so you can have class attention centered at one point.

1. Which word rhymes with *high*? (fly) *bone*? (shone) *bees*? (trees) *near*? (clear) *leak*? (week)
2. Which word is the opposite of *together*? (apart)

3. Which word means—
   a. made? (formed)
   b. all the things that were made? (creation)
   c. the sky? (heaven)
   d. seven days? (week)
   e. to love and praise God? (worship)
   f. forward? (forth)
4. Which are number words? (one, two, three, four, five, six, seven)
5. Which review word do you see in a learn word? (special)
6. Which word has—
   a. 4 syllables? (especially)
   b. 3 syllables? (creation)
   c. 2 syllables? (apart, heaven, worship, special, seven)

II. Reader

After the workbook exercises are done, tell the children to study the poem silently three times. Then conduct oral reading class. Give explicit directions on how to sit or stand and how to handle the books.

The children may remember the poem from first grade. You may want to let the class read it in unison a few times then see if they can say it without looking. Perhaps they can respond with the second line to each verse after you say the first.

Ask the children how many days the poem tells about. "What do we call seven days? What is the title of the poem? Why do we call it the first week? There were no weeks before that. There were no days before that. There was no earth before that. There were no people, no houses, no trees, no animals, no plants, no sky. There was nothing but God.

"All the things we see are here because God wanted to make them. How long did it take Him to make everything? What did He make the first day? The second day? The third day? The fourth day? The fifth day? How did He make these things? What did He make on the sixth day? What are beasts? Do you know how God made the beasts? Do you know how He made man? *Man* means people. We are all man, whether we are men or women or children.

"What was the seventh day for? Who rested? Who worshiped?"

III. After You Read the Poem

Workbook Exercises

Turn to the workbooks again and discuss the directions for the exercises under *After You Read the Poem*, doing a few examples in each of the sections. Let the children finish on their own.

ANSWER KEY

Before You Read the Poem

1. shone

2. a. week
   b. trees
   c. clear
   d. seas

3. fly

4. apart

5. for, for (circled)
   a. forth
   b. formed

6. plants

7. special (circled)
   especially

8. creation

9. one   two   three
   four   five   six
   seven

10. a. heaven   e. worship
    b. earth   f. light
    c. first   g. special
    d. brought

After You Read the Poem

A. 3 *land*   3 *trees*
   5 *birds*   1 *earth*
   1 *heaven*   2 *sky*
   3 *plants*   3 *grass*

   1 *light*   6 *man*
   4 *stars*   4 *moon*
   3 *seas*   5 *fish*
   6 *beasts*   4 *sun*

B. 1. c   8. k
   2. f   9. l
   3. d   10. i
   4. a   11. j
   5. e   12. h
   6. b
   7. g

C. Praise the LORD, all ye nations: praise him, all ye people. Psalm 117:1

EXTRA ACTIVITY

Have the children list the numbers from one to seven and print beside each number the things God made on that day.

LESSON 2
The Best Part

I. Before You Read the Story

A. Vocabulary

Let the children try reading the word lists and mark an X for each word they cannot say. Then go through the first exercises with the children. Help them to recognize the limit the directions give them by saying whether the answer should be a *Sound, Key, Learn,* or *Review* word. As you discuss each question and the children locate the answers, let them mark the words in the list with the numbers of the questions they answer.

Tell the children to read the phrases silently this time until they think they can read them well as groups of words. Give opportunity for them to read the phrases orally.

Assign the vocabulary exercises as seatwork.

B. Oral Vocabulary Drill

1. Use new or review words in these sentences.
   a. A bone in my side is a ——. (rib)
   b. Water runs in ——. (streams, rivers)
   c. Sometimes the sky is full of ——. (clouds)
   d. Men, women, boys, and girls are ——. (people)
   e. Cows, elephants, and mice are ——. (animals)
   f. Daisies, roses, and tulips are ——. (flowers)
2. Which word(s)—
   a. describe things we like? (lovely, beautiful, wonderful, pretty)
   b. name things people do? (woke, share, breathed, love, decided)
   c. mean more than one? (streams, rivers, clouds, flowers, people, animals)
3. Which word means the opposite of *slept*? (woke) *hate*? (love) *man*? (woman)

C. Reading Incentive

"What do you think is the very best thing that God made?"

II. Reader

Review the points of good posture and handling of the book for oral reading class.

Review the things God created on the first five days. Ask the children again what God made on the first, second, third, fourth, and fifth days. "What did God make on the sixth day? Beasts are animals that are not fish or birds. How many kinds of animals can you name? [You may or may not want to take time to compile a list of some animal names. There are about 6,000 kinds of reptiles, about 3,000 kinds of amphibians, and about 4,000 kinds of mammals.] There are many more kinds of animals than we could name. Who did name them all? He not only said their names, he thought of the names to call them.

"How did God make Adam? How did He make Eve? Why do you think God made Adam and Eve in a different way than He made all the rest of creation? Adam and Eve were special. Why were Adam and Eve the best part of God's creation?"

III. After You Read the Story
Workbook Exercises

Discuss the directions for the remaining workbook exercises. Part C is a review of the order of creation. Suggest that the children refer to the poem in Lesson 1 if they cannot remember the order.

You may prefer to do exercise D in class, drawing from the children's discussion the reason one word does not fit in each row.

ANSWER KEY

Before You Read the Story

1. a. streams
   b. breathed

2. a. woke
   b. share

3. a. shaped
   b. breathed

4. a. rivers
   b. rib

5. six th   cloud s   love ly

6. b
   a

7. a. beautiful
   b. flowers

8. a. pretty
   b. wonderful

9. a. Adam   e. six
   b. woman   f. decided
   c. animals   g. love
   d. people   h. cloud

After You Read the Story

A. 1. sixth
   2. sixth
   3. dust

4. rib
5. name the animals
6. Adam
7. Adam
8. Adam and Eve

B. *Accept interchanged answers unless you have directed the children to take them as found in the first paragraph of the story.*
1. wonderful
2. lovely
3. beautiful
4. pretty

C. 5 *fish and birds*
3 *land with plants*
1 *heaven, earth, light*
6 *beasts and man*
2 *sky*
4 *sun, moon, stars*

D. 1. animal
2. decided

E. Praise the LORD, all ye nations: praise him, all ye people. Psalm 117:1

LESSON 3
The Garden of Eden

I. Before You Read the Story

A. Vocabulary

Do the workbook exercises as a class activity again if you think the children still need the guidance. This time instead of taking an oral answer immediately, pause for each child to find and number his answer. This is a step toward independent work, but close guidance can be given by then discussing the answer chosen and letting the children change any wrong choices.

Encourage silent practice of the phrases and let the children prove their diligence when given a chance to read them aloud.

B. Oral Vocabulary Drill

1. Which word(s)—
   a. have the /o͞o/ sound? (cool, fruit)
   b. have two syllables? (rested, Eden, seventh, except, holy, seven, garden, water, obeyed)
   c. ends with *ed* that sounds /d/? (obeyed)
   d. ends with *ed* that sounds /t/? (blessed)
   e. ends with *ed* that sounds /ed/? (rested)
2. Which word means—
   a. did what one was told to do? (obeyed)
   b. something to eat that grows on a tree? (fruit)
   c. a place where plants grow? (garden)
   d. a place to live? (house)
   e. without any sin? (holy)
   f. a time when the weather gets rough? (storm)
   g. yet or but? (except)
3. a. How do the words *one* and *first* fit together? Find two words in the list that go together in the same way. We can say, "*One* is to *first* as *seven* is to *seventh*."
   b. How do the words *eat* and *food* go together? What goes with *drink* in the same way? We can say, "*Eat* is to *food* as *drink* is to *water*."

C. Reading Incentive

"Do you know what was used to build your house? Do you know what was used to build our school? What are some other kinds of houses? [stone, brick, log, block, adobe, tent, igloo, thatch] What kind of home do you think Adam and Eve had? Would you like to live in a home like theirs?"

II. Reader

Ask the children to demonstrate the proper way to sit or stand and hold the book and turn pages.

"What did God do on the seventh day? Was it the seventh day for Adam and Eve? Why not?

"What kind of home did Adam and Eve have? Do you have a garden at home? What is your garden like? Do you have trees in your garden? Do you think the Garden of Eden was like the gardens we make? Do you think the Garden of Eden had weeds in it?

"Did it rain on the Garden of Eden? How did the plants get water? Why did Adam and Eve not need a house?

"What did Adam and Eve eat? What were they not supposed to eat? What would happen if they did?

"What did Adam and Eve do in the Garden of Eden? What did they do in the cool of the day? When do you think that was? What is the cool part of the day? Do you like to go outside early in the morning when there is still dew on the grass and flowers? Do you like to sit outside with your family in the evening of a summer day after the work is done and the day is getting cool and dark? The times when God came and talked with Adam and Eve must have been special times for them."

III. After You Read the Story

Workbook Exercises

See if the children can follow the directions themselves and do the questions without using the reader.

ANSWER KEY

Before You Read the Story

1. Eden

2. a. cool
   b. Eden
   c. rested

3. seven th

4. b
   c
   a

5. a. holy   e. cool
   b. seventh   f. rested
   c. except   g. Eden
   d. fruit

6. a. house   e. garden
   b. seven   f. water
   c. blessed   g. obeyed
   d. storm   h. lives

After You Read the Story

A. 1. all things
   2. seventh
   3. a home
   4. from a river

5. fruit
6. a tree
7. one
8. they would die
9. the plants and trees
10. in the cool of the day

B. 1. Eden   6. river
   2. God   7. garden
   3. Adam   8. house
   4. Eve   9. plants
   5. fruit   10. tree

C. Praise the LORD, all ye nations: praise him, all ye people. Psalm 117:1

Gradebook: 45 points for all written work including two points for perfect printing of the memory verse.

EXTRA ACTIVITY

Give the children paper on which to draw a picture of Adam and Eve's home.

LESSON 4
The First Sin

I. Before You Read the Story

A. Vocabulary

Let the children handle the workbook exercises on their own if they are able.

B. Oral Vocabulary Drill

1. Print the words on the board and go around the class having each child in turn say the next word in the list.
2. Which word means—
   a. great sadness? (sorrow)
   b. to put something out of sight? (hide)
   c. a part of the body? (belly)
3. Which two words name the same kind of animal? (snake, serpent)
4. Which two words name the same kind of plant? (thistles, thorns)
5. Which words make you think of using your mouth? (answered, talked, promised, says)
6. a. How do the words *goes* and *toes* fit together? What word fits with *let* in the same way? *Goes* is to *toes* as *let* is to *sweat*.
   b. *Goes* is to *toes* as *song* is to ——. (long)
   c. How do the words *eyes* and *look* fit together? Which word fits with *ears* in the same way? *Eyes* is to *look* as *ears* is to ——. (listen)
   d. How do the words *alive* and *dead* fit together? *Alive* is to *dead* as *joy* is to ——. (sorrow)

C. Reading Incentive

"What is sin? Sin is disobedience and wickedness. Sin is what makes all the troubles and unhappiness in the world. There was no sin in the Garden of Eden where Adam and Eve lived. But something happened that spoiled their sinless lives. What was it?"

II. Reader

Ask for a demonstration of proper posture and handling of the book in oral reading class.

"What is the title of your story? Who sinned? What was their sin? Why did they do it? Who was the snake? It was Satan that wanted Adam and Eve to disobey God. Satan made the snake say those things. Satan hates God and he wants people to be wicked so they will not love God. Satan tells lies. What was the lie he told Eve?

"When Satan said Adam and Eve would be like gods, he meant they would be greater than ordinary people. He did not mean they could be like the God who created them. They would be able to understand about right and wrong things. God knew it was best for them to be as He made them. He did not want them to have anything to do with wrong.

"How did Adam and Eve feel after they had eaten some of the fruit? Why? Do you think the fruit made them sick? Why did they want to hide from God? Isn't that what you feel like if you have done something you were told not to do? If you take something to eat that you were not supposed to have, it does not taste very good, and you want to hide from the person that told you not to do it.

"What did God have to do about the sin?

"What was the punishment for the serpent?

"What was the punishment for Eve?

"What was the punishment for Adam?

"What punishment was for both Adam and Eve?

"Did God hate Adam and Eve now? When we do wrong things, we need to be punished too. But that does not mean that our parents or teachers or whoever punishes us hates us. They love us. They punish us because they love us and want us to learn to do good things."

III. After You Read the Story

Workbook Exercises

Go over the exercises the children have done before reading, letting them say the answers they have written and correct any wrong ones. Discuss the directions for the second part of the lesson and assign the exercises.

ANSWER KEY

Before You Read the Story

1. coats, long

2. hide, snake, long

3. snake, serpent

4. gods

5. coats, gods, thorns

6. belly

7. a. long
   b. listen

8. b
   c
   a

9. a. sweat
   b. Thistles
   c. says

10. a. Jesus   e. listen
    b. answered   f. long
    c. punished   g. promised
    d. sorrow   h. talked

After You Read the Story

A. 1. snake
   2. disobey God
   3. good
   4. yes
   5. the snake
   6. Adam
   7. Eve
   8. thistles
   9. no
   10. Jesus

B. 1   4   6   7
   2   3   5   8

C. 1. b
   2. d
   3. c
   4. a
   5. e

D. Praise the LORD, all ye nations: praise him, all ye people. Psalm 117:1

LESSON 5
Cain and Abel

I. Before You Read the Story

A. Vocabulary

Encourage independence as the children do the first part of the workbook lesson.

B. Oral Vocabulary Drill

1. Print the words on the board and have the children say them in unison as you point to the words, going down the list, up the list, and choosing words at random.

2. Use new and review words in these sentences.

    a. In our family we have sisters and ——. (brothers)

    b. A word that rhymes with *ought* is ——. (brought)

    c. When we give God something, we bring an ——. (offering)

    d. We do not want to feel ——. (angry)

    e. A baby ——. (cries)

    f. Very young children are ——. (babies)

    g. A name of a man is ——. (Abel)

    h. You need your feet to ——. (stand)

    i. If we sin, we need ——. (punishment)

    j. Ray put a black spot on his shirt. He put a —— on it. (mark)

    k. A child that is lost in the woods will —— about. (wander)

    l. I —— my hand to ask the teacher a question. (raised)

    m. Our neighbor —— a large crop of pumpkins. (raised)

    n. We tried not to —— on the flowers. (tramp)

    o. A —— just tramps around on the road. (tramp)

3. a. How do the words *said* and *bed* fit together? Which word fits with *closed* in the same way? We can say *said* is to *bed* as *closed* is to *supposed*.

    b. How do the words *green* and *grass* fit together? What word fits with *red* in the same way? We can say *green* is to *grass* as *red* is to *blood*.

    c. *Write* is to *wrote* as *bring* is to ——. (brought)

    d. *Hungry* is to *full* as *happy* is to ——. (angry)

C. Reading Incentive

"Do disagreements arise in your family sometimes? In this lesson you will read about the first family there ever was. How do you suppose things went in that family?"

II. Reader

As the children read silently, observe their habits. Do they mouth the words as they read? Do they point to each word? These habits hinder progress in reading with speed and smoothness.

Call the children to oral reading class. Instead of reminding them of posture and book handling, pause a moment as though waiting for something. Do they think of the request before you say it? Give the reminder if you need to.

Ask the children to point to the title of their story. Ask them to point to a margin. Ask them to point to an indented line. "Each indented line marks a new section of your story. What do we call those sections? [paragraphs]" Let the children read by paragraphs.

"Who was in the first family? Who were the parents? The children? Do you know if there were any other children? [There were other children later.]

"Cain and Abel grew up. What work did they do when they were men?

"How did things go in this family? What started the trouble? Did it get better or worse when God talked to Cain? Where were Cain and Abel one day? What terrible thing did Cain do? What did God ask Cain? What was Cain's answer? Was that true?

"Did God know where Abel was? What did He tell Cain? Was Abel dead? Could Abel cry? What did God mean? Abel wasn't crying with his voice, but God knew anyway what had happened to him, and it bothered Him as much as it would if someone was in trouble and was crying out loud.

"God had to punish Cain for what he had done. What was the punishment?"

III. After You Read the Story
Workbook Exercises

Go over the first part of the workbook lesson, having the children say the answers they chose and correct any mistakes using pen or colored pencil.

Let the children silently read the directions for the rest of the lesson and tell you what they understand them to mean. Make sure they realize that more than one answer is to be underlined in Part C.

The directions to Part D should be a reminder to the children to study the verse until they can say it well. Arrange a time to hear the recitations and tell the children when that will be.

ANSWER KEY

Before You Read the Story

1. a. raised
   b. cries

2. Abel, punish

3. Abel's

4. punishment

5. d, b, a, c

6. a. wander
   b. terrible
   c. supposed
   d. driven

7. a. driven
   b. terrible
   c. wander
   d. supposed

8. a. offering
   b. babies
   c. angry
   d. instead
   e. brothers
   f. punish
   g. Abel
   h. blood
   i. brought

After You Read the Story

A. 1. Cain   7. Cain
2. Cain   8. Cain
3. Abel   9. Cain
4. Cain   10. Abel
5. Abel   11. Cain
6. Abel   12. Cain

B. 2   4   6   7   10
1   3   5   8   9

C. *Answers to be underlined:*
a, c, d, e

EXTRA ACTIVITY

Designate certain phrases from the phrase practice section in the workbook. Have the children find them in the reader and print on paper the sentences containing those phrases.

LESSON 6
The Big Flood

Be Prepared

The ark measured about 450 feet long by 75 feet wide and 45 feet high. Do some calculating and estimate how many buildings the size of your school or lengths of your playground would equal ark dimensions.

I. Before You Read the Story

A. Vocabulary

Let the children work independently on the first part of the workbook lesson.

B. Oral Vocabulary Drill

1. Which word rhymes with—
   a. cry? (high)
   b. best? (rest)
   c. feast? (beast)
   d. bowl? (whole)
   e. could? (wood)
   f. woke? (broke)
   g. cried? (side)
   h. which? (pitch)
2. Find two words in the list that rhyme. (fountains—mountains)
3. Which words have suffixes? (creep*ing*, rest*ing*, brok*en*, high*er*, fountain*s*, mountain*s*, cover*ed*)
4. Which word means the opposite of *make*? (destroy) *working*? (resting) *valleys*? (mountains)
5. Find new or review words to fit in these sentences.
   a. We drink at drinking ——. (fountains)
   b. We can see through a ——. (window)
   c. A name of a man is ——. (Noah)
   d. In the fireplace we burn——. (wood)
   e. Two halves make a ——. (whole)
   f. John is lying on the sofa. He is ——. (resting)
   g. A horse is a ——. (beast)

h. There is a cabin in the ——. (mountains)
6. a. *Fast* is to *running* as *slow* is to ——. (creeping)
   b. *Snow* is to *storm* as *water* is to ——. (flood)
   c. *Beautiful* is to *lovely* as *animal* is to ——. (beast)

C. Reading Incentive

"We want to learn to read well. It will help you to read well if you learn to read without moving your lips for every word that you see when you read silently. Keep your lips closed and read the first sentence in your story. What did the sentence say? Read the first sentence in the second paragraph without moving your mouth. What does that sentence say?

"Keep your lips closed as you read the whole story through silently.

"I wonder if you can find a zoo in the story as you read."

II. Reader

"How many paragraphs are in your story? [7] Which paragraph tells about something we might call a zoo? [4 or 5] In which paragraph can you find words that someone said? They are marked with quotation marks. [2 or 3] What made God sad? What did God decide to do? Was He going to destroy everybody? Why not? Who was the man who was godly? What did God tell him to do? And what else? [Build the ark. Take the animals into the ark. Gather all kinds of food.]"

Impress upon the children what an awesome task Noah had. "How many kinds of animals would he have to take into the ark? How big would he have to make the ark to hold them all? How many kinds of food would he have to gather? The Bible says how big Noah made the ark. [Give a comparison of the ark size with the size of your school or playground.] We do not know how many kinds of animals were in the ark or what all the kinds of food were that Noah gathered, but it was surely a great big job.

"How long did it rain? How high did the water go? What happened to the animals and people and things that were not in the ark?"

III. After You Read the Story

Workbook Exercises

Review and correct the first part of the workbook lesson. Let the children tell you what they understand from the directions for the rest of the lesson.

ANSWER KEY

Before You Read the Story

1. rest, resting
2. creeping
3. beast
4. wood

5. Pitch
6. side
7. broke, broken
   a. broken
   b. broke

8. high, higher
   a. high
   b. higher

9. mountains

10. fountains

11. whole

12. a. Noah
    b. flood
    c. covered
    d. destroy
    e. sorry
    f. window
    g. along

After You Read the Story

A. 1. bad
   2. sorry
   3. flood
   4. Noah
   5. did
   6. Seven

7. Two
8. God
9. forty
10. covered
11. safe
12. of a mountain

B. 1. Many
   2. Most
   3. One
   4. a, three
   5. a, a
   6. some, seven
   7. two
   8. seven
   9. All
   10. Every
   11. forty, forty

C. For his merciful kindness is great toward us. Psalm 117:2

LESSON 7
After the Flood

I. Before You Read the Story

A. Vocabulary

Have the children do the first part of the reading workbook lesson. This routine exercise will not be repeated in the daily lesson plans.

B. Oral Vocabulary Drill

1. Say the words to the children and have them locate them in the list printed on the board.
2. Which word rhymes with—
   a. glove? (dove) d. haven? (raven)
   b. season? (reason) e. true? (flew)
   c. killed? (build) f. chief? (leaf)
3. Which words have suffixes? (decid*ed*, wait*ed*, par*ts*, thank*ful*, build*ing*, chang*ed*)
4. Which words have prefixes? (*a*round, *be*cause)
5. Which is a compound word? (understand)

6. Find the right words for these sentences.
   a. The bird —— away. (flew)
   b. We speak the English ——. (language)
   c. We should remember to be ——. (thankful)
   d. Do you have a good —— for what you did? (reason)
   e. Did you help —— the new barn? (build)
   f. A —— is part of a tree. (leaf)
   g. A word that means "to complete" is ——. (finish)
   h. A word that means "not the same" is ——. (different)

C. Reading Incentive

"Do you remember how long Noah and his family were in the ark before the rain began? Do you remember how long it rained? How long do you think Noah and his family stayed in the ark? You can find out when you read this story. Remember to keep your mouth still and read with just your eyes and mind."

II. Reader

"How many paragraphs are in your story? [5] How many sentences are in the first paragraph? [11]

"Can you tell me how long Noah and his family were in the ark?"

Call the children to oral reading class and wait for them to respond to the unspoken reminder of posture and proper book handling. Let them read by sentences.

"It rained forty days, but Noah and his family were in the ark over a year. A year is more than nine times as long as forty days. What was happening some of the rest of the time? They waited in the ark seven days before it started to rain. Then after the rain stopped the ark floated around a long time while the water was going down. Finally the water was down far enough that the ark stopped on the top of a mountain. Still they waited in the ark. What did Noah do one day? What did he let go out of the window? Where did the raven go? What else did Noah let go out of the window? What did the dove do? Why? How long did they wait in the ark until the next time Noah sent the dove out? What happened that time? How long did they wait again? By that time a whole year had passed since they had gone into the ark and God shut the door. Now it was time for them to come out and begin life on the land once again. There was nobody in the world besides Noah and his family.

"What did Noah do when they went out of the ark?

"What did God do?

"After a time there were many people on the earth again. Where did the people come from? [Noah's family grew. His sons and their wives had children. They grew up and had families until there were many people.] Did all those people love God?

"What did some of these people get together to do? What did God think about what they were doing? What did God do to the people? Can you imagine trying to work together with someone when you cannot understand a thing that the others are saying? What did the people do?"

III. After You Read the Story

Workbook Exercises

Correct the first part of the workbook lesson and go over the directions for the second part. You may want to do some oral samples of exercise B in class.

ANSWER KEY

Before You Read the Story

1. a. parts
   b. flew
   c. leaf

2. a. flew
   b. leaf
   c. parts

3. a. wait
   b. waited

4. a. thank
   b. thankful

5. d
   c
   a
   b

6. a. changed
   b. build
   c. building
   d. language

7. a. dove
   b. gone

8. a. around
   b. understand
   c. raven
   d. because
   e. reason
   f. decided
   g. finish
   h. different

After You Read the Story

A. 1. raven
    2. no
    3. dove
    4. yes
    5. seven
    6. one year
    7. made an offering to God
    8. no
    9. rainbow
    10. no

B. 1. g
    2. f
    3. e
    4. a
    5. c
    6. b

C. For his merciful kindness is great toward us. Psalm 117:2

Gradebook: 46 points for all written work including two points for perfect printing of the memory verse

EXTRA ACTIVITY

Give the children paper on which to draw a picture for paragraph 1 of the lesson.

LESSON 8
Abram and Lot

I. Before You Read the Story

A. Oral Vocabulary Drill

1. Go around the class having the children say in turn the words as you point to them, down the list, up the list, and in random order.
2. Which word(s)—
   a. tells how we should not be? (selfish)
   b. means the opposite of *country*? (city)
   c. means the same as *fight*? (quarrel)
   d. name cities? (Ur, Sodom)
   e. names a country? (Canaan)
   f. have suffixes? (cit*ies*, mov*ed*, worship*ed*, self*ish*)
   g. names a woman? (Sarah)
   h. tells what you did if you changed from one place to live in another place? (moved)
   i. names a place where burnt offerings were offered? (altar)
3. a. *Study* is to *studied* as *choose* is to ——. (chose)
   b. *Ur* is to *city* as *Canaan* is to ——. (country)
   c. *Wife* is to *Sarah* as *husband* is to ——. (Abram)
4. Discuss the various meanings of *country* such as "rural areas," or "a nation."

B. Reading Incentive

"I wonder how many reasons you can find in the story for Abram to be moving from one place to another.

"Remember to read with your eyes and mind only. Do you need your hands to read? Can you read a paragraph without using your finger or a marker to show your eyes where to go? Try it."

II. Reader

Conduct oral reading class.

"Where did Abram live at first? Who else moved when he moved away from there?

"Who told Abram to move the next time? Who would show him where to go? Who went with him that time? Where did they go?

"Why was it easy for Abram to move around from place to place in the land of Canaan? Why would he want to move? [Abram had many animals and he probably moved around to new places to find grass to feed his animals.] What did he do every time he moved?

"Why did Abraham move to a strange land?

"Why did he move back to Canaan?

"What was the reason for the next move? There was trouble between Lot's servants and Abram's servants. What was the problem? Who suggested that they move apart? Who decided which way they would go? Why did Lot choose the part he did? What was in the land that Lot chose? Was that good for him and his family?

"What did God promise to Abram after Lot made his choice and left? Would Abram get the land that Lot had chosen too? There is a lesson for us in that. We will usually find that if we are selfish and choose what we think is best, it does not bring happiness. We often find that if we are unselfish and let others have the best, we will feel happier than we thought we would.

"We will find out in the next lesson how it went with Lot."

III. After You Read the Story
Workbook Exercises

Check the first part of the workbook lesson and make sure the children understand the directions for the second part.

ANSWER KEY

Before You Read the Story

1. Ur
2. chose
3. city, build
4. a. cities
   b. built
5. selfish
6. Sodom
7. country
8. a. Abram
   b. Sarah
   c. Canaan
9. a. altar, worshiped
   b. quarrel
   c. moved

After You Read the Story

A. 1. Sarah
   2. Lot
   3. rich
   4. worshiped God
   5. crops
   6. tent
   7. quarrel
   8. did not
   9. Lot
   10. wicked cities
   11. family
   12. Abram

B. 3, 5
   7 paragraphs

C. For his merciful kindness is great toward us. Psalm 117:2

LESSON 9
Abraham Prays

I. Before You Read the Story
A. Oral Vocabulary Drill

1. Let the children say the words in unison as you point to them on the board.

2. Which word(s)—
   a. have the /ô/ sound? (salt, thought, warn)
   b. have suffixes? (hard*ly*, marri*ed*, final*ly*, angel*s*)
   c. makes you think of heaven? (angels)
   d. means "at last"? (finally)
   e. means the opposite of *easily*? (hardly) *ahead*? (behind)
   f. tells what you did with your mind? (thought)
3. Find the correct words for these sentences.
   a. A —— is a person you like to be with. (friend)
   b. We put —— on our food. (salt)
   c. Your mother is —— to your father. (married)
   d. Ten tens is one ——. (hundred)
   e. A man's name is ——. (Isaac)
   f. Mother will —— you to stay away from danger. (warn)
   g. *Above* is to *below* as *doubt* is to ——. (believe)
   h. *Still* is to *storm* as *before* is to ——. (behind)
   i. *Few* is to *four* as *many* is to ——. (hundred)

B. Reading Incentive

"See if you can find out something about Abraham's wife and something about Lot's wife when you read the story.

"Read without pointing to the words or moving your mouth."

II. Reader

"What did you learn about Abraham's wife? What did you learn about Lot's wife?

"Find a question mark in your story. How should a sentence sound when there is a question mark at the end of it? Read the sentence so that it sounds like someone asking a question. [Demonstrate if you need to.]

"Find an exclamation mark. [Help them locate the one in the second paragraph.] How should a sentence sound with an exclamation mark at the end? Read that sentence. Try to make it sound the way you think Abraham felt when he thought about Lot in the city that God was going to destroy."

Conduct oral reading class. Is the proper posture and book handling becoming automatic?

"How old was Abram when God changed his name? What was his new name? *Abraham* means 'the father of many nations.' Was Abraham a father yet? What did God promise Abraham and Sarah? What was surprising about that? [They were so old.]

"What was the name of the wicked city that God wanted to destroy? Do you know why Lot was living there? [He chose to move that way because he selfishly wanted the best land.]

"What did Abraham ask God? What was God's answer? What did Abraham say next? What did God say? Abraham kept changing his mind until

God finally promised to save the city for how many godly people?

"Were there ten godly people in the big city of Sodom? Did that mean Lot would be destroyed? What did God do about Lot? Lot was not very quick to obey. What did God have to do to save him? Who went out of the city with Lot? What happened to Lot's wife? Why? What happened to the city?

"What is the title of our story? Did Abraham pray in this story? Can you find a sentence in which Abraham prayed? Abraham talked to God. That is what praying is."

III. After You Read the Story

Workbook Exercises

Correct the first part of the workbook lesson and discuss the directions for the second part.

ANSWER KEY

Before You Read the Story

1. hardly, hard
   hard, hardly

2. c
   b
   a

3. a. Finally
   b. warn
   c. married

4. behind, believe

5. angels

6. hundred

7. thought

8. friend

9. Isaac

10. Salt

11. a. Angels
    b. married
    c. behind
    d. hardly
    e. Finally
    f. believe
    g. warn
    h. Salt
    i. friend
    j. hundred
    k. Isaac
    l. thought

After You Read the Story

A.
1. no
2. yes
3. no
4. yes
5. no
6. yes
7. no
8. no
9. no
10. yes

B.
1. God
2. God
3. God's friend
4. Lot was there
5. she did not obey (or) she looked back

C. For his merciful kindness is great toward us. Psalm 117:2

EXTRA ACTIVITY

Find in the reader the phrases listed in the workbook and mark each one with the paragraph number.

LESSON 10
A Test for Abraham

I. Before You Read the Story

A. Oral Vocabulary Drill

1. Call on several individuals to say the whole list of words, some forward and some backward.
2. Which word(s)—
   a. begin with consonant blends? (*br*ush, *pr*omises, *pr*ove, *pr*omise)
   b. begins with a silent consonant? (*k*nife)
   c. tells how many? (most)
   d. tells when? (early)
   e. have suffixes? (Sarah's, promise*s*, will*ing*, call*ing*, fear*ed*)
   f. names something sharp? (knife)
   g. means "tied up"? (bound)
3. Find the correct words for these sentences.
   a. We —— the mouse in a trap. (caught)
   b. Did you —— your hair? (brush)
   c. Little trees, bushes, and weeds are called ——. (brush)
   d. You can —— to me that you know your reading lesson. (prove)
   e. Something positive is ——. (sure)
   f. *Happy* is to *enjoyed* as *afraid* is to ——. (feared)
   g. *Run* is to *ran* as *mean* is to ——. (meant)
   h. *Now* is to *later* as *few* is to ——. (most)
   i. *Sew* is to *needle* as *cut* is to ——. (knife)

B. Reading Incentive

"How do we worship God? Do you know how people worshiped God in Abraham's time? One thing they often did was to pile stones up for an altar, then kill an animal and burn it on the altar. God wanted them to worship Him that way. We will read about a very special offering in this story. Do you know what was offered?"

II. Reader

"Find the exclamation marks in the lesson. An exclamation mark marks the end of a sentence just as a period or question mark. How do you think these sentences should sound when we read them?

"Find the quotation marks on the same page. Quotation marks show that somebody said the words that we are reading. Think about what the person said and think how they would say it. Try to read it the way you think the person would say the words.

"How old was Abraham when his little boy was born? Do you know how old your parents are? Do you know how old your grandparents are? Do you know anybody that is 100 years old? It was a very special thing for some-one so old to have a baby. But God had promised that they would have a son, and God always keeps His promises.

"Did Abraham and Sarah love Isaac? What did God ask Abraham to do to Isaac? Would he want to do that if he loved Isaac? Why would he do it? [God told him to, and if Abraham loved God best, he would do what God told him to do.]

"Where was Abraham supposed to go to offer Isaac to the Lord? How far away was that? Who went along with Abraham and Isaac? Did they go the whole way?

"What stopped Abraham from killing Isaac? Didn't Abraham offer an offering after all? What did he offer?

"Do you love your parents? What is a test that proves whether you love them? [obedience to what they say]"

III. After You Read the Story

Workbook Exercises

Note the sets of three sentences in Part B and consider with the children the order of the first three sentences.

Make sure the children understand what a column is and work Part C in columns.

Plan for a time to hear the memory verses.

ANSWER KEY

Before You Read the Story

1. a. brush
   b. calling
   c. bound

2. feared, calling, willing

3. a. promise
   b. Sarah
   c. move

4. Sarah's

5. promises

6. prove

7. a. meant, ready
   b. sure
   c. caught
   d. most

8. a. Sarah's
   b. Sarah
   c. sure
   d. feared

e. ready / willing / sure
f. most
g. early
h. meant
i. knife
j. caught
k. calling
l. bound
m. brush

After You Read the Story

A. 1. 100
   2. yes
   3. to prove Abraham's love for God
   4. kill him
   5. God
   6. no
   7. an angel
   8. yes
   9. an animal caught in a bush

B. 2 4 8 11
  1 6 9 10
  3 5 7 12

C. *Words to be crossed out are—*
 1. animal (The others name people.)

2. mountain (The others are verbs.)
3. heard (The others pertain to speaking.)

Gradebook: 54 points for all written work

LESSON 11
A Wife for Isaac

I. Before You Read the Story

A. Oral Vocabulary Drill

1. Call the children's names at random to have them say the next word in the list as it appears on the board. Do not point to the words so each child will need to pay attention to the list to be able to say the correct word when you call on him.

2. Which word(s)—
 a. begins with a silent consonant? (*w*hole)
 b. have three syllables? (invited, grandfather, Rebekah)
 c. have suffixes? (woman*'s*, invit*ed*, camel*s*, follow*ed*)
 d. means the opposite of *master*? (servant) *man*? (woman)
 e. names animals? (camels)
 f. names a way we can feel? (afraid)
 g. is a compound word? (grandfather)
 h. name a sister and brother? (Rebekah, Laban)

3. Find the correct words for these sentences.
 a. Two halves make a ——. (whole)
 b. Mother —— company for dinner. (invited)
 c. *Daughter* is to *mother* as *grandchild* is to ——. (grandfather)
 d. *Talk* is to *listen* as *lead* is to ——. (follow)
 e. *Boy* is to *lad* as *worker* is to ——. (servant)
 f. *Sad* is to *unhappy* as *all* is to ——. (whole)
 g. *Created* is to *made* as *asked* is to ——. (invited)

B. Reading Incentive

"Now Isaac, the baby who was born to the old people and the child who was almost killed, is grown up already! In this lesson we will read about the time when Isaac was married. Do you know how they decided who should be his wife?"

II. Reader

Have the children skim the lesson to find quotation marks and discuss the expression of the quotations in reading.

"How old was Isaac when his mother died? What was Abraham concerned about? What did Abraham plan to do about the problem?

"How did the man travel? What did he do when he got to the land from which Abraham had come? What did the servant ask God? How long did he have to wait until God answered his prayer?

"Who was the woman? What was her brother's name?

"What did the servant have to do before he ate? What did Rebekah's family say?

"Where did Rebekah live when she was Isaac's wife?"

III. After You Read the Story

Workbook Exercises

Explain the meaning of the Bible verse in a literal sense. The things we reap are exactly what we have planted.

ANSWER KEY

Before You Read the Story

1. woman, followed

2. woman's (any noun)

3. follow

4. invited

5. a. afraid, Laban
   b. whole, followed
   c. Rebekah
   d. grandfather, servant

6. a. grandfather
   b. Afraid
   c. Camels
   d. woman
   e. servant
   f. whole

7. l *afraid*   c *grandfather*
   h *camels*   k *invited*
   i *follow*   b *Laban*

      a *Rebekah*   d *woman*
      g *servant*   f *woman's*
      j *whole*   e *women*

After You Read the Story

A. 1. thirty-seven
2. a servant
3. to his country
4. ten
5. by a well
6. the camels
7. Rebekah
8. Laban
9. to his mother's tent

B. 1. Abraham
2. Rebekah
3. Laban
4. Isaac
5. Sarah
6. Rebekah / Laban
7. Isaac
8. Rebekah
9. Laban
10. Abraham
11. Rebekah

C. Whatsoever a man soweth, that shall he also reap. Galatians 6:7

EXTRA ACTIVITY

"List all the words you can find in the story that name people." The list should include names with capital letters and other words such as *servant*, *woman*, *wife*, etc.

The children may also pick up pronouns such as *they*, *he*, *I*, etc.

Isaac	man
mother	women
Sarah	brother
Abraham	grandfather
wife	family
people	Rebekah
servant	Laban
woman	

LESSON 12
The Twins

I. Before You Read the Story

If you have not been practicing the analogies in the oral vocabulary drill, discuss the last few sentences in number 7 with the class. Get the children to state the relationship between the pairs of words instead of saying *is to*. (*Big* is the opposite of *little*. *Wrong* is the opposite of ——.)

A. Oral Vocabulary Drill

1. Go around the class having the children say the words as you point to them on the board.
2. Which word means the same as—
   a. plenty? (enough)   d. seek? (hunt)
   b. stew? (soup)   e. envious? (jealous)
   c. argument? (quarrel)   f. correct? (right)
3. Which word means the opposite of *wrong*? (right) *same*? (different) *wondered*? (knew) *agree*? (quarrel)
4. Which words are compound words? (birthright, birthday, because)
5. Find correct words for these sentences.
   a. We do not like —— in our food. (dirt)
   b. Two babies born the same day are ——. (twins)
   c. When something is lost we —— it. (hunt)
   d. —— and —— were twins. (Jacob, Esau)
   e. If I give you something for which you give me something in return, we ——. (trade)
   f. We shivered —— the sun was shining. (although)

B. Reading Incentive

"Did you ever say, 'I have a right to do something?' To have a right to something means it is fair and just for you to have something or do something. Because you belong to your parents, you have a right to eat at their table.

"Esau could say, 'I have a right to have most of my father's things when he dies.' In those days when a father died, his things were divided among his sons. The son who was born first always got more of the things than the others did. That was his right. It was called his birthright.

"See what happens to Esau's birthright as you read this story."

II. Reader

"Find the exclamation mark. How should that sentence sound? Find a period. What does a period mean? Find a comma. A comma does not mark the end of a sentence, but it tells you to stop for a short time. Sometimes sentences make better sense if you stop between some of the phrases.

"For what did Isaac ask the Lord? What did the Lord give them?

"What were these twins like? What did they do when they grew up?

"What kind of soup did Jacob make one day? What was Esau doing that day? Why did Esau ask Jacob to give him some soup? What did Jacob say Esau had to give him first? What was the birthright? Do you think it was a fair trade? Why did Esau say Jacob could have the birthright?

"What happened in the land where Isaac's family lived? How did Isaac become rich? What did some other people act like when Isaac became rich? Why did they do those things? How should we feel when we see that someone else has a lot of things? We should be glad for them and be content with the good things that we have. We only make ourselves unhappy if we feel jealous of someone else.

"How did Isaac act toward the men who were mean to him? How many times did he dig another well? [3] How should we act if other people are mean to us?"

III. After You Read the Story
Workbook Exercises

Follow the directions.

ANSWER KEY

Before You Read the Story

1. birthday, right, birthright

2. a. though
   b. enough
   c. soup

3. although

4. jealous

5. Esau, Jacob

6. knew

7. a. birthday
   b. twins
   c. dirt
   d. enough
   e. trade
   f. hunt
   g. though
   h. Soup
   i. different
   j. right
   k. trade
   l. quarrel

After You Read the Story

A. 1. d   5. f
     2. e   6. g
     3. a   7. c
     4. b   8. h

B. 2	4	9	10	15
3	6	8	11	13
1	5	7	12	14

C. a. good   c. good
     b. red   d. rich

D. Whatsoever a man soweth, that shall he also reap. Galatians 6:7

LESSON 13
How Jacob Got the Blessing

I. Before You Read the Story

The workbook exercises again include some analogies at the end of number 5. Help the children to identify the relationships between the words if you have not been using oral activities of this type.

A. Oral Vocabulary Drill

1. Let the children respond in unison as you point to the words in any order.
2. Which word(s)—
   a. ends with *ed* that sounds /d/? (puzzled)
   b. ends with *ed* that sounds /t/? (fixed)
   c. ends with *ed* that sounds /ed/? (sounded)
   d. means "if"? (whether)
   e. begin with consonant blends? (*br*inging, *bl*ind, *cl*othes)
   f. means the opposite of *taking*? (giving)
   g. rhymes with *mix*? (fix)   *would*? (could)   *find*? (blind)
      word? (heard)
3. Find the correct words for these sentences.
   a. Mother sewed some new —— for us. (clothes)
   b. If someone wants to know how old you are, they ask, "What is your ——?" (age)
   c. Isaac could not see because he was ——. (blind)
   d. Crops are planted in a ——. (field)
   e. *Seeing* is to *blind* as *sure* is to ——. (puzzled)
   f. *Eat* is to *food* as *wear* is to ——. (clothes)
   g. *Grain* is to *stalk* as *meat* is to ——. (deer)

B. Reading Incentive

"Close your eyes. If you were blind, and someone came into our room, how could you tell who it was? There is a blind man in our lesson who wanted to know who somebody was. Read the story to see what happened."

II. Reader

"Find a question mark. Find quotation marks. Find a period. Find a comma. What does a comma mean? Find an apostrophe. An apostrophe is at the top of the letters instead of at the bottom. When you see a word with an apostrophe and an *s* at the end, it shows that something belongs to someone. What belonged to Esau? [clothes]

"Who was the blind man in the story? Why do you think he was blind? What did he want to do before he died? What did he tell Esau to do? Who else heard what he said? What did she plan?

"Why was Jacob afraid to do what his mother said? What did Rebekah do so that Isaac would think Jacob was Esau? What did Isaac think? How do you know Isaac didn't quite believe it was Esau?

"Find a sentence Jacob said that was a lie.

"Did Jacob get the blessing? Do you think he felt blessed? Do you feel good if you lie to get something? Jacob sowed something that day that he had to reap later. We will read about some of it in the next lessons."

III. After You Read the Story

Workbook Exercises

In class discussion, help the children to formulate answers that will make good sentences for Part B.

ANSWER KEY

Before You Read the Story

1. a. fixed
   b. fix
   c. deer
   d. age
   e. bringing

2. a. give, giving
   b. sound, sounded

3. puzzled

4. a. became, field, really
   b. whether
   c. clothes
   d. give
   e. blind
   f. clothes
   g. heard, whether
   h. could
   i. sound

5. a. Blind
   b. Clothes
   c. deer
   d. field
   e. puzzled
   f. fixed
   g. fix
   h. age
   i. sounded
   j. whether
   k. really
   l. became
   m. giving
   n. heard
   o. could

After You Read the Story

A. 1. blind
   2. meat
   3. did
   4. Before
   5. felt
   6. the blessing

B. 1. bless Esau.
   2. get him some meat.
   3. Rebekah

4. Isaac would find out he was not Esau. (or) Isaac would ask God to give him bad things.
5. so quickly.
   like Esau and sounded like Jacob.
6. Jacob

C. Whatsoever a man soweth, that shall he also reap. Galatians 6:7

EXTRA ACTIVITY

Have the children print original sentences about the picture in the reader.

LESSON 14
Jacob Leaves Home

I. Before You Read the Story

A. Oral Vocabulary Drill

1. Spell words orally and let the children identify the word for which you have given the letters.
2. Which word—
   a. rhymes with *face*? (place)
   b. names something to climb? (ladder)
   c. means "shook"? (trembled)
   d. means the opposite of *rich*? (poor)
   e. makes you think of something soft? (pillows)
3. Find the correct words for these sentences.
   a. We should not feel ——. (angry)
   b. Your mother's brother is your ——. (uncle)
   c. Something unusual is ——. (strange)
   d. Girls are ——. (daughters)
   e. God's home is in ——. (heaven)

B. Reading Incentive

"See if you can find in this lesson some reaping that Jacob had for being untruthful."

II. Reader

"Find an apostrophe in the lesson. What does an apostrophe show? [You may want to explain the second use of the apostrophe in forming the word *don't* from *do not*.]

"Find a comma, an exclamation mark, and a question mark. [Discuss the expression for the questions and exclamation.]

"Look back in Lesson 13. What did Isaac ask when Jacob came in with the meat? Now look in Lesson 14. What did Isaac ask when Esau came in with the meat? He asked the same question. Do you think he sounded the same when he asked it? How do you know Isaac was upset?

"How did Esau feel?

"Couldn't Isaac say good things for Esau as well? Some of the things Isaac had said in the blessing Jacob got were asking God to make him great so that the other people in his family would serve him, and asking God to give him the best of the riches of the earth. Only one person could be the greatest and have the best, so Isaac could not say those things for Esau too.

"What kind of blessing did Isaac give Esau? He said Esau would have some of the good things of the earth too, but he would have to serve his brother.

"What did Esau decide to do to Jacob? Do you think that was reaping for Jacob? Who thought of a way to keep Jacob from being killed? What did she plan? Who was Laban? Why did Isaac think it was a good idea?

"Jacob started out to go to Laban's home. Where did he sleep that night? What happened while he was sleeping? What did God promise to Jacob? Do you remember to whom He made a promise like that before? [Abraham]

"Why do you think Jacob felt afraid when he woke up? People who do wrong things are afraid of God. But Jacob promised to serve God. God will forgive those who are sorry for the wrong things they did."

III. After You Read the Story

Workbook Exercises

Follow the directions.

Gradebook: 38 points for all written work counting two points for the memory verse

ANSWER KEY

Before You Read the Story

1. poor	7. strange
2. Pillows	8. already
3. uncle	9. angry
4. Trembled	10. decided
5. place	11. daughters
6. ladder	12. heaven

After You Read the Story

A. 1. just after Jacob left
    2. a small one
    3. angry
    4. kill him
    5. to Laban
    6. stones
    7. a ladder
    8. angels
    9. God
    10. afraid

B. | | |
|---|---|
| 1. Esau | 6. Isaac |
| 2. Issac | 7. Esau |
| 3. Esau | 8. Rebckah |
| 4. Isaac | 9. God |
| 5. Esau | 10. Jacob |

C. *Words to be crossed out:*
    1. blessing (The others express the undesirable.)
    2. wife (The others pertain to night rest.)
    3. daughters (The others indicate time relation.)
    4. Lord (The others name men.)

D. Whatsoever a man soweth, that shall he also reap. Galatians 6:7

LESSON 15
Jacob Works for Laban

I. Before You Read the Story

You may again want to discuss the analogies at the end of number 7.

A. Oral Vocabulary Drill

1. Go around the class having the children say the words in the list.
2. Which word(s)—
   a. means the opposite of *everything*? (nothing)   *small*? (large)
      young? (old)   *play*? (work)   *started*? (finished)
   b. means "money earned for work"? (wages)
   c. is a way to measure time? (month)
   d. have suffixes? (play*ed*, wage*s*, roll*ed*, old*er*, marri*ed*, young*er*, fin-ish*ed*)
   e. name two sisters? (Rachel, Leah)
3. Find the correct words for these sentences.
   a. *Rolled* is to *bold* as *carry* is to ——. (marry)
   b. *Brush* is to *paint* as *pencil* is to ——. (draw)
   c. *Father* is to *daughter* as *Laban* is to ——. (Rachel or Leah)
   d. *Older* is to *younger* as *start* is to ——. (finish)

B. Reading Incentive

"See if you can find some more reaping for Jacob as you read this lesson."

II. Reader

Have the children find apostrophes, commas, quotation marks, periods, and question marks.

"What did Jacob see when he reached the land where Laban lived? Do you think it was the same well where Abraham's servant met Rebekah? We do not know. What did Jacob ask the men at the well? Who was coming with some sheep at that time? What did Jacob do for her?

"What did Laban do when he heard that Rebekah's son had come?

"How long did Jacob stay with Laban before he started working for wages? What did Jacob want for his wages? Was Laban pleased with what Jacob asked? How long did Jacob work for Rachel? How old are you? Do you think seven years is a long time? Did seven years seem like a long time to Jacob? Why not?

"When seven years were gone, what did Laban do? Do you think that was reaping for Jacob? Do you remember a time when Jacob tricked someone else?

"Could Jacob not marry the wife he wanted? Some things were different in those days. Some men had more than one wife. Laban said Jacob could marry Rachel too. And that is what he did. Which wife did Jacob love more? How many more years did he work for her?

III. After You Read the Story
Workbook Exercises

Follow the directions.

ANSWER KEY

Before You Read the Story

1. month

2. played, played

3. draw, draw

4. a. old, older
   b. finish, finished
   c. marry, married

5. a. younger
   b. work
   c. old
   d. nothing
   e. large
   f. finish

6. Leah, Rachel

7. a. finished
   b. older (*younger* may also be given as a sensible answer without having the story as a basis)
   c. rather
   d. Wages
   e. rolled
   f. month
   g. old
   h. work
   i. large

After You Read the Story

A. 1. early
   2. mouth
   3. Rachel
   4. sheep
   5. one month
   6. two
   7. seven years
   8. Leah
   9. seven

B.
2	6	7	11
1	5	9	10
3	4	8	12

C. 1. he loved Rachel.
   2. we must not give the younger one before the older one."

EXTRA ACTIVITY

Have the children print original sentences using some of the phrases in the workbook under *Phrase Practice*.

Reminder

Remember that the class drills and discussions included in this manual are optional. Do not tie yourself to them, but tailor them to the needs of your class and demands of your schedule. One balance may be to spend time with vocabulary practice one day, and discussion on comprehension of the story the next. Develop your own teaching method and skill.

LESSON 16
Jacob Leaves Laban

I. Before You Read the Story

A. Oral Vocabulary Drill

1. Call on several individuals to read the complete list of words.
2. Which word(s)—
    a. mean more than one? (tents, idols, family, eleven)
    b. has a consonant digraph? (cat*ch*)
    c. have vowel digraphs? (*goo*d-bye, l*ea*ve, l*ea*ving)
    d. have three syllables? (family, eleven)
    e. have prefixes? (*be*longed, *be*long)
    f. have suffixes? (tent*s*, leav*ing*, belong*ed*, idol*s*)
    g. names false gods? (idols)
    h. rhymes with *match*? (catch)
    i. means the opposite of *come*? (leave)
3. Find the correct words for these sentences.
    a. *Hello* is to *arriving* as *good-bye* is to ——. (leaving)
    b. *Chickens* are to *flock* as *people* are to ——. (family)
    c. *Truth* is to *lie* as *paid* is to ——. (stole)

B. Reading Incentive

"Jacob thought someone should die. See if you can find out why and who it was."

II. Reader

Continue to have the children find various punctuation marks and discuss them until the children are familiar with the marks and their purposes. Read by sentences.

"Why did Jacob say someone should die? Who was it? Did Jacob find out who it was? Did she have to die?

"How big was Jacob's family? Where did Jacob want to go? Why didn't Laban want him to go? Why did he go anyway?

"Why didn't Laban know it when Jacob left? What did he do when he found it out? How long did it take to catch up with Jacob?

"Why did Jacob go without telling Laban? Who were Laban's daughters?

"Where did Laban look for his idols? Why did he not find them?

"How did Jacob feel about Laban's coming after him? How did they feel toward each other when they parted?"

III. After You Read the Story

Workbook Exercises

Follow the directions.

ANSWER KEY

Before You Read the Story

1. stole

2. catch

3. leave, belong

4. a. leaving
   b. belonged

5. good-bye

6. a. eleven   h. leaving
   b. family   i. good-bye
   c. tents   j. Tents
   d. idols   k. leave
   e. belong   l. catch
   f. family   m. eleven
   g. stole

After You Read the Story

A. 1. yes   5. no
2. no   6. yes
3. yes   7. yes
4. no   8. no

B. 1. God made things go better for Laban when Jacob was there.
2. Jacob did not know she had them.
3. a. Laban had not been very nice to Jacob.
   b. God had told Jacob to leave.
4. Jacob was afraid Laban would take his daughters.

C. Call upon me in the day of trouble. Psalm 50:15a

LESSON 17
Jacob Is Afraid

I. Before You Read the Story

A. Oral Vocabulary Drill

1. Let the children respond in unison as you point to the words.
2. Find the word that means the same as—
   a. gift. (present)   d. struggled. (wrestled)
   b. thigh. (hip)   e. leading. (ahead)
   c. covered. (buried)   f. puzzled. (wondered)
3. Which word(s)—
   a. name things you do in your mind? (expect, wondered)
   b. names a place? (Bethel)
   c. names a boy? (Benjamin)
   d. is a number word? (twenty)
   e. names part of the body? (hip)
   f. makes you think of a grave? (buried)
4. Find correct words for these sentences.
   a. *Girl* is to *Susan* as *boy* is to ——. (Benjamin)
   b. *Two* is to *four* as *ten* is to ——. (twenty)
   c. *Arm* is to *shoulder* as *leg* is to ——. (hip)
   d. *Dark* is to *light* as *doubt* is to ——. (expect)

B. Reading Incentive

Print these sentences on the board for consideration of expression.

1. Would it be safe for him to go home?
2. He is coming with four hundred men to meet you.
3. Poor Jacob did not know.
4. Jacob did not know who it was.
5. He knew that God would help him.

Ask the children to find a sentence that fits with a fearful feeling. (2 or 4) Can they read it with an expression that shows that feeling? You may want to demonstrate for them and let them practice by copying your voice.

Can they find a sentence that fits with a worried feeling? (1 or 3)

Find a sentence that fits with a feeling of trust and confidence. (5)

"Think about how the people felt as you read this story."

II. Reader

"What did Jacob think about on the way home? What did he do to try to make things better? What did the men tell him when they came back to him? How did that make Jacob feel? What did he do when he was afraid? What should we do when we are afraid?

"Did God answer his prayer? How did it happen? When did Jacob stop being afraid?

"What did Esau do when they met?

"Where did God want Jacob to move? What did he have his family do first? What had happened at Bethel before?

"What happened when they left Bethel? Do you remember what Jacob had said about whoever stole Laban's idols? Did it come true?

"Who else died? How long was that after the time he wanted to bless Esau because he thought he was going to die soon?"

III. After You Read the Story

Workbook Exercises

Discuss Part B with the children and do some of the numbers together if you think they need the help.

ANSWER KEY

Before You Read the Story

1. hip
2. expect
3. buried, wondered, wrestled
4. Benjamin
5. Bethel
6. wrestled
7. twenty
8. ahead
9. a. expect
   b. hip
   c. joint
   d. present
   e. buried
   f. wondered
   g. wrestled

After You Read the Story

A. 1. men
2. four
3. kill
4. animals
5. morning
6. hip
7. Israel
8. kissed

B. 1. a, b
2. b, c
3. a, b
4. b, c
5. a, b

C. Call upon me in the day of trouble. Psalm 50:15a

LESSON 18
Joseph's Dreams

I. Before You Read the Story

A. Oral Vocabulary Drill

1. Go around the class letting the children say the words in turn.
2. Find the correct words for these sentences.
   a. Joseph tied a bundle of grain into a ——. (sheaf)
   b. Change the answer if it is ——. (wrong)
   c. Jean can fold the towels ——. (nicely)
   d. Jacob's field was full of ——. (sheaves)
   e. Toby's big bone made the other puppies ——. (jealous)
   f. We want to make a —— card for grandmother. (nice)
   g. We drive —— miles to town. (eleven)

B. Reading Incentive

Print these sentences on the board for studying expression.
1. This made them jealous.
2. They hated him all the more.
3. Shall I and your mother and brothers bow down to you?
4. His sheaf stood up, and his brothers' sheaves stood around his sheaf and bowed down to it.

"Which sentences should be read in a way to sound hateful? [1, 2] Which sentences should sound amazing or disbelieving? [3, 4]"

II. Reader

Have the children read by paragraphs.

"Whom did Jacob love most of all his sons? Why do you think he might have loved him the best? How could the other brothers tell that their father loved Joseph? How did they like it? How did they treat Joseph because of it?

"Were Joseph's brothers good men? How did their father find out about some of the bad things they did? Was Joseph a tattle-tale? You can tell parents about wrong things without being a tattle-tale. If someone is doing dangerous things or something that will make them worse and worse, parents should know about it so they can help the person to do right. If we tell about the bad things people do because we are angry with them and we want them to get into trouble, we are being tattle-tales. We should not do that.

"What did Joseph dream? What did his brothers think it meant? Did they like that? What was Joseph's second dream? What did his father think that one meant?

"Did his father believe it? It seems as if he could hardly believe it. But he remembered it. He was going to wait and see."

III. After You Read the Story

Workbook Exercises

Help the children formulate a complete sentence answer for number 3 in Part B.

ANSWER KEY

Before You Read the Story

1. nice, nicely

2. sheaf, sheaves

3. jealous

4. eleven

5. wrong

6. nicely, nice, jealous

7. sheaves

8. wrong

9. a. nice
   b. nicely
   c. sheaf
   d. sheaves
   e. eleven
   f. jealous
   g. wrong

After You Read the Story

A. 1. Joseph
   2. a coat of many colors

3. jealous
4. Joseph
5. sheaves
6. the sun, moon, and eleven stars
7. his brothers
8. his father

B. 1. their father loved Joseph more than them.
   2. a. Joseph to be a great man.
      b. to bow down to him.
   3. Joseph's dreams made his brothers more jealous and hateful.

C. 1, 4, 6

D. Call upon me in the day of trouble. Psalm 50:15a

Gradebook: 37 points for all written work counting two points for number 3 in Part B and the memory verse

LESSON 19
A Wicked Plan

I. Before You Read the Story

A. Oral Vocabulary Drill

1. Call the children's names at random to have them say the words of the list in order.
2. Which word(s)—
   a. have suffixes? (nearer, minds, expected, expects, finds, thoughts)
   b. have three syllables? (expected, Israel)
   c. has the /ô/ sound? (thoughts)
   d. has the /ōō/ sound? (true)
   e. tells where thoughts are? (minds)
   f. means "very"? (quite)
3. Find the word which means the opposite of *false.* (true) *far.* (near) *full.* (empty) *holy.* (wicked)

B. Reading Incentive

Print the following sentences on the board for discussion of expression.
   1. They decided to kill him.
   2. Poor Joseph was coming nearer and nearer.
   3. They were not where he expected to find them.

"In which sentence should your voice show the feeling of pity? [2]

"Which sentence should show the sound of a mean feeling? [1]

"Which sentence should show a puzzled feeling? [3]

"Think of the feelings in the story and think how you will read the sentences."

II. Reader

"Who was Israel? What was the errand Israel sent Joseph to do? What problem did Joseph have? Who helped him?

"Were the brothers glad to see him coming? What did they plan to do? Who said not to kill Joseph? What did he plan to do?

"What happened when Joseph reached his brothers? Were you ever down in a hole in the ground? Imagine just ground walls around you, too high for you to climb out. Nothing but dirt and stones under you, and nothing but sky above. And the only people that could hear you cry for help would be someone who hates you and does not care that you will stay there until you die.

"What were the brothers doing while Joseph was feeling like this? How unkind!"

III. After You Read the Story

Workbook Exercises

Follow the directions.

ANSWER KEY

Before You Read the Story

1. near, nearer

2. expects, expected

3. finds, minds

4. quite

5. thoughts

6. empty

7. Israel

8. a. true
   b. wicked
   c. near
   d. nearer
   e. finds

9. a. minds
   b. quite
   c. expected
   d. expects
   e. Israel
   f. wicked
   g. thoughts
   h. near
   i. empty
   j. true

After You Read the Story

A. 1. brothers
2. man
3. a long way off
4. kill
5. pit
6. oldest brother
7. coat

B. 1. b   6. g
2. c   7. j
3. a   8. f
4. e   9. h
5. d   10. i

C. 1. wicked
2. bad
3. oldest
4. dry / empty

D. Call upon me in the day of trouble. Psalm 50:15a

EXTRA ACTIVITY

Let the children draw a picture to illustrate paragraph 3.

LESSON 20
Joseph Is Sold

I. Before You Read the Story

A. Oral Vocabulary Drill

1. Call on pairs of children to say the words in the list by alternating turns.

2. Find the word that means the same as—
   a. thought. (idea)   d. ripped. (torn)
   b. crowd. (group)   e. worker. (servant)
   c. unusual. (strange)   f. parts. (pieces)

3. Find the correct words for these sentences.
   a. *Thirsty* is to *water* as *hungry* is to ——. (soup)
   b. *Town* is to *Bethlehem* as *land* is to ——. (Egypt)

c. *Cold* is to *hot* as *lie* is to ——. (truth)

d. *Sold* is to *fold* as *horse* is to ——. (course)

e. *Bottom* is to *top* as *servant* is to ——. (chief)

f. *Wet* is to *water* as *bright* is to ——. (silver)

B. Reading Incentive

Print these sentences on the board for discussion of expression.

1. One of the brothers got an idea.
2. A bad animal has eaten him.
3. Joseph is torn in pieces.
4. And his own brothers had done this to him.

"Which sentence should be read with a tone of voice to sound like a terrible thing? [2, 3] Which should be read in an excited tone? [1] Which should be made to sound like a shameful thing? [4]"

II. Reader

"The brothers had seen Joseph coming a long way off. Now they saw something else. What was it this time?

"What did one of the brothers suggest? Why did that seem like a good idea to him? They would get rid of Joseph whether he was dead or sold, and this way they would get some money besides. How much money did they get for Joseph?

"Which do you think would be worse, being left alone in a pit to die, or being sold to strange men to be carried off as a slave?

"What had the oldest brother wanted to do to Joseph? Why didn't he stop the others from selling him?

"How did the brothers trick their father? What did they say that was a lie? Did they find the coat? I suppose you could say they found it on Joseph. But when they said it that way, they wanted Israel to believe that they came to it on the ground somewhere. That was as bad as saying the words, 'We came to this lying on the ground.' It was a lie.

"Have you ever been tempted to answer a question with some words that are partly true, but saying it that way will make your parents think something that is not true? If we say such things on purpose to make other people think something that is not true, we are telling a lie.

"What did Israel think? Is that what the brothers wanted him to think? Can you imagine how sad Israel felt?

"Where was Joseph? What was happening to him there? Though it may have seemed like terrible things happened to him, God was with him and God blessed him."

III. After You Read the Story

Workbook Exercises

In Part B the children are to print their own answer sentences. You may want to discuss the answers with the children and help them to formulate sentences. The questions may be answered as well by copying sentences from the reader.

ANSWER KEY

Before You Read the Story

1. soup, group
   soup, group

2. Egypt

3. chief

4. torn

5. a. farther   c. truth
   b. servant   d. strange

6. course

7. silver

8. idea

9. pieces

Matching and Underlining

1. d, Egypt	a. truth
2. f	b. torn
3. b	c.
4. e	d.
5. a	e. silver
6. c, group	f. chief

After You Read the Story

A. 2   4   9   10   14
   3   6   7   11   13
   1   5   8   12   15

B. 1. Joseph's oldest brother was not there.
   2. We found this.
   3. a. A bad animal has eaten him.
      b. Joseph is torn in pieces.
   4. Joseph's master could see that God was with him.

C. 1. twenty (The others refer to mental processes.)
   2. camels (The others name people.)
   3. made (The others rhyme.)
   4. Israel (The others refer to the transaction of selling Joseph.)

LESSON 21
Joseph in Prison

I. Before You Read the Story

A. Oral Vocabulary Drill

1. Go around the class having the children say the words.
2. Which word(s)—
   a. has an *s* to show something belongs to someone? (master's)
   b. have an *s* to make them mean more than one? (prisoners, branches)
   c. name people? (master, prisoners, butler)
   d. names a building? (prison)
   e. means the opposite of *blessings*? (trouble)
   f. rhymes with *sent*? (meant)
   g. begin with consonant blends? (*pr*ison, *pr*isoners, *br*anches, *tr*ouble, *pr*essed)

3. A word that acts is a verb. Can you find a verb in the list? (pressed)

B. Reading Incentive

Print these sentences on the board. Discuss and practice suitable oral expression.

      1. He was angry with Joseph.

      2. Why do you look so sad today?

      3. We dreamed a dream, and no one can tell us what it means.

II. Reader

"Who got Joseph into trouble? Had Joseph been doing anything wrong? What did the master's wife do? What did Joseph's master do?

"Who else was in the prison where Joseph was? [the king's prisoners, the butler and the baker, God] Why did Joseph get to look after the other prisoners? [God made the prison keeper like Joseph.]" Take this opportunity to enlarge upon such characteristics as diligence, kindness, etc. which display trustworthiness and draw respect and appreciation.

"Who was sad one morning? Why were they sad? What did Joseph tell them?

"What was the butler's dream? [Sketch the objects on the board as you discuss them.] What did the dream mean?" Refer to the pictures as you discuss the significance of each of the things.

III. After You Read the Story

Workbook Exercises

Point out that the new verse is part of the same verse the children studied last. Have them say the two parts together in the daily recitation. "Who is in the day of trouble in our story?"

ANSWER KEY

Before You Read the Story

1. master's (any noun)

2. prison

3. meant

4. a. master, branches
   b. meant, pressed
   c. prison, prisoners
   d. trouble, butler

5. prisoners, branches

6. a. branches   f. pressed
   b. butler   g. master
   c. master   h. trouble
   d. trouble   i. branches
   e. meant   j. butler

k. master

l. prisoners

m. trouble

After You Read the Story

A. 1. wicked
   2. sin
   3. that Joseph sinned
   4. God
   5. into prison
   6. grapes
   7. Joseph
   8. three

B. 1. he believed what his wife told him.
2. looked after the other prisoners.
3. the king became angry with them.
4. no one could tell them what their dream meant.

C. 1. a, c
2. a, b
3. b, c
4. a, c

D. I will deliver thee, and thou shalt glorify me.
Psalm 50:15b

Gradebook: 45 points for all written work

EXTRA ACTIVITY
Have the children print on paper all the action words they can find in the story.

LESSON 22
The King Dreams

I. Before You Read the Story

A. Oral Vocabulary Drill

1. Let the children respond in unison as you point to words in the list.
2. Which word(s)—
   a. name more than one thing? (baskets, ears)
   b. have suffixes? (ears, stolen, baskets, happened)
   c. is a compound word? (birthday)
   d. are verbs? (hope, stolen)
3. Find the correct words for these sentences.
   a. Corn grows on a ——. (stalk)
   b. Every year you have a ——. (birthday)
   c. *Good* is to *nice* as *expect* is to ——. (hope)
   d. *Grapes* are to *bunches* as *corn* is to ——. (ears)
   e. *Milk* is to *bottles* as *fruit* is to ——. (baskets)
   f. *Breeze* is to *wind* as *snack* is to ——. (feast)
   g. *Soil* is to *field* as *water* is to ——. (river)

B. Reading Incentive

Print these sentences on the board for discussion of oral expression.
1. When you are back in the king's house, tell the king about me.
2. Everything happened to the butler and baker just as Joseph said.
3. The butler forgot about Joseph.
4. Two years went by.
5. In the morning the king was troubled.

Review the whole verse of Psalm 50:15. "Do you think Joseph was trusting that God would deliver him? How do you think God might do it?"

II. Reader

"What did Joseph think might give him a chance to get out of prison? Did he deserve to be in prison? What do you think the baker was expecting when he told his dream? What was his dream? [Sketch the objects on the board as you discuss them.] What did the dream mean?" Refer to your sketches as you discuss the significance of each one.

"What day came three days later? What all happened on that day? What was the butler supposed to do when he got back to the king's house? Did he do it?

"What do you think Joseph was thinking in prison as he waited a few days and the days kept going by? Maybe he thought the king was not interested in him. Maybe he guessed that the butler forgot. How long did Joseph wait in prison?

"What happened two years later? What was the king's dream? How did the king feel in the morning? Whom did he ask to tell him the meaning of his dream? Could they?

"What did the butler remember? Why do you think he thought of it?"

III. After You Read the Story

Workbook Exercises

Follow the directions.

ANSWER KEY

Before You Read the Story

1. a. happened, baskets
   b. river
   c. feast, ears
   d. hope, stolen
   e. stalk

2. stalk

3. a. river
   b. feast
   c. stalk
   d. ears

4. a. hope
   b. birthday
   c. stolen
   d. happened
   e. ears, stalk
   f. baskets
   g. feast
   h. river

After You Read the Story

A. 1. b, c   4. c, d
   2. a, c   5. a, b
   3. a, d   6. c, d

B. 1. butler   6. butler
   2. baker   7. Joseph
   3. Joseph   8. king
   4. king   9. king
   5. baker   10. wise men

C. 1. The king made a feast for his birthday.
   2. The butler remembered Joseph because the king had a dream.

D. I will deliver thee, and thou shalt glorify me.
   Psalm 50:15b

LESSON 23
Joseph Helps the King

I. Before You Read the Story

A. Oral Vocabulary Drill

1. Choose several individuals to say the whole list.
2. Which word(s)—
   a. have suffixes? (cloth*es*, open*ed*, hurri*ed*, gather*ed*, rul*er*)
   b. are verbs? (opened, hurried, gathered)
   c. means the same as *two times*? (twice) *but*? (except) *king*? (ruler)
   d. means the opposite of *closed*? (opened) *servant*? (ruler)
      scattered? (gathered) *went slowly*? (hurried)
3. Find the correct words for these sentences.
   a. We read the lesson ——. (twice)
   b. Many people starved in the ——. (famine)
   c. Mother asked if I had —— meat. (enough)
   d. I told her I had ——. (plenty)
   e. I missed some of the dirt because I ——. (hurried)
   f. The king wore very ordinary ——. (clothes)
   g. He traveled to every part of his ——. (kingdom)
   h. Sue found a five dollar bill when she —— the book. (opened)
   i. The storm came after the farmer had —— all his crops. (gathered)

B. Reading Incentive

Review the content of the king's dreams. "Do you know the meaning of his dreams? You should be able to explain their meaning after you read the story."

II. Reader

"What did the butler say that made the king think that Joseph could tell what dreams mean? What did Joseph have to do before he went to the king? Why do you think that was necessary? [Prison life was unclean, uncomfortable, and distasteful. Any prisoner would have been unfit to appear before the king as they were in prison.]

"Did God deliver Joseph? Did Joseph glorify God or take honor to himself?

"How were the king's two dreams alike? How were they different? Why did Joseph say the dream is one? What did the dream mean? Why did the king dream twice?

"What did the king give to Joseph? What did Joseph do in the seven good years? What did he do when the seven poor years came? Who came to buy food from him?"

III. After You Read the Story

Workbook Exercises

Make sure the children realize that there are two answers for each of the questions in Part C. You may want to help them to separate the two answers and word each one in a separate sentence.

ANSWER KEY

Before You Read the Story

1. twice

2. kingdom

3. famine

4. a. gathered
   b. opened
   c. hurried

5. enough, plenty

6. except

7. a. ruler   f. opened
   b. hurried   g. famine
   c. gathered h. kingdom
   d. Twice   i. plenty
   e. clothes   j. except

After You Read the Story

A. 1. Joseph
    2. seven years
    3. Joseph
    4. a wife
    5. two
    6. houses
    7. seven
    8. seven
    9. in every land
   10. Joseph

B. 1. the king
    2. Joseph
    3. God
    4. God
    5. wise man
    6. God was with him
    7. Joseph
    8. sold

C. 1. a. Joseph cleaned up.
       b. Joseph put on other clothes.
    2. a. The dream was from God.
       b. God would soon make the dream happen.

D. I will deliver thee, and thou shalt glorify me.
Psalm 50:15b

EXTRA ACTIVITY

Have the children recall or re-read the story of Joseph's dreams and print the dreams in their own words.

LESSON 24
Joseph Sees His Brothers

I. Before You Read the Story

A. Oral Vocabulary Drill

1. Go around the class having the children say the words.
2. Which word(s)—
   a. are verbs? (run, bowing, trust, lose, bow, buy)
   b. are describing words? (sorry, youngest)

3. Find the correct words for these sentences.
   a. Do you have enough money to —— the book? (buy)
   b. Be careful not to —— your money. (lose)
   c. This picture is for my —— sister. (youngest)
   d. We were all —— to hear about the accident. (sorry)
   e. The heavy snow made all the trees ——. (bow)
   f. Some branches were —— to the ground. (bowing)
   g. How fast can a deer ——? (run)
   h. We do not need to be afraid because we —— God. (trust)

B. Reading Incentive

"Why were people coming to Egypt? People came from other lands, and Joseph sold food to them all without any trouble. When Joseph's brothers came from Canaan to buy food, what made trouble for them?"

II. Reader

"What did Israel hear about Egypt? Whom did he send to Egypt? Who did not go? Why not? What did the brothers do when they got to Egypt? Do you think Joseph thought of his dreams?

"Did the brothers think of the dreams? Why not? How do you think Joseph knew his brothers if they did not know him? [They probably appeared much as he remembered them—same kind of clothes, same language, and their number. Joseph was much changed—Egyptian clothes, Egyptian language.]

"What did Joseph not know? How was he going to find out? What did he ask the men? How did he act when they answered? Do you know what he pretended that he did believe? He said the men came to find out how bad things were in Egypt so that their land could fight against Egypt.

"What would prove that the brothers were telling the truth? What did Joseph do to make sure the brothers would come back?"

III. After You Read the Story

Workbook Exercises

Follow the directions.

ANSWER KEY

Before You Read the Story

1. bow, bowing

2. trust

3. buy, sorry

4. a. sorry
   b. run, trust, youngest
   c. buy
   d. lose
   e. bowing, bow

5. a. bow   c. buy
   b. bowing   d. trust

6. a. run   c. youngest
   b. lose   d. buy

After You Read the Story

A. 1. food   4. Joseph
   2. Benjamin   5. tests
   3. Ten   6. prison

B. 1. yes   6. no
   2. no   7. yes
   3. no   8. yes
   4. yes   9. no
   5. no   10. no

C. 1. Israel was afraid something might happen to him.
   2. bowed down to Joseph.

3. whether he could trust them.
4. bring their youngest brother with them.

D. I will deliver thee, and thou shalt glorify me.
Psalm 50:15

LESSON 25
The Brothers Go Home

Be Prepared

Bring an assortment of grains to make the definition of corn real to the children. Wheat, barley, millet, lentils, and dried beans are native to Bible lands.

I. Before You Read the Story

A. Oral Vocabulary Drill

1. Choose individuals to say all the one-syllable words or two-syllable words or three-syllable words.
2. Which word rhymes with—
   a. funny? (money)   e. post? (most, almost)
   b. ship? (trip)   f. they? (gray)
   c. borrow? (sorrow)   g. there? (hair)
   d. tax? (sacks)
3. Which word—
   a. names a feeling? (sorrow)
   b. names a part of the body? (hair)
   c. names a color? (gray)
   d. names a man? (Simeon)
   e. has the word *cover* in it? (discovered)
   f. means the same as *a gift*? (present)   *cleaned out*? (emptied) *found*? (discovered)

B. Reading Incentive

"Find the little star on the first page of the lesson. Which word does it mark? Find the matching star at the bottom of the page. There is a note to tell you something about the word *corn*. [Show the children some various grains and tell them that this is what was put into the brothers' sacks when they bought food.] Do you know what else went into their sacks?"

II. Reader

"What was in the one brother's sack? When did he find it? How did it make them feel? Why would they be afraid? Why do you think they said God did it to them? They remembered the terrible thing they had done to Joseph and they knew God remembered it too. They knew they deserved to be punished. When they got into trouble in Egypt, they thought God was letting those things happen to them for punishment.

"What did the brothers find when they got home? Who else was afraid when he saw the money? Were they guilty of stealing? Did it seem like the man in Egypt believed what they said before? Would he likely believe them if they said they did not steal the money?

"Why was Israel sad? How sure were the brothers that Benjamin would be safe with them? How bad would it be if something happened to Benjamin? What did Israel mean when he said they would bring down his gray hair with sorrow to the grave? [His sorrow would be so great he would die.]

"Why did Israel finally let Benjamin go along? What all did he send with the brothers? What else did he do so that things would go well for them?"

III. After You Read the Story

Workbook Exercises

Follow the directions.

ANSWER KEY

Before You Read the Story

1. all, most
   almost

2. empty, emptied

3. discovered

4. Simeon

5. a. sorrow
   b. empty
   c. emptied
   d. all

6. a. trip
   b. almost
   c. hair, gray
   d. present
   e. sacks
   f. money
   g. discovered

After You Read the Story

A. 1. corn, money (line between)
   2. afraid (an X after)
   3. Joseph (circled)
   4. Simeon (underlined)
   5. Benjamin (line above)
   6. a present (an X before)

B. 1. they opened it to feed their animals.
   2. they emptied their sacks at home.
   3. the food was almost gone.
   4. to help them so Simeon and Benjamin could come back home.

C. 1. sacks (The rest are food.)
   2. Jacob (The rest are his sons.)
   3. gray (The rest describe unpleasant emotions.)
   4. brother (The rest are verbs.)

Gradebook: 37 points, counting two points for each sentence answer (1 for answer content and 1 for sentence form)

EXTRA ACTIVITY

Have the children find and copy the sentence in the story that fits best with the picture in the reader.

LESSON 26
The Brothers Eat With Joseph

I. Before You Read the Story

A. Oral Vocabulary Drill

1. Name the children at random for turns to say the words as they come in the list.
2. Find the correct words for these sentences.
   a. *Late* is to *early* as *dead* is to ——. (alive)
   b. *Love* is to *hate* as *sickness* is to ——. (health)
   c. *Inches* are to *sizes* as *years* are to ——. (ages)
   d. *Animals* are to *barn* as *people* are to ——. (house)
   e. *Water* is to *wipe* as *dirt* is to ——. (wash)
   f. *Exact* is to *carefully* as *rush* is to ——. (hurried)

B. Reading Incentive

"Who was going to Egypt? Who was there waiting for them? Can you imagine how you would feel if you were waiting to see someone you loved very much whom you had not seen for many years? How did Joseph feel when he finally saw Benjamin?"

II. Reader

"What plans did Joseph make when he saw that Benjamin was with his brothers? What did the brothers think of the plans? What did they try to explain to Joseph's helper?

"What did the helper do for the brothers?

"What did Joseph ask when he got home? How did he feel when he saw Benjamin?

"What puzzled the brothers when they sat down to eat? How do you think Joseph's helper knew how to arrange them?

"Who got more food than anybody else? Why do you think Joseph did that? Do you remember how the brothers felt when their father loved Joseph best and gave him a special coat? This was a test to see if the brothers would be jealous of Benjamin."

III. After You Read the Story

Workbook Exercises

Discuss the new verse on sowing and reaping. Apply it to the grief that led to joy in Joseph's life.

ANSWER KEY

Before You Read the Story
1. alive
2. health
3. wash
4. house
5. ages
6. hurried

After You Read the Story
A. 1. eat with him
   2. Joseph's house
   3. afraid
   4. feet
   5. cry
   6. five

B. 1. They were afraid they would be punished for taking money.
   2. He cried because he was so happy to see Benjamin.
   3. Joseph told his helper how to seat them.

C. 1. a, c
   2. b, c
   3. a, c
   4. a, b
   5. b, c

D. They that sow in tears shall reap in joy. Psalm 126:5

LESSON 27
Joseph Tests His Brothers

I. Before You Read the Story

A. Oral Vocabulary
1. Go around the class having the children say the words.
2. Which word(s)—
   a. are verbs? (loaded, carry, starting, brought, start, follow, marry)
   b. begin with consonant blends? (*st*arting, *br*ought, *st*art)
   c. have three syllables? (whomever, idea)
   d. have two syllables? (loaded, carry, follow, starting, marry, safely)
3. Which word means the same as *without any harm*? (safely)
   a thought? (idea) *beginning*? (starting) *anyone*? (whomever)

B. Reading Incentive

   "How had Joseph tested his brothers so far? [He made them prove they were telling the truth about their family by bringing the younger brother to Egypt. He tested their honesty by putting the money back in their sacks. He tested their feelings toward Benjamin by giving him more than the others.] What did he think of next to test them?"

II. Reader

   "What did Joseph direct his helper to do? Did he blame the brothers for stealing the money the first time it was put back in their sacks? What did he plan to do this time?

"When did the brothers start for home? What stopped them? What did the man blame the brothers for? What did they say about it? Do you think they would have said that if they had known where the cup was? What did the man say would happen to the one who had it? Where did the man look for the cup? What do you think he saw in all the sacks? [their returned money] And where was the cup? Would Benjamin be killed like the brothers said? Would Benjamin have to stay and be a servant because he had the cup? What about the promise to bring him back to their father? This was a test indeed. Did they love Benjamin and their father too much to go home without him? What did they do?"

III. After You Read the Story

Workbook Exercises

Follow the directions.

ANSWER KEY

Before You Read the Story

1. loaded, load

2. whomever

3. marry, carry

4. a. starting
   b. start

5. a. brought
   b. start

6. a. safely
   b. brought
   c. start
   d. idea
   e. whomever

7. a. brought   f. loaded
   b. follow   g. marry
   c. safely   h. start
   d. idea   i. whomever
   e. carry

After You Read the Story

A. 1. money / food
   2. his silver cup
   3. light
   4. die
   5. stay and be a servant

6. Benjamin's

7. Benjamin

8. promised

9. very sad

10. back to Joseph

B. 1. d
   2. b
   3. e
   4. c
   5. a

C. 1. silver
   2. next
   3. Benjamin's / first / each
   4. great
   5. poor

D. They that sow in tears shall reap in joy. Psalm 126:5

EXTRA ACTIVITY

"Draw and color a picture of Benjamin's open sack." (The money and cup should be shown, as well as the sack full of grain.)

LESSON 28
Joseph Makes Himself Known

I. Before You Read the Story

A. Oral Vocabulary Drill

1. Let the children respond in unison as you point to words in the list.
2. Which word(s)—
   a. is a compound word? (outside)
   b. begin with silent letters? (*k*nown, *k*now)
   c. is the name of a man? (Judah)
3. Find the correct words for these sentences.
   a. Grandfather will come —— it rains too much. (unless)
   b. We will go even —— it is raining. (though)
   c. Do you —— my cousin Leon? (know)
   d. The writer of this poem is not ——. (known)
   e. Do you know what —— when water freezes in a jar? (happens)
   f. When did the accident ——? (happen)

B. Reading Incentive

Review the dilemma in which Joseph's brothers found themselves. "What solution did Judah suggest, and why?"

II. Reader

"Had anyone stolen the cup? Why did they not tell Joseph that they were not guilty? Why did they say they would all stay and be servants? Perhaps they thought that was how God wanted to punish them for what they had done to their brother Joseph.

"How did Joseph say he wanted it to be?

"Who was the brother that talked to Joseph? What can you tell me about Judah? What did Judah explain to Joseph? And what did Judah offer to do at the end of his explanation?

"What did this show to Joseph about his brothers? Did they pass his test? What did he do when he was satisfied that they were no longer wicked?

"How did the brothers feel when they knew who Joseph was? Why were they afraid?"

III. After You Read the Story

Workbook Exercises

Follow the directions.

ANSWER KEY

Before You Read the Story

1. know, known	2. a. know	c. happen
happen, happens	b. known	d. happens

3. a. Judah
   b. Judah
   c. Judah
4. a. though
   b. unless
   c. know
   d. Judah
   e. outside
   f. know
   g. though / know

After You Read the Story

A. 2 6 7
   1 5 9
   3 4 8

B. 1. Benjamin would not go home.
   2. Judah said he would stay and be a servant.
   3. Joseph learned that they were not wicked any more.

4. They were afraid.
5. They thought he might punish them.

C. 1. Judah
   2. Joseph
   3. Benjamin
   4. Joseph
   5. Jacob / Israel
   6. Judah
   7. Joseph
   8. Joseph
   9. Benjamin
   10. Joseph

D. They that sow in tears shall reap in joy. Psalm 126:5

Gradebook: 49 points, counting two points for sentence answers and the memory verse

LESSON 29
Good News for Israel

I. Before You Read the Story

A. Oral Vocabulary Drill
1. Call on several individuals to read the whole list.
2. Which word(s)—
   a. mean more than one? (clothes, wagons)
   b. are describing words? (eager, special)
   c. begin with consonant blends? (*spr*ead, *cl*othes, *sp*ecial)
3. Which word rhymes with *social*? (special) *said*? (spread) *traps*? (perhaps)
4. Which word means the opposite of *ordinary*? (special) *feast*? (famine) *dreading*? (eager) *surely*? (perhaps)

B. Reading Incentive
   "What is the title of our story? What do you think is the news? Did you ever hear something that was so wonderful you did not think it was true?"

II. Reader
   "Were the brothers sorry for what they had done to Joseph? Were they

supposed to be angry with themselves for doing it? Why not? Why did God want Joseph to be in Egypt? How many years of famine would there be yet? How many years had there been already? How many does that make in all?

"What did Joseph want his father and brothers to do?

"What did the other people in Egypt think when they heard who these men were? What did the king tell Joseph to give them?

"How did the brothers get their father to believe them when they got home?"

III. After You Read the Story

Workbook Exercises

Discuss how fitting the memory verse is to the experience in this story.

ANSWER KEY

Before You Read the Story

1. Perhaps

2. b
   a

3. a. eager
   b. spread

4. a. spread
   b. spread
   c. spread

5. special

6. a. eager
   b. clothes
   c. famine
   d. special
   e. eager
   f. wagons
   g. spread
   h. Perhaps
   i. wagons
   j. perhaps
   k. clothes

After You Read the Story

A. 1. kind
   2. God
   3. Egypt
   4. happy
   5. The king
   6. a special present
   7. eager
   8. Joseph
   9. believe it
  10. die

B. 1. God sent Joseph to Egypt.
   2. God wanted Joseph to save the people from dying.
   3. There would be five more years of famine.

C. 3, 7

D. They that sow in tears shall reap in joy. Psalm 126:5

EXTRA ACTIVITY

Print the long vowel symbols across the top of a paper and look for words in the story containing the sound to list under each vowel.

LESSON 30
Israel Moves to Egypt

I. Before You Read the Story

A. Oral Vocabulary Drill

1. Go around the class having the children say the words in the list.
2. Which word means the same as *hurt*? (harm) *hide*? (bury)
   another time? (again) *problems*? (troubles) *did mean*? (meant)
3. Which word(s)—
   a. have two syllables? (again, bury, troubles)
   b. has three syllables? (seventeen)
   c. is ten plus seven? (seventeen)
   d. names the hard parts inside our bodies that help us to stand up?
      (bones)

B. Reading Incentive

"Where did Israel want to be buried? Where did Joseph want to be buried? Can you think of any reasons why they would want to be buried there?"

II. Reader

"Why did Israel and his family stop on the way to Egypt? What did God tell Israel that night? Who went ahead to show the way to Egypt? What did Joseph do when they were coming? What did Israel say when he saw Joseph? Did he really want to die? He was very happy to see Joseph again. It made him so happy that he was satisfied that he had all the good things that he wanted in life. He would be satisfied to die anytime because there was nothing missing in his life.

"What did the king suggest for Joseph's family?

"What did Israel tell his sons before he died? Did his sons do what he wanted? Why were the brothers afraid after their father died? Of what did Joseph remind them?

"Where did Joseph want to be buried? Why do you think he wanted to be buried in Canaan? He had lived most of his life in Egypt. Remember that God had promised to give the land of Canaan to Israel and his family. Now all of his family was living in Egypt. Joseph knew that Canaan was the place for his family and he wanted to be buried there. Joseph knew that sometime God would lead them all back to Canaan. Maybe he thought it would help the people to remember that, if he told them to bury him there. Did they carry him to Canaan and bury him like they did for Israel? No, he just told them to keep his bones and take them along when they go back to Canaan."

III. After You Read the Story

Workbook Exercises

Follow the directions.

ANSWER KEY

Before You Read the Story

1. a. troubles
   b. harm
   c. seventeen
   d. meant
   e. bury, bones
   f. again, again
   g. seventeen
   h. bones
   i. troubles

After You Read the Story

A. 1. yes   6. yes
2. yes   7. yes
3. yes   8. no
4. yes   9. no
5. no   10. no

B. 1. offer an offering to God.
2. Judah went ahead and
3. "Now let me die, for I have seen you and you are still alive."
4. seventeen years.
5. in Canaan.
6. one hundred ten years old.

C. 1. a, c
2. b, c
3. a, c
4. a, b
5. b, c

Reading Test   Unit 1

Have the children take the unit test, either as an additional part of the lesson or as the total reading activity on another day.

ANSWER KEY

A. 1. six
2. in the Garden of Eden
3. all the wicked people
4. Jacob and Esau
5. Leah and Rachel

B. 1. no
2. no
3. no
4. yes
5. no
6. no
7. no
8. yes
9. yes
10. yes

C. 1. d   6. h
2. e   7. f
3. a   8. i
4. b   9. j
5. c   10. g

D. *Possible sentence:* Joseph dreamed that his brothers' sheaves bowed down to his sheaf.

Gradebook: 27 test points, counting two points for the sentence answer

Unit 2

UNIT 2
General Plan

Reader

The thirty lessons of Unit 2 are stories from Exodus, Leviticus, and Numbers.

The Bible memory verses are a short form of the Ten Commandments. A new commandment may be introduced every third day, or they can be fitted into six one-week sections if you take numbers 4 and 5 the same week, then study numbers 6, 7, and 8 together, and 9 and 10. The workbook does not provide the exercise of printing the verses to give liberty to schedule the rate of learning the passage as you please. The children can practice the verses by daily printing them on writing paper.

You may find it profitable to put the commandments up as a bulletin board display. Printing each commandment on a large cut-out number should help the children associate and remember the number of each commandment. Use your board for daily oral drill, pointing to the number as the children recite the commandment. After each commandment is thoroughly learned, you may want to cover or replace the verse with a plain number cut-out to enforce recitation by memory.

Workbook

Remove and file the unit tests before you distribute the workbooks.

The words presented at the beginning of each lesson do not include review words as in Unit 1. Pronunciations are given with the new words using bold print for accented syllables. Most of the lessons include crossword or acrostic puzzles with new word exercises.

Every fifth lesson includes an exercise in understanding word meanings by context. This is not necessarily related to the understanding of the story, but is an exercise to build comprehension skill.

Use the map at the beginning of the workbook frequently in class discussion. Locate the setting of the stories as you study them.

Teacher's Manual

I. Before You Read the Story

Oral vocabulary exercises are included for some lessons. If your schedule permits and the class benefits by the practice, continue to drill regularly, making your own questions for those lessons which do not provide some in the manual.

The reading incentive discussion may be used to introduce the story. Some additional pointer questions are also given for each story. These may be useful especially in a multigrade setting. A question or two may be printed on the board, and the children can independently read the lesson and prepare answers for discussion or on paper while you conduct other classes.

II. Reader

In this section some of the discussion details are omitted. Jot down your own questions or underline good question material as you read in preparation for class. Include questions that stimulate the children's minds beyond the exercise of finding something that is plainly stated in the story. Lead them in discussions of cause and effect or inference that may be gathered from what the story says. At this point such discussion will largely be your telling the class these things to train their thinking into such skills. Do not expect the children to readily answer insight questions.

III. After You Read the Story

Any workbook explanations and the answer key are given as in Unit 1.

Grading

Include evaluation of oral reading as part of the reading grade. Below is a suggested system in which oral reading represents 25% of the total reading grade.

Rate each of the following qualities on a scale from six to ten, letting ten equal A; nine equal B; eight, C; etc.

Volume—loud enough to be heard by an audience.
Smoothness—meaningful phrases instead of choppy word-by-word reading.
Expression—tone of voice that gives meaning.
Enunciation—pronouncing syllables clearly.
Correctness—reading exactly what appears on the page.

Record the total as a fraction of 50. A child given ratings of 8, 9, 7, 8, and 10 in the different areas would score 42/50 or 84%.

At the end of a marking period, average all oral grades and average all written grades. Add the oral average to three times the written average and divide by four for a final reading grade.

Reading Lessons　　Unit 2

LESSON 1
A Hard Time for God's People

I. Before You Read the Story

A. Vocabulary

Discuss the new way in which the words are presented at the beginning of the workbook lesson. Practice some two and three-syllable pronunciations consciously emphasizing the syllables in bold print.

B. Reading Incentive

"Who died in the story at the end of Unit 1? What was supposed to happen to his bones? Joseph's bones were stored in a coffin waiting for the time when the children of Israel would move back to Canaan. Do you know how long they waited? The story we will read today happened about 400 years after Joseph died."

C. Pointer Questions

1. Who wanted the babies to be killed?
2. Which babies were allowed to live?

II. Reader

Have the children turn to the table of contents. Find the page that lists the stories in Unit 1 and briefly notice the titles about Jacob and Joseph.

Turn to the page that lists the stories of Unit 2. Look at the first entry— *Bible Memory Verses*, and ask the children on which page to find the Bible verses. Turn to page 102 and introduce the memory passage.

Proceed to the story on the facing page.

"How did God's people come to be in Egypt? How many of them were there when they went to Egypt? How many of them were there now? Were they all Israel's children? Why were they called the children of Israel? Today when we talk about someone's children, we usually mean just the children that are born to one mother and father. But *children* can mean more than that. Israel's children grew up and had children, and they grew up and had children, and so on. When we talk about the children of Israel, we mean all of them.

"How were the children of Israel different from the people of Egypt? Why was the king afraid to have these different people in his land? What did he plan to do about it?

"Did his plan work? Why do you think it didn't work the way he wanted it to? Did you ever discover that if you have to work hard you get stronger? But why would there be more of the children of Israel when the Egyptians were mean to them? God was blessing the children of Israel. He would not let the king's plans hurt them.

"What were some of the kinds of work the children of Israel had to do?

Were there other kinds too? What do you think some of the other work might have been? They made mortar to hold the bricks together that they made. They built things for the king. They built whole cities.

"What did the king plan next to make the people weak? Why did that plan not work? Who helped the women?

"What did the king try next to get rid of some of the people?"

III. After You Read the Story

ANSWER KEY

Before You Read the Story

1. a. grandchildren
   b. anymore
   c. seventy
   d. bricks
   e. unhappy
   f. Egyptians
   g. becoming

2. a. 3   e. 3
   b. 3   f. 3
   c. 1   g. 3
   d. 3

After You Read the Story

A. 1. worship
   2. many
   3. Israel
   4. work hard
   5. boys
   6. river
   7. saved

B. 1. e   C. 1. c
   2. a   2. b
   3. d   3. a
   4. b   4. e
   5. c   5. d

D. 1. He was afraid they might try to kill him and his people.
   2. very hard
   3. They made bricks, and worked in the field, and did other work.
   4. no
   5. God helped them so that the king did not hurt them.

EXTRA ACTIVITY

Have the children draw pictures of the Israelites toiling at their work. You may want to describe the process of making bricks from mud or clay and drying them in the sun.

LESSON 2
The Baby in the Boat

I. Before You Read the Story

A. Oral Vocabulary Drill

1. Refer to the new way of listing vocabulary words in the workbook and again practice reading the pronunciations.

2. Which word(s)—
   a. have consonant digraphs? (amo*ng*, *th*rown)
   b. have consonant blends? (*fl*ags, herse*lf*, *pr*incess, *thr*own)
   c. is a compound word? (herself)
   d. names a man? (Moses)
   e. names a sister to Moses? (Miriam)
   f. names a plant that grows by the river? (flags)
3. Find the correct words for these sentences.
   a. A king's son is a prince. A king's daughter is a ——. (princess)
   b. When something is in the middle of many things, it is —— the things. (among)
   c. The box was —— so well we could not find it. (hidden)
   d. One baby boy was not —— into the river. (thrown)

B. Reading Incentive

"Did you ever have to watch a baby brother or sister? Did anything dangerous ever happen while you were taking care of them? Find out what happened while this girl was watching her little brother."

C. Pointer Questions

1. What was Miriam doing at the river?
2. What was the princess doing at the river?

II. Reader

Begin again at the table of contents. Read the title of the first story in Unit 2, then look at the title for Lesson 2, and find the lesson by the page number given.

"Do you know what the name *Moses* means? It means 'drawing out of the water.' The princess got him out of the water and gave him that name. He probably had a name before that, but when the princess took him for her child, she gave him the name she wanted him to have."

III. After You Read the Story

Workbook Exercises

Locate Egypt on the workbook map and let the children find the river that runs through the land.

Perhaps you know the poem in Part B as a song and can sing it with the class.

A help for unscrambling the words in Part D would be to scan the story for words that begin with the required letter. Consider each word found to see if it could refer to one or more people, and then check the letters to see if the word can be spelled with the letters given in the exercise.

ANSWER KEY

Before You Read the Story

1. Moses
2. Miriam
3. princess
4. flags
5. hidden
6. among

After You Read the Story

A. 1. months
2. boat
3. river
4. Miriam
5. The princess
6. The baby's mother
7. Moses

B. 1. boy
2. son
3. baby
4. king
5. mother
6. father
7. babies
8. family

9. child
10. sister
11. women
12. brother
13. children
14. princess

C. 1. basket (circled)
2. princess (underlined)
3. wept (an X after)
4. rushes (a line over)
5. His Word (a box around)
6. angels, Miriam

D. The princess gave the baby his name.

EXTRA ACTIVITY

Let the children print the conversation as they imagine it may have been when Miriam took the message of the princess to her mother.

LESSON 3
Moses Runs Away

I. Before You Read the Story

Tell the children the title of the story and ask them what they think Moses ran away from and why.

Pointer Questions

1. What did God want Moses to do?
2. What did one Israelite say when Moses wanted to help them?

II. Reader

Ask the children to tell you what we call the part in the front of the book that gives the names and the pages of the stories in the book.

"Think about how Moses' life was saved when he was a little baby. Many other boy babies were drowned at that time. But this was a special baby. God wanted him to do something special when he grew up. Do you know what God's plan was for Moses?

"Did Moses know what God wanted him to do? What did Moses do one day that may have been his idea of helping the children of Israel?

"Did the men of Israel know Moses would take them away from their great troubles in Egypt? How do we know they did not understand? [One man said, "Who made you a ruler over us?"]

"Why was Moses afraid? What did he do?

"Where did Moses sit down? Who came to the well? What did he do for them? What happened because of his kindness to the sisters? Sometimes you may be quite surprised by the blessings that come to you because you have been kind to strangers. Maybe nothing special will happen, but we should always be kind anyway because it is right."

III. After You Read the Story

Workbook Exercises

Locate the land of Midian on the workbook map as the home of Moses' wife and her family.

The children will need to consider four items at a time in working with the time order exercise in Part C.

ANSWER KEY

Before You Read the Story

1. drew	6. Egyptian
2. Jethro	7. two
3. hitting	8. two
4. yesterday	9. three
5. lead	10. three

After You Read the Story

A. 1. plan
   2. Egypt
   3. hitting
   4. sand
   5. fighting
   6. kill
   7. sisters
   8. Jethro
   9. wife
   10. the king of Egypt

B. 1. b
   2. c
   3. a
   4. e
   5. d

C.
2	5	12	14
3	6	10	15
1	7	11	16
4	8	9	13

D. 1. God wanted Moses to lead His people out of Egypt.
   2. no
   3. Who made you a ruler over us?

Gradebook: 44 points for the whole lesson

LESSON 4
Moses Sees Something Strange

I. Before You Read the Story

A. Oral Vocabulary Drill

1. Which word means—
   a. a large cane? (rod)

b. to give something you have to God? (sacrifice)

c. part of an animal's body? (tail)

2. Find the correct words for these sentences.

a. When God created the earth, He did many ——. (wonders)

b. Our friends came for a —— visit. (three-day)

c. *Hands* are to *gloves* as *feet* are to ——. (shoes)

B. Reading Incentive

"See how many things you can find in this story that made Moses afraid."

C. Pointer Questions

1. What was Moses doing on the Mountain of God?

2. Why did Moses take off his shoes?

3. What wonders did God do for Moses?

II. Reader

Turn to the table of contents and have the children locate the story title for today's lesson. Ask for the page number on which the story begins, then find that page.

Evaluate the oral reading of your class and determine in what aspect you should work for improvement. Teach by explanation, example, and encouragement on a daily basis. Work on one aspect until you see results, then work for improvement in another area.

For an explanation of a grading system for oral reading see the suggestions given at the end of the general plan for this unit.

III. After You Read the Story

Workbook Exercises

Locate the Mountain of God on the workbook map.

Note that Part B has five items to be put in order according to time. You may want to help the class find the first one or two. Have them consider the first two items and determine which precedes the other. Compare that one with the next possibility. Compare the first one of that set with the next possibility, and so on.

ANSWER KEY

Before You Read the Story

1. three-day

2. rod

3. shoes

4. tail

5. sacrifice

6. wonders

7. a. rod
   b. tail
   c. Wonders
   d. shoes
   e. sacrifice
   f. three-day

After You Read the Story

A. 1. took care of his sheep
   2. the Mountain of God
   3. a bush that did not burn up
   4. his shoes
   5. hid his face
   6. bring them out of Egypt
   7. a rod
   8. a snake

B. 4
  2
  5
  3
  1

C. 1. he was standing on holy ground.
   2. God wanted Moses to bring His people out of Egypt.
   3. "Who am I, that I should bring the children of Israel out of Egypt?"
   4. no
   5. no
   6. God would do all His wonders.

LESSON 5
Moses Goes Back to Egypt

I. Before You Read the Story

Look at the map. Find the land of Midian where Moses worked for Jethro. Find the land of Egypt where Moses' brother Aaron lived. Moses and Aaron did not plan it together, but Moses started back to Egypt, and Aaron started out to meet him. How do you think they found each other with all that wilderness between?

Pointer Questions

1. Why did God tell Moses to take his rod?
2. What happened at the Mountain of God in this story?

II. Reader

"Where is the table of contents in your reader? For what reason is it there? Use it to tell me on what page Lesson 1 of Unit 2 begins. On what page does Lesson 3 begin? On what page does Lesson 5 begin?

"What new reasons did Moses have to be afraid to go back to Egypt? How did God answer Moses?

"Whom did God send to meet Moses? How would Aaron help? What did Jethro say about Moses' going? Who went with Moses?

"What did God say He would do to the king when he does not let the people go?

"Where did Moses and Aaron meet? What did the children of Israel think when Moses and Aaron came and told them these things?"

III. After You Read the Story

Workbook Exercises

Remind the children how to help themselves by looking for the words in the reader if they get stuck in unscrambling the letters in Part D.

Explain that the children are to find out the meanings of the words in Part E by reading the paragraphs.

ANSWER KEY

Before You Read the Story

1. Aaron
2. deaf
3. father-in-law
4. deaf
5. father-in-law
6. Aaron

After You Read the Story

A. 1. no
2. no
3. yes
4. yes
5. yes
6. yes
7. yes
8. no
9. no
10. yes

B. 1. God
2. Aaron
3. wonders
4. God
5. Moses did not want to go.

C. 1. old
2. oldest
3. older

D. 1. talk
2. tell
3. told
4. said
5. say
6. speak
7. talking
8. promised
9. thanked

E. 1. edge
2. get
3. plants
4. king's daughter
5. work for
6. men who give people work to do
7. cried

EXTRA ACTIVITY

Have the children print the conversation as they imagine Moses may have talked to Aaron when they met.

LESSON 6
More Trouble for God's People

I. Before You Read the Story

A. Oral Vocabulary Drill

1. Which word(s)—
   a. has a controlled *a*? (straw)
   b. have the long *o* sound? (Pharaoh, scolded)
   c. have consonant digraphs? (*Ph*araoh, *th*emselves)
   d. begin with consonant blends? (*dr*ive, *sc*olded, *str*aw)
   e. is a compound word? (themselves)

2. Find the correct words for these sentences.
   a. If you have more pencils than you need, you have ——. (extra)
   b. Fred does not have a car because he cannot ——. (drive)
   c. The king of Egypt was ——. (Pharaoh)
   d. An ant is not ——. (lazy)
   e. The dog looked ashamed when he was ——. (scolded)
   f. After the wheat was harvested, the field was full of ——. (straw)
   g. The girls washed the dishes all by ——. (themselves)
   h. —— makes a good bed for a goat. (straw)

B. Reading Incentive

"What had God told Moses on ahead about the king? What did the king think when Moses and Aaron said the people want to go?"

C. Pointer Questions

1. What did Pharaoh say about God?
2. What did Moses and Aaron say the people wanted to do?

II. Reader

Discuss the brick-making method and use of straw.

III. After You Read the Story

Workbook Exercises

Tell the children that some of the speakers which they are to identify in Part A will be named by words other than by a name.

Printing a paragraph number for the information given is new as a written exercise. Make sure the children understand the directions for Part C.

ANSWER KEY

Before You Read the Story

1. drive, straw

2. extra, lazy, Pharaoh, scolded, themselves

3. Pharaoh

4. a. scolded
   b. straw
   c. themselves

5. drive, lazy, Pharaoh, scolded

6. themselves

7. a. lazy   e. themselves
   b. drive   f. extra
   c. straw   g. Pharaoh
   d. scolded

After You Read the Story

A. 1. Pharaoh
2. Pharaoh
3. Pharaoh
4. Moses and Aaron
5. Moses and Aaron
6. Pharaoh
7. Pharaoh
8. taskmasters (or) men who made Israel work
9. men of Israel
10. Pharaoh
11. Moses
12. Moses
13. God
14. God

B. 1. b, c
2. a, c
3. a, c
4. a, b

C. a. 1
b. 8
c. 5
d. 10

D. 1. bricks
2. straw
3. They had to go get the straw themselves.
4. Their masters beat them and scolded them.

5. They thought things would get better.
6. Things were worse instead of better.
7. The king would drive them out of his land.

EXTRA ACTIVITY

Use the statements in the workbook for which the children have identified the speakers, and have them tell to whom the words were said. That name may be printed after each statement.

LESSON 7
The First Wonder

I. Before You Read the Story

A. Reading Incentive

Review the story setting. "Who was afraid to talk? Who would do the talking for him? Together they went to Pharaoh. What did they say? What was Pharaoh's answer?

"In today's lesson they went to the king again. What happened this time?"

B. Pointer Questions

1. What land did God promise to give the children of Israel?
2. Why were they not happy about the promise?
3. What happened to the magicians' rods?

II. Reader

"What do we call the list of stories in the front of the reader? Use the table of contents to answer these questions.

"What story begins on page 123?

"What is Lesson 10 about?

"What story begins on page 148?

"Why do you think there are so many stories before the one about leaving Egypt? Our story today gives us an idea why it went so long.

"What things did God promise to the suffering children of Israel? Why did the people not listen to the promises?

"What did Moses and Aaron take with them when they went to the king? What happened when Aaron threw down his rod? What did the king's magicians do? What became of their rods? Did Pharaoh believe God then?

"What did Aaron do with his rod the next morning? What happened to the water when Aaron did that? What happened to the fish?

"Did Pharaoh know it was going to happen? How did the people of Egypt feel about the blood for water? Would the king let Israel go?"

III. After You Read the Story

ANSWER KEY

Before You Read the Story

1. a. magicians
   b. swallowed
   c. stink
   d. burdens

2. stink

3. burdens

4. swallowed

5. magicians

Puzzle Words

1. magicians
2. burdens
3. swallowed
4. stink

After You Read the Story

A. 1. Abraham, Isaac, and Jacob
   2. swallowed
   3. blood
   4. fish
   5. dug

B. 1. will / with
   2. bring
   3. give
   4. things / this
   5. him / his / hit
   6. in / it / is

7. king
8. still / stink
9. fish
10. drink
11. live

C. 1. c   6. h
   2. e   7. f
   3. a   8. i
   4. d   9. g
   5. b   10. j

D. 1. You will know that I am the Lord.
   2. I will give you this land.

Gradebook: 40 points for the whole lesson

EXTRA ACTIVITY

Have the children alphabetize their answers for exercise B in the workbook. The given order of letters in the exercise is in the order in which the answers may be found in the story.

LESSON 8
Frogs in Egypt

I. Before You Read the Story

A. Oral Vocabulary Drill
1. Which word(s)—
   a. names a time? (tomorrow)
   b. mean more than one? (frogs, ovens, piles)
   c. are verbs? (jump, serve)
2. Find the correct words for the sentences.
   a. When you work for someone, you —— them. (serve)
   b. We use a rope to play —— rope. (jump)
   c. There is an apple and a pear in the dish. I could have —— one. (either)
   d. We saw three —— jump from the pond bank. (frogs)
   e. Most stoves have —— in them. (ovens)
   f. We like to rake leaves into ——. (piles)
   g. The day after today is ——. (tomorrow)

B. Reading Incentive
   "What had Moses and Aaron taken with them when they went to the king? Do you remember what Aaron did with his rod so far? In this story Aaron does something else with his rod. A rod is not a big thing, but when God uses a rod, He can do great things with it."

C. Pointer Questions
   1. Where did the frogs go?
   2. What would Pharaoh know when the frogs go away?
   3. What made the land stink?

II. Reader
   Conduct oral reading and discussion.

III. After You Read the Story

Workbook Exercises
   The last question in Part C will probably be a difficult one unless you include it in the reader discussion.

ANSWER KEY

Before You Read the Story

1. ovens

2. four

3. tomorrow

4. piles, serve

5. jump

6. serve

7. a. Frogs
   b. piles
   c. tomorrow
   d. either

Puzzle Words

1. frogs
2. either
3. piles
4. jump
5. ovens
6. tomorrow
7. serve

After You Read the Story

A. 1. seven 6. Tomorrow
2. frogs 7. All
3. would 8. piles
4. everything 9. stink
5. destroyed 10. would not

B. land
bread
stink
go

C. 1. Aaron put his rod out over the water.
2. They also brought frogs over the land.
3. They wanted to show that they could do whatever Moses and Aaron could.

LESSON 9
Lice and Flies

I. Before You Read the Story

A. Reading Incentive

"Do the flies get pesty at your house sometimes? (Maybe they do at school.) What do you do about it when there are lot of flies? Can you ever kill them all? What was it like when there were flies in Egypt?"

B. Pointer Questions

1. What could the magicians not do?
2. Where would there be no flies?

II. Reader

Test the children's silent reading comprehension. Have them read one paragraph silently, then ask questions on it before any oral reading is done. You may want to follow the discussion with oral reading of the entire story.

Paragraph 1

"What did Aaron do with his rod this time? What happened? Have you ever seen lice? Some kinds of lice we can see crawling on plants. They are very tiny insects. Some kinds of lice crawl on animals. Some crawl on people. They are almost too tiny to see that they are insects. It is very unpleasant to have lice crawling on things. You have seen dusty places on the ground, haven't you? After you play in a place like that, you have dust on your skin and on your clothes. Imagine what it was like in Egypt when God made all the dust to be lice.

"What did Pharaoh's magicians do this time? Why could they not bring lice? This was a wonder from God, and God was not helping them."

Paragraph 2

"What would God do next if Pharaoh would not let the people go? Why would there be no flies in the land where the children of Israel lived? God would do it that way so Pharaoh would know that God is the Lord. No one but God could make a whole lot of flies in one place and not let one get in another place."

Paragraph 3

"Find a word that means a very large group. Have you ever had a lot of flies around you? I am sure that the swarms of flies in Egypt were much worse than any amount of flies we have ever seen."

Paragraphs 4 and 5

"What was Pharaoh ready to let the people do? What did Moses say it had to be?"

Paragraph 8

"What happened to the flies? How many were left? Just think how great God is! He could make the swarms of flies come thicker than we have ever seen them, and He could make them go away so completely that there was not one left. Not one!"

III. After You Read the Story

ANSWER KEY

Before You Read the Story

1. lice
2. flies
3. swarms
4. one
5. a. Flies
   b. Lice
   c. Swarms

Puzzle Words

Across
2. lice
3. swarms

Down
1. flies

After You Read the Story

A. 1. lice
2. magicians
3. flies
4. sacrifice
5. go very far away

6. mind
7. God
8. would not

B. 4	7	9
2	5	11
1	8	12
3	6	10
		13

C. 1. God told Moses to tell Aaron to hit the dust. (or) He hit the dust so it would become lice.
2. What Aaron did was from God.
3. Moses met the king at the water.
4. God did not send flies where his people were so Pharaoh would know God is the Lord.

D. 1. 102
  2. 126
  3. 3
  4. More Terrible Wonders
  5. 129

E. 1. king (The rest name troubles that came on Egypt.)
  2. dust (The rest tell when.)

  3. animals (The rest are people.)
  4. swarm (The rest are verbs.)
  5. knew (The rest refer to speech.)

EXTRA ACTIVITY

Have the children write in their own words the story of the first four wonders.

LESSON 10
More Terrible Wonders

I. Before You Read the Story

A. Oral Vocabulary Drill
  Complete these sentences.
  a. Colts are baby ——. (horses)
  b. Mother cooks dinner on a ——. (stove)
  c. If you are not careful when doing dishes, something may ——. (break)
  d. When sore spots appear on your skin, we say they —— out. (break)
  e. When you carry all you can hold, you are carrying ——. (handfuls)
  f. Mother asked me to bring two —— of clothes pins. (handfuls)
  g. We used the watering can to —— the flower beds. (sprinkle)
  h. Animals something like small mules are ——. (donkeys)

B. Reading Incentive
  "Did you ever have a boil? A boil is a very, very painful spot of infection with pus in it. Somebody in the story had boils. Who was it?"

C. Pointer Questions
  1. What was different for the animals of Egypt from the animals of Israel?
  2. What did Moses and Aaron use this time instead of a rod?

II. Reader
  Use discussion after silent reading of paragraphs to test comprehension.

III. After You Read the Story

ANSWER KEY

Before You Read the Story

1. handfuls	5. donkeys
2. sprinkle	6. stove
3. oxen	7. break
4. horses	

Crossword Puzzle

Across	*Down*
2. handfuls	1. donkeys
4. oxen	3. sprinkle
6. break	5. horses
7. stove	

After You Read the Story

A. 1. so they could serve the Lord
2. all the Egyptians' animals
3. all
4. not one
5. ashes
6. boils

B. 1. ashes
2. disease

C. 3
4
1
5
2
6

D. 1. cows   5. camels
2. oxen   6. horses
3. sheep   7. donkeys
4. cattle   8. animals

E. 1. e   4. b
2. a   5. c
3. f   6. d

Gradebook: 42 points for the whole lesson

LESSON 11
Thunder, Lightning, and Hail

I. Before You Read the Story

A. Reading Incentive

Read the following sentence to the children from paragraph 1. "I will at this time send all My troubles on you and your servants and on all your people so that you will know that there is no one like Me in all the earth."

"That was God's message to Pharaoh. What terrible things had God already done to them? Think how fearful it would be to have God say that he was going to send more terrible wonders! What will happen next? Will it make Pharaoh change his mind?"

B. Pointer Questions

1. Why did God say everything should be gathered in from the fields?
2. What did Pharaoh say when it hailed?

II. Reader

Paragraph 1

Have the children read the paragraph silently. "What time of day did Moses go to the king? What was the reason God was going to send great troubles? What did he say was going to happen? What time of day was the hail going to come? How bad would it be? Have you ever seen a hailstorm? Sometimes hail tears the plants in the gardens and breaks the crops in the fields and even breaks windows and makes marks on metal roofs. But this hail would be so terrible that it would kill any animals and people that stayed outside. How was God kind to the Egyptians in this? [He gave forewarning and instruction for those who would believe Him.]"

Paragraphs 2 and 3

"Who made their servants and animals get into houses? Why? Why did some let their servants and animals out in the field?"

Paragraph 4

"What did Moses do to make the hail start? What else was in the storm? What happened in the storm? Can you imagine such a storm? What do you think it sounded like? [thunder cracking, cattle bawling, hail clattering, fire crackling, trees crashing] Then how did Pharaoh talk?" (Paragraph 5)

Paragraphs 6, 7 and 8

"What did Moses do to stop the hail? Where did he go to do it? And then what did the king do?"

Ask the children to tell you the number of the paragraph—
    a. that describes the hailstorm. (4)
    b. in which Pharaoh called for Moses and Aaron. (5)
    c. that tells about some Egyptians that believed God. (2)
    d. that tells what Moses did to stop the hail. (6 or 7)

III. After You Read the Story

ANSWER KEY

Before You Read the Story

1. a. thunderings
   b. thunder, thunderings
   c. flax
   d. hail
   e. spoiled
   f. mixed
   g. barley
   h. mighty
   i. lightning
   j. stop

2. flax

3. thunder, thunderings

4. lightning

5. 5

Crossword Puzzle

Across	Down
3. mighty	1. hail
5. thunder	2. mixed
6. spoiled	4. thunderings
7. barley	8. flax
9. lightning	
10. stop	

After You Read the Story

A. 1. no   7. no
2. yes   8. no
3. no   9. no
4. yes   10. yes
5. yes   11. yes
6. no (some were   12. yes
    taken in)

B. 1. Moses was to go early in the morning.
   2. God was going to send troubles so they would know there is no one like God.
   3. Moses put out his hand toward heaven.
   4. Moses spread out his hands to the Lord.

C. 1.
   2.
   3.
   4.
   5. thunder
   6. hail
   7. sinned

LESSON 12
Locusts

I. Before You Read the Story

A. Oral Vocabulary Drill

1. Which word(s)—
   a. has a *w* that is a vowel? (blow)
   b. have suffixes? (sign*s*, thick*ly*)
   c. have consonant digraphs? (bo*th*er, stret*ch*, *th*ickly)
   d. have silent consonants? (si*g*ns, stre*t*ch)
   e. tells what you do to make bubbles? (blow)
   f. is the opposite of *thinly*? (thickly)
2. Find the correct words for these sentences.
   a. If something gets bigger when you pull it, it can ——. (stretch)
   b. When you are touching something, you are —— it. (against)
   c. To make trouble for someone is to —— them. (bother)
   d. —— tell us something if we read them. (signs)
   e. A whistle is made to ——. (blow)
   f. We put leaves on the flower bed to cover it ——. (thickly)
   g. Sometimes we hunt for letters on the —— along the road. (signs)
   h. A rubber band is easy to ——. (stretch)

B. Reading Incentive

"Do you know what locusts are? They are little animals like grasshoppers, that can fly or jump. The next thing God sent to trouble Pharaoh and his people was locusts. What do you think was so terrible about that? What did the locusts do?"

C. Pointer Questions

1. What stories did the people of Israel tell their children?
2. What happened to the crops the hail had not spoiled?
3. What made the locusts come?

II. Reader

After reading and discussion, have the children tell in which paragraph certain information can be found.

III. After You Read the Story

ANSWER KEY

Before You Read the Story

1. a. go
   b. father
   c. pines
   d. quickly

2. a. signs
   b. stretch
   c. blow

3. a. blow
   b. stretch

4. 3

5. a. thickly
   b. against
   c. bother

6. stretch

Crossword Puzzle

Across
1. signs
2. against
3. bother
5. thickly

Down
1. stretch
4. blow

After You Read the Story

A. 1. all
   2. servants
   3. east
   4. west
   5. Red
   6. it was dark in the daytime.

B. 4
   6
   10

C. 1. Their God was a great God.
   2. He could do great things for them.

D. disease, thunder, locusts

E. 6 *boils*
   2 *frogs*
   1 *blood*
   8 *locusts*
   5 *cattle died*
   7 *hail*
   4 *flies*
   3 *lice*

LESSON 13
The Thick Darkness

I. Before You Read the Story

A. Reading Incentive

"Nighttime is a lovely time. We like to see the stars in the sky like little candles. We like to see the moon. Have you ever been out in the night when you could not see the moon or stars? That seems pretty dark. Now put your hands over your eyes. That seems even darker. When you are in the dark and reach out your hands, can you feel anything? Darkness is not something you can touch—not usually. But God made it darker in Egypt than what we have ever seen. It got so dark with a thick darkness that the people could feel the darkness. It was dark like that in the daytime. How long did it stay dark? What did the people do?"

B. Pointer Questions
1. What did Moses do to bring the darkness?
2. From whom did the children of Israel borrow things?
3. What would happen at midnight?

II. Reader

Paragraphs 1 and 2
Let the children read the paragraphs silently. "How long did the darkness last? What did the people do those three days? Where was it not dark?"

Paragraph 3
"Pharaoh had driven Moses and Aaron away the time before. What did he do now? What did he say to Moses?"

Paragraph 4
"For what did Moses say they had to take their cattle? How do you think they used their cattle to serve the Lord?"

Paragraphs 5, 6, and 7
"How did the king like what Moses said? What did he say to Moses? It was getting close to the time when the people would finally go away and Moses would never see Pharaoh again. What did the Lord say He would do yet?"

Paragraph 8
"What did God want the children of Israel to do? Why did the Egyptians give things to them gladly?"

Paragraph 9
"What was the last terrible thing that God was going to do to the Egyptians?"

Paragraph 10
"Why would the people of Israel not be hurt?"

Ask the children which paragraph—
a. tells about borrowing from the Egyptians? (8)
b. describes the darkness? (1 or 2)
c. tells about the last terrible thing God would do to the Egyptians? (9)
d. has Moses' answer to Pharaoh about taking the animals? (4)

III. After You Read the Story

ANSWER KEY

Before You Read the Story

1. midnight

2. firstborn, midnight

3. a. midnight
   b. firstborn
   c. neighbors
   d. herds
   e. borrow
   f. thick

Crossword Puzzle

Across	*Down*
3. neighbors	1. herds
4. thick	2. firstborn
5. borrow	
6. midnight	

After You Read the Story

A. 1. felt   4. borrow
   2. three   5. midnight
   3. see   6. firstborn

B. 1. midnight
   2. firstborn
   3. terrible
   4. glad
   5. cry
   6. again
   7. Lord
   8. king / Pharaoh

C. 1. c   4. b
   2. a   5. f
   3. e   6. d

D. 1. God
   2. Pharaoh
   3. Moses
   4. Pharaoh
   5. Moses

Gradebook: 40 points for the whole lesson

LESSON 14
What Happened at Midnight

I. Before You Read the Story

A. Oral Vocabulary Drill

Which word(s)—

   a. makes you think of a fence? (posts)
   b. make you think of counting? (tenth, fourteenth)
   c. makes you think of money? (spend)
   d. makes you think of great things? (important)
   e. makes you think of an animal? (lamb)
   f. makes you think of food? (yeast)
   g. has three syllables? (important)
   h. has a silent consonant? (lam*b*)
   i. have vowel digraphs? (f*ou*rteenth, y*ea*st)

B. Workbook Notes

   Teach the children how to do the acrostic puzzle. "The first word is easy. There is only one word in the list that begins with *p*." Have the children note for the second word that it will be a word with just four letters and the second letter has to be *a*. See if they can tell you which word belongs in the third row. When two words fit the same space, use a word that was not used before.

C. Reading Incentive

"Did you ever move? Suppose you were moving to another country. How might you travel? Do you think you would sleep the night before you left?

"The children of Israel were moving to another land. What did they do the night before they left? God told them exactly what to do."

D. Pointer Questions

1. What kind of lamb was each family to take?
2. Why would the Lord skip some houses when He went through the land?

II. Reader

After discussion and oral reading, have the children tell in which paragraph certain information may be found.

III. After You Read the Story

ANSWER KEY

Before You Read the Story

1. a. yeast
   b. lamb
   c. tenth
   d. fourteenth
   e. important
   f. spend
   g. posts

2. 5

3. 1

4. important

5. posts, yeast

6. lamb, spend, tenth

7. a. lamb
   b. important
   c. spend
   d. tenth
   e. fourteenth
   f. yeast

Acrostic Puzzle

1. *P* osts
2. l *A* mb
3. yea *S* t
4. *S* pend
5. f *O* urteenth
6. t *E* nth (or) y *E* ast
7. impo *R* tant

After You Read the Story

A. 1. lamb
   2. year
   3. neighbors
   4. fourteenth
   5. evening
   6. door
   7. bitter
   8. bread
   9. house
   10. firstborn
   11. bowed
   12. obeyed

B. 1. There was someone dead in every house.
2. No one died in the houses with blood on the door.
3. They wanted Israel to leave quickly.
4. They were afraid the Lord would kill all of them.

C. *Answers may be interchangeable unless you require them to be in proper order.*
1. blood
2. frogs

3. lice
4. flies
5. disease
6. boils
7. hail
8. locusts
9. darkness
10. death of each firstborn

D. plagues

EXTRA ACTIVITY
Have the children memorize the poem on the ten plagues.

LESSON 15
The People Leave Egypt

I. Before You Read the Story

A. Reading Incentive
"Close your eyes and think of the largest church meeting you ever attended. Imagine such crowds of people walking down the road. Imagine so many people walking that the big long line would reach as far as you could see and farther.

"The crowd of people we will read about today is more than you ever saw together at one time. Try to imagine the great crowd as you read."

B. Pointer Questions
1. How many people left Egypt?
2. What would the people do to remember this night?
3. How did the people know where to go?

II. Reader
Have the children read **paragraph 1**.

"How many men went out of Egypt? How many people were there all together? What did they take along?"

Paragraph 2
"Where were the children of Israel going? What unusual thing did they take along?"

Paragraph 3
"God wanted His people always to remember the night they left Egypt. What were they to do so that they would remember?"

Paragraph 4

"How did the people know where to go when they started out? Where did the cloud lead them?" Look at the workbook map and find the beginning of their journey, going to the sea.

Paragraph 5

"What did the king decide to do? Why did he want them back? About what did he forget?"

III. After You Read the Story

Workbook Exercises

You may want to explain exercise B to the children. They will need to read one paragraph, then consider the titles and chose the best one for the paragraph they have read.

The review words in exercise D are from Lessons 5 and 10, Part E.

ANSWER KEY

Before You Read the Story

1. dough

2. million

3. one-half

4. easily

5. pillar

6. one-half, whenever

7. a. missed
   b. pillar
   c. million
   d. one-half
   e. dough
   f. missed

After You Read the Story

A. 1. gold, silver, clothes
   2. over a million
   3. Joseph's
   4. a cloud
   5. fire
   6. the Red Sea
   7. go after the children of Israel and bring them back
   8. what a great God the children of Israel had

B. *Paragraph 1*
How Many People Left Egypt

Paragraph 2
Why Israel Took Joseph's Bones Along

Paragraph 3
How God Helped His People to Remember

Paragraph 4
How God Led His People

Paragraph 5
What the King Decided to Do

C.	**D.**	
1. c	1. c	6. h
2. a	2. e	7. j
3. b	3. d	8. f
4. e	4. b	9. l
5. d	5. a	10. g
		11. i
		12. k

EXTRA ACTIVITY

Let the children draw a picture for one of the paragraphs, then see if the rest of the class can identify the part of the story illustrated.

LESSON 16
God Helps His People

I. Before You Read the Story

A. Oral Vocabulary Drill

1. Which word(s)—
   a. has a suffix? (camping)
   b. has two modified vowels? (forward)
   c. has a consonant digraph? (*ch*ariot, campi*ng*)
   d. names a person? (captain)
   e. are verbs? (camping, lift)

2. Find the correct words for these sentences.
   a. Living outside is ——. (camping)
   b. A two-wheeled cart in which to ride is a ——. (chariot)
   c. A building has more than one ——. (wall)
   d. The box was so heavy only Father could —— it. (lift)
   e. The opposite of *backward* is ——. (forward)
   f. The leader of your team is your ——. (captain)

B. Reading Incentive

"Do you remember where God led the children of Israel when they left Egypt? [Refer to the map and find the Red Sea.] Do you remember what King Pharaoh decided to do? The children of Israel thought they were trapped. The sea stopped them from going forward, and Pharaoh and his army were coming from behind. God had led them there. He knew the Egyptians would come after them. Should the people have trusted God? Did they? What happened?"

C. Pointer Questions
   1. What did the children of Israel see that made them afraid?
   2. Who was going to fight the Egyptians?
   3. What was dark and light at the same time?

II. Reader

Conduct oral reading and discussion.

III. After You Read the Story

Workbook Exercises

Discuss the questions in Part C. Help the children to choose answers by evaluation rather than by finding information in the story.

ANSWER KEY

Before You Read the Story

1. forward
2. wall
3. chariot
4. captain
5. camping
6. lift
7. camping

Crossword Puzzle

Across

2. captain
4. forward

Down

1. camping
2. chariot
3. lift
5. wall

After You Read the Story

A. 1. God told the children of Israel to go forward.
2. He was to hold his rod over the sea.
3. God put the pillar of cloud between Israel and Egypt.
4. A strong wind made the waters go back.
5. They walked on dry ground.

B. 1. six hundred (underlined)
2. by the Red Sea (box around)
3. afraid (line above)
4. the Lord (circled)
5. be quiet (cross after)

C. 1. b
2. c
3. a
4. a

D. The picture should show a cloud between the two groups, colored bright on the left and dark on the right.

EXTRA ACTIVITY

Have the children print original sentences with the unused words of the answer list in Part B.

LESSON 17
What Happened to the People of Egypt

I. Before You Read the Story

A. Reading Incentive

"How do armies fight? Who was going to fight for Israel? Do you know how the Lord fought? Did He use swords, or did He hit the people? When you read the story, see what the Lord did to fight for Israel."

B. Pointer Questions

1. What made the Egyptians want to get away from Israel?
2. What did Israel see on the seashore?
3. What trouble did the children of Israel have next?

II. Reader

Paragraph 1—Have the children read the paragraph silently. Ask the class to close their books and think about what they have read. "What was it about? What was the main idea of the paragraph? Can you think of a good title for that paragraph?" Help them to summarize the discussion in a title such as "How God Fought" or "The Egyptians in the Sea."

Paragraph 2—Have the children read the second paragraph and think about the content. Summarize the thought in a title such as "God Tells Moses What to Do."

Paragraph 3—All the Egyptians Die
Paragraph 4—Israel Sings a Song
Paragraph 5—Bitter Water
Paragraph 6—God's Cure
Paragraph 7—God's Promise
Paragraph 8—A Good Place to Camp

III. After You Read the Story

Workbook Exercises

Locate Marah (place of bitter water) and Elim (place of 12 wells and 70 palms) on the workbook map.

You may want to discuss Part E with the children to help them summarize the story in one sentence.

ANSWER KEY

Before You Read the Story

1. seashore
2. wheels
3. pull
4. healthy
5. palm
6. path
7. a. traveled
   b. grumbled
   c. sang
   d. song
   e. sweet
   f. fast

5. horses
6. seashore
7. hand (back)
8. morning
9. sea
10. Egypt
11. true
12. wonderful
13. long
14. happy
15. afraid

B. 1. yes   7. no
    2. yes   8. yes
    3. yes   9. no
    4. no   10. no
    5. no   11. no
    6. no   12. yes

C. 1. c   4. b
    2. f   5. e
    3. a   6. d

D. What Happened to the People of Egypt

E. *Possible sentence:* The people of Egypt tried to follow Israel and drowned in the Red Sea.

Crossword Puzzle

Across	*Down*
4. seashore	1. fast
5. sweet	2. traveled
6. grumbled	3. wheels
7. pull	4. sang
8. song	7. path
9. healthy	

After You Read the Story

A. 1. dry
    2. hard
    3. middle
    4. chariot

Gradebook: 59 points for the whole lesson counting two points for the sentence in Part E

EXTRA ACTIVITY

"Draw a picture of the camping place described in paragraph 8."

LESSON 18
God Feeds His People

I. Before You Read the Story

A. Oral Vocabulary Drill

1. Which word(s)—
   a. have modified vowels? (des*e*rt, waf*e*rs)
   b. has a vowel digraph? (qu*ai*ls)
   c. has a consonant digraph? (Sabba*th*)
   d. have little words in them? (*man*na, *melted*, Sab*bath*)
   e. names a kind of bird? (quails)
   f. names a place? (desert)
   g. names a day? (Sabbath)
   h. names food? (manna, wafers)
2. Find the correct words for these sentences.
   a. Crackers are ——. (wafers)
   b. The ice cream ——. (melted)
   c. Many plants cannot grow in the ——. (desert)
   d. The children of Israel were not to work on the ——. (Sabbath)

B. Reading Incentive

"If you were among the children of Israel, do you think you would ever want to go back to Egypt? Why not? What was it like where they were camping? But they are traveling and must keep moving on. What do you think they could come to that would make them wish they were back in Egypt?"

C. Pointer Questions

1. What did the children of Israel grumble about?
2. On which day did no manna fall?

II. Reader

Discuss the story by paragraphs again, helping the children to identify the main idea of the paragraphs. (Using titles from Part C of the workbook lesson will prepare the children to do that exercise on their own.)

III. After You Read the Story

Workbook Notes

Locate the Wilderness of Sin (where people grumbled for food).

ANSWER KEY

Before You Read the Story

1. quails
2. manna
3. desert
4. Sabbath
5. melted
6. wafers

Acrostic Puzzle

1. Sabbat *H*
2. waf *E* rs (or) des *E* rt
3. qu *A* ils
4. d *E* sert (or) m *E* lted
5. ma *N* na

After You Read the Story

A. 1. grumbled
   2. eat
   3. heaven
   4. manna
   5. in the morning
   6. seventh
   7. white
   8. melted

B. 1. The people were traveling.
   2. They could not find enough wild animals.
   3. God made bread rain down from heaven.
   4. They were to rest on the seventh day.
   5. They would eat what they had gathered on the sixth day.

C. *Paragraph 1*   b
   Paragraph 2   a
   Paragraph 3   b
   Paragraph 4   c
   Paragraph 5   b
   Paragraph 6   c
   Paragraph 7   a

EXTRA ACTIVITY

Have the children write sentences telling all the things they can think of which God had done for His people since they left Egypt.

LESSON 19
God Gives Water to His People

I. Before You Read the Story

A. Reading Incentive

"Did you ever take a trip that took longer than one day to get to the place where you were going? Where did you sleep for the night when you were traveling? What was the longest trip you ever took? How many days did it take? How long do you think the children of Israel were traveling? Where did they sleep when night came?"

B. Pointer Questions

1. How long did the children of Israel eat manna?
2. Why was Moses angry with some of the people?
3. Why did the people scold Moses?

II. Reader

Have the children read paragraph 1, then discuss traveling with tents. Try to summarize the discussion with a title for the paragraph such as "Tent Homes."

Paragraph 2

Discuss the food they had while traveling. How did they get it? The paragraph could be summarized with a title "Food for their Families."

Paragraph 3

Discuss the transgression of doing more than one is supposed to do, and that of doing less than one is supposed to do. Summarize the paragraph with a title such as "The People Who Would Not Obey."

Paragraphs 4-7

"What was the next thing that the children of Israel grumbled about? Should they have grumbled? Why not? What did they blame Moses for doing? What were the people almost ready to do?"

Paragraphs 8 and 9

"What was God's direction to Moses? What was he supposed to take along? When had Moses used it to hit a river? [When the plague of blood was brought upon the Egyptians.] What was Moses supposed to hit this time? What happened when he did it? What do you think the people thought of such a wonderful thing? It should have reminded them that God was with them and made them realize that Moses had done the right thing, as it did when God fought for them at the Red Sea."

III. After You Read the Story

Workbook Exercises

Practice orally making the sentences for the riddle in Part C. Discuss the form for the last sentence of the riddle, comparing the riddle given in Part B.

ANSWER KEY

Before You Read the Story

1. breakfast
2. thirst
3. overnight
4. worms
5. stank
6. breakfast, overnight
7. thirst, worms, overnight

Acrostic Puzzle

1. *W* orms
2. bre *A* kfast
3. s *T* ank
4. ov *E* rnight (or) br *E* akfast
5. thi *R* st

After You Read the Story

A. 1. tents
   2. manna
   3. forty
   4. overnight
   5. worms
   6. sixth
   7. seventh
   8. scolded
   9. stone
   10. rock

B. tents

C. *Possible sentences:*
It was white.
It tasted like wafers made with honey.
It came from heaven.
It melted when the sun came out.
The children of Israel ate it forty years.
It was ——.

D. 3　　　　6
2　　　　8
4　　　　10
1　　　　9
　　　　　7
　　　　　5

E. 1. rock (The rest relate to water.)
2. cattle (The rest are people.)
3. manna (The rest name meals.)
4. ahead (The rest indicate abundance.)
5. evening (The rest are unpleasant responses.)
6. forty (The rest are ordinal numbers.)

EXTRA ACTIVITY
Let the children print original riddles about something of their own choice in the schoolroom.

LESSON 20
God Fights for His People

I. Before You Read the Story

A. Oral Vocabulary Drill
1. Which word(s)—
   a. has a vowel digraph? (h*ea*vy)
   b. has a consonant digraph? (Jo*sh*ua)
   c. has a modified vowel? (H*ur*)
2. What little words can you find in the new words?
3. Find the correct words for these sentences.
   a. An elephant is very ——. (heavy)
   b. A mountain is a very high ——. (hill)
   c. Two men's names are —— and ——. (Hur, Joshua)
   d. When Jane got her father's slippers, the slippers were —— by Jane. (gotten)
   e. My dog likes to run. He does not like to be ——. (held)
   f. We will be happy even if we do not —— the game. (win)
   g. *Tall* is to *short* as *lose* is to ——. (win)
   h. *Up* is to *down* as *dropped* is to ——. (held)
   i. *Woman* is to *Mary* as *man* is to ——. (Hur or Joshua)
   j. *Pie* is to *sky* as *rotten* is to ——. (gotten)
   k. *Flat* is to *plain* as *high* is to ——. (hill)

B. Reading Incentive

"Hold both your hands up in the air, and keep them up. Somebody in the story held up his hands. Why do you think he was doing it? How long does it go until your arms are tired and you would like to put them down? Keep them up. Do you think you could last all day? The person in your story did. How do you think he could do it? You may put your hands down now, and read your story."

C. Pointer Questions

1. What would Moses do while others fight the battle?
2. How could Moses hold up his hands all day?
3. What was Moses doing that Jethro thought was not good?

II. Reader

Turn to the table of contents and look over the titles of Lessons 15 to 20. Let the children briefly explain what God did in each situation named. What wonderful care God gave to them in every trouble they faced. Our God is the same God today, and He cares for us just the same.

Treat the new lesson by paragraphs, helping the children to express the main ideas.

III. After You Read the Story

Workbook Exercises

Let the children explain to you what they understand the directions to mean.

ANSWER KEY

Before You Read the Story

1. Hur
2. Joshua
3. gotten
4. a. win
   b. hill
   c. heavy
   d. held

Crossword Puzzle

Across
4. hill
5. gotten
6. Hur

Down
1. held
2. win
3. Joshua
4. heavy

After You Read the Story

A. *Order interchangeable:*

a. (2) God fought for the children of Israel at the Red Sea.
b. (5) God gave the children of Israel manna from heaven to eat.
c. (6) When men came out to fight with the children of Israel, God fought for them.
d. (8) God led the children of Israel with a cloud so that they could know where to go.
e. (9) God gave the children of Israel water to drink.

B. 1. fight 6. hands **C.** 1. c 5. h
2. Joshua 7. win 2. d 6. e
3. the rod 8. an altar 3. b 7. f
4. Hur 9. father-in-law 4. a 8. g
5. stone 10. God

LESSON 21
How God Speaks to His People

I. Before You Read the Story

A. Reading Incentive

"Were you ever on a mountain? Some mountains are so high that it is always cold at the top. No trees can grow there, and there is always snow on the mountain. Do you know the names of any mountains? Some of the big mountains are called Mt. Everest, Mt. Whitney, Mt. Hood. The children of Israel came to a mountain when they were traveling. This was not the first time Moses had been to this mountain. Do you know which mountain it was? Do you know when Moses was there before?"

B. Pointer Questions

1. How would the Lord come to talk to Moses?
2. What did the people do to be ready for God to talk to them?
3. What happened to the mountain when God was on it?

II. Reader

Follow Israel's travel on the map.

"When had Moses been to this mountain before?

"Where did Moses talk to God? What did God want Israel to be to Him? What would they have to do to be His treasure? What did the people think of it?

"God is very great and holy. People should be very serious and careful when they plan to meet with God. What did God tell the people to do to be ready to hear Him talk to them? How long were they to be getting ready?

"When God came down on the mountain, it was a very important time. If you had been there, what could you have seen? What could you have heard? What could you have felt? What do you suppose you would have thought? What would have happened if anybody touched the mountain when God was on it? God is that great and mighty. Who was allowed to go up on the mountain?

"Notice how careful God was to protect the people from harm. How many times did He tell Moses to warn the people against touching the mountain? God never punishes without giving fair warning for people to understand."

III. After You Read the Story

ANSWER KEY

Before You Read the Story

1. treasure

2. trumpet

3. myself

4. Mount Sinai, 2, long

5. edge, d, e

6. shake

After You Read the Story

A. 1. travel
   2. long
   3. fire, burn
   4. Egypt
   5. treasure
   6. earth
   7. again
   8. called, told, said, answered, says
   9. thick
   10. clean
   11. edge
   12. die
   13. three

B. 1. Sinai
   2. long
   3. obey
   4. thick
   5. wash
   6. mountain
   7. die

C. 1. To be prepared just so.
   2. All those would die that do.
   3. Descended with the Lord.
   4. And felt the shaking ground.
   5. "We'll keep His every word."

D. 2   5
   4   6
   3   8
   1   7

Gradebook: 48 points for the whole lesson

EXTRA ACTIVITY

Draw and color a picture to show what the mountain might have looked like.

LESSON 22
The First Four Commandments

I. Before You Read the Story

A. Oral Vocabulary Drill

1. Which word(s)—
   a. mean more than one? (commandments, countries)
   b. mean "you"? (thee, thou)
   c. means "your"? (thy) Use it with a word to name something that is yours. (thy coat, thy name, thy house, etc.)
   d. means "shall"? (shalt)

    e. have a vowel digraph? (th*ee*, v*ai*n)
    f. begins like *gray*? (graven) *Graven* means "carved or cut out."
    g. rhymes with *pain*? (vain) *Vain* means "useless and not good."
    h. means "a shape or form"? (image)
    i. means something to learn? (lesson)
2. Which two words mean the same thing? (rules, commandments)
3. Find the correct words for these sentences.
    a. Canada, United States, and Egypt are names of ——. (countries)
    b. He can answer every question in the ——. (lesson)
    c. We should never worship an ——. (image)
    d. The turtle was gone, and we looked for him in ——. (vain)
    e. A statue is an ——. (image)

B. Workbook Notes

   Discuss the different form of the acrostic puzzle. Clues are given for the words as for a crossword puzzle. One word down will appear in the shaded blocks when the answers are written.

C. Reading Incentive

   "What are some rules that we have in games we play? What are some rules we have in school? Do you know some rules that the government has made for our land? Why do we have rules? See if you can find out when you read the lesson."

D. Pointer Questions

    1. Of what are images made?
    2. What were they not to do on the Sabbath Day?

II. Reader

III. After You Read the Story

ANSWER KEY

Before You Read the Story

1. commandments	6. thee, thou
2. rules	7. thy
3. image	8. shalt
4. vain	9. countries
5. graven	10. lesson

Acrostic Puzzle

1. commandments	6. rules
2. countries	7. image
3. thou	8. lesson
4. graven	9. shalt
5. thee	10. vain

                  Mount Sinai

After You Read the Story

A. 1. gods
       2. graven
       3. vain
       4. Sabbath

B. 1. Remember the Sabbath Day, to keep it holy.
       2. Thou shalt have no other gods before Me.
       3. Thou shalt not take the Name of the Lord thy God in vain.
       4. Thou shalt not make unto thee any graven image.

C. 1. God gave the Ten Commandments at Mount Sinai.
2. An image is something made
to look like a real thing.
3. The Sabbath Day was the
seventh day.
4. God has given us rules for
our own good.

LESSON 23
The Last Six Commandments

I. Before You Read the Story

A. Reading Incentive

"Who have we been reading about in our stories? [children of Israel]
How many of them are there? [over a million] Where were they camping?
[Mount Sinai] What special thing happened at this mountain? [Com-
mandments were given.] How many commandments did we have in the last
lesson? How many more commandments are there? The first four commandments tell how Israel was to worship God. The last six are all about
the way they were to act toward each other. As you read the lesson think
about how many are like the rules that we have."

B. Pointer Questions

1. What will help us learn to love and obey God?
2. When are people likely to kill others?

II. Reader

"Find and read the commandment that told the people of Israel how
they should treat their parents. Find and read the commandment that told
them what married people should not do. Find and read the commandment
that told them what they should not do with their tongues. Find and read
the commandment that told them not to take the life of anyone else. Find
and read the commandment that told them not to want what belonged to
others. Find and read the commandment that told them not to take what
belonged to others.

"When Jesus talked about the commandments, He said, 'Thou shalt love
thy neighbor as thyself.' When people love others, they will do these commandments without being told. Would you disobey your parents or talk
back to them if you love them? Would a person kill someone he loves? Would
a person take a man's wife away from him if he loved the man? Would a
person steal from someone he loves? Would a person want someone else's
things if he loved him? Would a person tell lies about someone he loves?
God gave these commandments to help His people live together happily."

III. After You Read the Story

ANSWER KEY

Before You Read the Story

1. false

2. honor

3. adultery

4. bear

5. commit

6. witness

7. covet

Crossword Puzzle

Across	*Down*
2. commit	1. honor
5. adultery	3. bear
6. covet	4. witness
7. false	

After You Read the Story

A. 1. love
2. hate
3. live
4. steal
5. true
6. want

B. 1. Honor thy father and thy mother.
2. Thou shalt not bear false witness.
3. Thou shalt not kill.
4. Thou shalt not covet.
5. Thou shalt not steal.

C. 1. a, c   4. b, c
2. a, b   5. a, c
3. a, c   6. b, c

LESSON 24
How the People Worshiped God

I. Before You Read the Story

A. Reading Incentive

"Where was God when He gave the Ten Commandments to the people? What was it like on the mountain? Do you know how the people felt after they heard God talking?

"After that Moses went up on the mountain and God talked to Moses alone. God and Moses talked together forty days and forty nights. What do you think they talked about? See if you can find out when you read."

B. Pointer Questions

1. What would the children of Israel be tempted to do?
2. What would help them not to do it?
3. How did the people worship God?

II. Reader

"How did the people feel after they heard God talk? What did they think might happen to them? Did God want the people to be afraid? Of what did He want them to be afraid? What was it like on the mountain when Moses went up on it?

"What were God and Moses talking about? What kind of house would they have for God's house?

"What would the children of Israel be tempted to do? Why would they be tempted with that? What was God going to do to help them not to worship idols?

"Where was the tent that was God's house to be set up? What were some things from which the tent was made?

"How did the children of Israel worship God? How do we worship God? [prayer, praise, singing, reading the Bible] Why do we worship God in a different way than they did? [They lived before Jesus died; we live after Jesus died.]

"What did God give Moses? What was on the stones? How did God put the commandments on the stone? Did you ever write with your finger? You can do it in loose ground or sand. You can do it on a dusty place or a steamed window. But God wrote on stone with His finger. God can do anything!"

III. After You Read the Story

ANSWER KEY

Before You Read the Story

1. finger
2. write
3. tempted
4. tempted
5. write
6. finger
7. (Individual work)

After You Read the Story

A. 1. listen
2. talk
3. to, do, be, so
4. sin
5. mountain
6. dark
7. forty
8. things, wanted, traveling, moved, (or) God's
9. special
10. better

B. 1. God
2. dark
3. forty
4. tent
5. idols
6. stone
7. finger
8. two

C. 1. People should be afraid when they sin.
2. They would be tempted to worship idols.
3. God's house would be a tent so it could be moved.
4. They gave gold and silver to help make God's house.
5. They worshiped God by offering a lamb.

EXTRA ACTIVITY

Have the children print sentences to tell how we worship God.

LESSON 25
The People Sin

I. Before You Read the Story

A. Oral Vocabulary Drill
1. Which word(s)—
   a. have suffixes? (danc*ing*, sing*ing*)
   b. means "very small"? (fine)
   c. means "very good"? (fine)
   d. names a baby animal? (calf)
   e. names a part of your leg? (calf)
2. Find the correct words for the sentences.
   a. *Hungry* is to *ate* as *thirsty* is to ——. (drank)
   b. *Love* is to *kindness* as *hate* is to ——. (war)
   c. *Rocks* are to *large* as *dust* is to ——. (fine)
   d. *Cat* is to *kitten* as *cow* is to ——. (calf)
   e. *Sad* is to *crying* as *happy* is to ——. (singing)
   f. *Tired* is to *sitting* as *lively* is to ——. (dancing)
   g. *Ice* is to *cold* as *pillow* is to ——. (soft)

B. Reading Incentive
"In this story the children of Israel broke something, and Moses broke something. What did they break, and who did it first?"

C. Pointer Questions
1. Whom did the children of Israel want to lead them?
2. How did Moses find out about the people's sin?

II. Reader

III. After You Read the Story

ANSWER KEY

Before You Read the Story

1. a. drank
   b. soft
   c. calf
   d. dancing
   e. war
   f. singing
   g. fine

2. dancing

3. calf

Crossword Puzzle

Across
1. soft
2. dancing
4. war
5. fine

Down
1. singing
2. drank
3. calf

After You Read the Story

A. 1. first
   2. gold
   3. calf
   4. gods
   5. feast
   6. Moses
   7. angry
   8. commandments
   9. calf
   10. drink

B. 1. Moses   5. Joshua
   2. Aaron   6. Moses
   3. Aaron   7. Moses
   4. Moses

C. 1. c   5. e
   2. b   6. h
   3. a   7. g
   4. d   8. f

D. a. 3 / 8
   b. 7
   c. 6
   d. 8

LESSON 26
The People Are Punished

I. Before You Read the Story

A. Reading Incentive

"What is the title of your story? What had the people done that they needed to be punished? Who got the blame for their sin? What was the punishment?"

B. Pointer Questions

1. Who was on the Lord's side?
2. What were they supposed to do?
3. How long did Moses stay on the mountain this time?

II. Reader

"Whom did Moses say had brought the sin upon the people? What was Aaron's answer? What did he say that was not the whole truth?

"What did Moses ask the people? Who was on the Lord's side? What did God want the people to do that were on His side? How many men were killed that day?

"What did Moses ask the Lord to do? What was Moses willing to do for the people? What was God's answer?

"What did God tell Moses to get? What was He going to do with them? Where did Moses go? How long was he there? Did the people worship other gods again? Why not?

"If you had been there when Moses came down from the mountain what would you have seen? Why do you think his face was shining? What did Moses have to do so that the people could come near him? Just think how glorious God Himself must be, if the people could not look at Moses after he was with God for a while!"

III. After You Read the Story

ANSWER KEY

Before You Read the Story

1. veil
2. Levi
3. tribe
4. shining
5. gate
6. long
7. (Picture of something shining)

Acrostic Puzzle

1. tribe
2. shining
3. Levi
4. veil
5. gate

After You Read the Story

A. forgive

B. 1. upon
2. great
3. fire
4. gods
5. gold
6. calf
7. swords
8. three thousand
9. Lord's
10. sin, sinned
11. go
12. whether
13. gold, told
14. suffer
15. people, gods

C. a. 3
b. 3
c. 2
d. 7
e. 9
f. 9

D. 1. The tribe of Levi came to Moses.
2. Three thousand men were killed that day.
3. He said the calf came out of the fire.
4. Moses went forty days and nights without food or water.
5. Moses' face was shining.
6. He put a veil over his face.

E. They had learned their lesson.

Gradebook: 50 points for the whole lesson counting two points for each sentence in Part D.

LESSON 27
The People Leave Sinai

I. Before You Read the Story

A. Oral Vocabulary Drill

1. Which word(s)—
   a. is a compound word? (throughout)
   b. has a suffix? (grumbling)
   c. is a naming word? (tabernacle)
   d. is a verb? (grumbling)
   e. has the letters *ou*? (throughout) What sounds do these letters make?
2. Let the children compose sentences with the new words.
3. Find the correct words for these sentences.
   a. No one likes to hear you ——. (grumbling)
   b. When it snowed all night, we say it snowed —— the night. (throughout)

    c. The children of Israel made a special tent in which to worship God. It was called the ——. (tabernacle)

4. Review some vocabulary words by practicing the lists at the back of the reader.

B. Reading Incentive

"How do you start a fire? The children of Israel used fire to burn the animals in their offerings, but they did not need to start a fire each time. How did they get their fire? See how many fires you can find as you read the story. The children of Israel did not make any of them."

C. Pointer Questions

1. What was the special work of the tribe of Levi?
2. How did the children of Israel know when it was time to move?
3. What made the fire go out that was sent to punish the people?

II. Reader

Discuss God's choice of the tribe of Levi in relation to their choice to be on the Lord's side.

III. After You Read the Story

ANSWER KEY

Before You Read the Story

1. tabernacle
2. throughout
3. grumbling
4. grumbling
5. throughout
6. tabernacle
7. grumbling
8. throughout
9. tabernacle
10. throughout

After You Read the Story

A. 1. Levi
2. go out
3. God
4. another fire
5. a year
6. built the tabernacle
7. a cloud
8. eating manna

B. 1. The tribe of Levi came to be on the Lord's side.
2. He chose them because they wanted to be on the Lord's side.
3. a. They took care of the house of God.
b. They looked after the offerings.
4. Aaron was the high priest.
5. Aaron was of the tribe of Levi.

C. 1. yes   6. no
2. no   7. no
3. yes   8. no
4. yes   9. yes
5. yes   10. yes

D. 1. b   6. h
2. a   7. j
3. e   8. f
4. c   9. g
5. d   10. i

LESSON 28
The Sin of Aaron and Miriam

I. Before You Read the Story

A. Reading Incentive

"Who is the leader for the children of Israel in the stories we are reading? What do you know about the time when Moses was a baby? What did his sister Miriam do? How do you think she felt toward him at that time? Now they are both grown up. How did she feel toward him at this time? What happened because of it?"

B. Pointer Questions

1. Why did Miriam and Aaron find fault with Moses?
2. Why could the people not travel for seven days?

II. Reader

Read and discuss the story by paragraphs, summarizing each one with a title.

Paragraph 1—Aaron and Miriam Find Fault
Paragraph 2—What God Thought of the Faultfinding
Paragraph 3—God Talks to the Three
Paragraph 4—The Lord Scolds and Punishes
Paragraph 5—The Disease of Leprosy
Paragraph 6—Aaron Is Sorry
Paragraph 7—Miriam Is Healed

Follow Israel's travels on the map.

III. After You Read the Story

ANSWER KEY

Before You Read the Story

1. allowed

2. hasn't

After You Read the Story

A. 1. brother, sister
   2. jealous
   3. Miriam
   4. fault, because
   5. heard
   6. think
   7. pleased
   8. trying
   9. three
   10. cloud
   11. door
   12. looked, saw
   13. a. up
       b. after
       c. terrible
       d. asked
   14. leprosy, disease
   15. who
   16. one

B. 1. Aaron and Miriam
2. making his work harder
3. tabernacle
4. cloud
5. leprosy
6. sinned
7. Moses
8. seven
9. traveled

C. *Paragraph 1*   b
Paragraph 2   c
Paragraph 3   a
Paragraph 4   c
Paragraph 5   b
Paragraph 6   a
Paragraph 7   a

D. (Individual work)

LESSON 29
Ten Wicked Men and Two Faithful Men

I. Before You Read the Story

A. Oral Vocabulary Drill

1. Which word(s)—
   a. can describe people? (brave, faithful, weak, taller)
   b. can name people? (Caleb, enemies, giants, leader)
2. Which word means the opposite of—
   a. afraid? (brave)
   b. safety? (danger)
   c. winning? (losing)
   d. follower? (leader)
   e. dwarfs? (giants)
   f. dropped? (carried)
   g. unfaithful? (faithful)
3. Find the correct words for these sentences.
   a. *Cold* is to *hot* as *strong* is to ——. (weak)
   b. *Dark* is to *light* as *end* is to ——. (beginning)
   c. *Young* is to *short* as *older* is to ——. (taller)
   d. *Love* is to *friends* as *hate* is to ——. (enemies)
   e. *Woman* is to *Martha* as *man* is to ——. (Caleb)
   f. *Birds* are to *robins* as *insects* are to ——. (grasshoppers)
   g. *Corn* is to *ear* as *grapes* are to ——. (bunch)
   h. *Bread* is to *baked* as *fruit* is to ——. (ripe)
   i. *Door* is to *gate* as *post* is to ——. (pole)

B. Reading Incentive

"When you are traveling to a place that is far away, what do you begin asking after a while? ["Are we soon there?"] The children of Israel must surely have wondered when they would be getting to the promised land. In this lesson they were very close to the land God had promised them. They were so close that Moses sent some men ahead to see what it was like. Were the people excited? Did they get to go into the land?"

C. Pointer Questions

1. What did the men bring back from the promised land?
2. The men said they were like what beside the giants of the land?

II. Reader

Follow Israel's travels on the map and observe their closeness to Canaan.

III. After You Read the Story

ANSWER KEY

Before You Read the Story

1. carried
2. weak
3. Giants
4. Brave
5. Caleb
6. leader
7. enemies
8. danger
9. bunch
10. Grasshoppers
11. Overcome
12. beginning
13. taller
14. faithful
15. ripe
16. losing
17. pole

Acrostic Puzzle

1. faithful
2. bunch
3. beginning
4. ripe
5. overcome
6. grasshoppers
7. enemies
8. giants
9. losing
10. brave
11. carried
12. Caleb
13. weak
14. danger
15. leader

Shaded blocks: the promised land

After You Read the Story

A. 1. grapes
2. Egypt
3. grasshoppers
4. Caleb
5. walls
6. right away
7. a. forty
   b. good
   c. big
   d. high
   e. big / strong / taller

B. 1. They would know better where and how to take the rest of the people into the land.
2. They were afraid of the big men.
3. He knew God would help them fight their enemies.
4. They grumbled because Moses and Aaron brought them to this land.

C. 3   5
1   8
4   7
2   6

EXTRA ACTIVITY

Draw and color a picture for paragraph 3.

LESSON 30
More Sin in the Camp

I. Before You Read the Story

A. Workbook Notes

Having no new words for Lesson 30, the first part of the workbook lesson need not be done before the story is read. The activity reviewing word meanings may be done before reading the lesson though, to fit the routine schedule. The review words are from Lessons 20 and 25, Part C.

B. Reading Incentive

"Did you ever make a gift for someone? How would you feel if you gave the gift and the person would say, 'I don't like it. I don't want it'? What did God want to give the children of Israel? What did they say about it?"

C. Pointer Questions

1. What did the people want to do to Joshua and Caleb?
2. Who would go into the good land?

II. Reader

Have each paragraph read, then discussed and summarized.

      Paragraph 1—What Joshua and Caleb Said
      Paragraph 2—What the People Wanted to Do
      Paragraph 3—The Lord's Punishment
      Paragraph 4—What Happened to the Twelve Men
      Paragraph 5—The People Change Their Minds
      Paragraph 6—Moses' Warning
      Paragraph 7—The People Disobey

III. After You Read the Story

ANSWER KEY

Before You Read the Story

1. sore	12. charged
2. midst	13. gaze
3. chided	14. perish
4. host	15. molten
5. hoar	16. stiff-necked
6. even	
7. pitched	
8. murmured	
9. descended	
10. ascended	
11. quaked	

After You Read the Story

A. 1. b
    2. a
    3. a
    4. a
    5. c
    6. b
    7. c
    8. c
    9. a
   10. b

B. 1. wicked
2. is
3. listen
4. died
5. end
6. war
7. need
8. help
9. sinned
10. sinning

C. wilderness

D. 1. Moses
2. Jethro
3. Joshua
4. Miriam
5. Aaron
6. The children of Israel
7. God
8. Twelve men
9. Joshua and Caleb
10. Hur

Reading Test   Unit 2

ANSWER KEY

A. 1. boys
2. river
3. The princess
4. an Egyptian
5. Jethro
6. snake
7. palm
8. manna

B.
2	6	14
4	8	11
5	9	13
1	7	12
3	10	15

C.
1. e	8. l	15. o
2. f	9. j	16. s
3. a	10. k	17. p
4. b	11. n	18. q
5. d	12. i	19. t
6. g	13. h	20. r
7. c	14. m	21. u

D. 1. When the pillar of cloud went up, they traveled. When it rested, they stayed in camp.
2. Moses held his arms up so Israel would win the battle.
3. Miriam got leprosy.
4. The were afraid of the giants in the land.

Gradebook: 52 test points for written work counting two points for each sentence in Part D

Unit 3

UNIT 3
General Plan

Reader

Unit 3 contains stories from Numbers, Deuteronomy, Joshua, and Judges. The Bible memory work is a series of verses that begin with the word *blessed*.

Workbook

Every fifth lesson in the workbook introduces a new Bible memory verse. The lessons include daily practice of printing the verse.

As in Unit 2, every fifth lesson includes an exercise in understanding word meanings by context.

Make frequent reference to the workbook map.

Remove and file the unit test before distributing the workbooks.

Teacher's Manual

I. Before You Read the Story

Oral vocabulary drill is not included in the daily lesson plans. Prepare your own exercises or formulate the usual questions on the spot when you have time for class drill.

As in Unit 2, a bit of discussion for reading incentive and a few pointer questions are included with each lesson. (See instructions in the general plan for Unit 2.)

II. Reader

The story discussion questions suggested in some lessons are such that involve a bit of independent thinking. Continue to prepare detail questions for most of the stories. (Underline details that relate to important concepts of the story, or jot questions in the margin as you read, for a guide to class discussion.) At other times you may omit such questions and direct the children in consideration of principles, or cause and effect, or inference questions. Always discuss any pointer questions you have assigned.

III. After You Read the Story

Any workbook explanations and the answer key are given in this section.

Reading Lessons   Unit 3

LESSON 1
A New Thing

I. Before You Read the Story

A. Reading Incentive

"Can thinking get you into trouble? What kind of thoughts did some people in this story have, and what kind of trouble did it bring them? Who else got into trouble because of those thoughts? [their families]"

B. Pointer Questions

1. Whose fault was it that the children of Israel were not in Canaan?
2. What new thing happened?

II. Reader

"Why do you think some men felt Moses and Aaron tried to make themselves great? [Moses and Aaron were the leaders, and they were telling the people what to do.]"

"When Moses called for the men to come to him, what did they do? What does that show about their feeling toward Moses? [They were not going to obey him as their leader.]"

"What were the two sides of the argument? [Either God had not sent Moses to be the leader, or God was not pleased with the men who talked against Moses.] Which side was right? How do we know?"

III. After You Read the Story

ANSWER KEY

Before You Read the Story

1. wilderness
2. hole
3. closed
4. screamed, screaming
5. e
   c
   d
   b
   a
6. (Individual sentences)

After You Read the Story

A. 3   8
    1   7
    4   6
    2   9
        5

B. 1. b
2. c
3. a
4. b
5. c

C. 1. God had not sent Moses to be their leader.
2. God did send Moses. (or) God was not pleased with what the men did.

D. 1. The, ungodly
2. The, counsel
3. in, the, of, ungodly, not, blessed
4. man, that, in, the, in, the

E. Blessed is the man that walketh not in the counsel of the ungodly. Psalm 1:1

EXTRA ACTIVITY

Have the children list all the action words they can find in the story.

LESSON 2
More Sin

I. Before You Read the Story

A. Reading Incentive

"What happened to some people in the story we read yesterday? Why did that happen to them? What did all the other people know after that had happened? Do you think they would always honor and obey Moses after this? When you read Lesson 2, see how long it went until more people found fault with the leaders, and find out what God did this time."

B. Pointer Questions

1. What did the people say Moses and Aaron had done?
2. What would remind the people that God had chosen Aaron for special work?

II. Reader

"Who had killed some of the men of Israel? So with whom were the people really finding fault?

"Of what were rods made? A stick of wood can grow buds and blossoms and nuts if it is part of a tree. But this was an old stick that Aaron had been using as a rod for a long time. Could such a stick grow? Because something impossible happened, the people knew that it was really God's doing. Moses and Aaron could never have made that happen."

III. After You Read the Story

ANSWER KEY

Before You Read the Story

1. bloom, displeased, laid

2. chosen

3. a. displeased
   b. nuts
   c. remind

4. bloom, probably

5. a. chosen

b. remind
c. displeased
d. bloom
e. nuts
f. laid
g. probably

After You Read the Story

A. 1. b
   2. a
   3. b

4. a
5. c
6. a
7. c

B. 1. Moses, Aaron
2. rods
3. tabernacle
4. blooming, nuts
5. Miriam

C. 1. God had called Aaron to this special work.
2. He was supposed to keep it in the tabernacle.
3. It was to stay there to remind the people that God had chosen Aaron.

D.

E. 1. f   4. e
2. d   5. b
3. a   6. c

F. Blessed is the man that walketh not in the counsel of the ungodly. Psalm 1:1

Gradebook: 44 points for the entire lesson counting two points for each sentence in Part C and only one point for correctly copying the memory verse

LESSON 3
Water and Snakes

I. Before You Read the Story

A. Reading Incentive

"What is the title of your story? What do you think might happen in the story? God sent water to His people in the wilderness, and God sent snakes to His people in the wilderness. Can you think why He would send those things? See if you can find out as you read."

B. Pointer Questions

1. Why was Moses punished?
2. What was his punishment?
3. What happened on the mountain?

II. Reader

"What did the children of Israel do when they could not find water to drink? How had God given them water before? Was God giving them food? Had God kept them safe from their enemies? What do you think they should have done now in their need for water?

"Why did they think they would die?"

III. After You Read the Story

ANSWER KEY

Before You Read the Story

1. bit, bitten

2. anger

3. brass

4. hung

5. a. bit
   b. bitten
   c. hung
   d. brass
   e. Anger

6. a. bite   g. hang
   b. bit   h. hung
   c. bitten   i. found
   d. chosen   j. find
   e. chose
   f. choose

After You Read the Story

A. 1. water
   2. fault
   3. died, drink, do
      did, done, die
   4. together, animals
   5. faces
   6. rod
   7. rock
   8. water
   9. forty
   10. good, hard

B. a. 6
   b. 8 / 9
   c. 5
   d. 7

C. 1. grumbled (an X before)
   2. speak (circled)
   3. hit (first letter circled)
   4. water (underlined)
   5. Aaron (first letter under-
      lined)
   6. grumbled (an X after)
   7. snakes (line over)
   8. brass (last two letters circled)
   9. a pole (two lines under)
   10. look at (box around)

D. 1. Moses did not follow direc-
      tions because he was angry.
   2. Moses could not go into the
      good land.
   3. Aaron's son was the high
      priest.
   4. They had manna to eat.
   5. They were tired of eating
      manna.

E. Blessed is the man that walketh
   not in the counsel of the
   ungodly. Psalm 1:1

LESSON 4
Balaam Called

I. Before You Read the Story

A. Reading Incentive

"What did God do when the children of Israel grumbled about the food they had? Do you think God liked having bad things happen to His people? In our new story, someone wanted to bring trouble to the children of Israel. How do you think God felt about that? Find out who wanted to bring trouble on them and how he thought he was going to do it."

B. Pointer Questions

1. How was Balaam going to decide what to do?
2. What did the king promise Balaam?

II. Reader

Locate the land of Moab, where Israel was camping at this time.

"How did the king think it would help him to have Balaam curse Israel? [If he could get God to be against them, they could not be strong, and he could kill them.]

"Was it true that the children of Israel covered the earth? There were so many of them that when one was up on a hill where he could look out over the tents of the children of Israel it must have looked like there was no end to them.

"What did God say when Balaam asked to go? What does that tell us about the way God felt toward His people?

"How did Balaam tell his answer to the men? Does that give you an idea how he felt about it?

"What did Balaam think about the king's promises? Did you ever beg for something that you had been told you could not have? Sometimes people get that for which they beg, but they get into a lot of trouble because of it. We are much happier if we give up what we should not have, and be satisfied."

III. After You Read the Story

ANSWER KEY

Before You Read the Story

1. curse

2. anyway, tonight

3. a. Balaam
   b. Balaam

4. tonight

5. anyway

6. Balaam

7. curse

After You Read the Story

A. 1. yes   6. yes
   2. no   7. yes
   3. yes   8. yes
   4. no   9. yes
   5. no   10. no

B. 1. curse   5. Canaan
   2. bless   6. Egypt
   3. servants   7. probably
   4. donkey   8. tonight

C. 1. There were so many of them. (or) He had heard about the great things God had done for them.
   2. He was not supposed to curse them because they were blessed.
   3. He wanted the things the king promised to give.

D. 1. sin, therein
      king, thing
      cost, lost

2. God
3. the king
4. the king's
5. no

E. Blessed is the man that walketh not in the counsel of the ungodly. Psalm 1:1

EXTRA ACTIVITY

Print these letter combinations on the board and let the children rearrange the letters to make words found on the first page of the lesson in the reader.

1. a a a B l m (Balaam)
2. a a a C n n (Canaan)
3. a a d i r f (afraid)
4. r i c h l e n d (children)
5. s c r u e (curse)
6. c l e a l d (called)
7. s c u b e e a (because)
8. l e e p o p (people)

LESSON 5
The Donkey Talks

I. Before You Read the Story

A. Reading Incentive

"Where was Balaam going? Why? How was he traveling? Three times on the way this donkey did something strange. And then it did something that you never heard an animal do. What do you think it was? What would you do if an animal started talking to you? How could that happen?"

B. Pointer Questions

1. Who told Balaam why his donkey did those strange things?
2. What did Balaam do to Israel?

II. Reader

"Why do you think the angel told Balaam to go on? What kind of things did Balaam say about Israel? Do you think the king asked Balaam again to curse Israel? Do you think he might have asked Balaam again if he had gone back home after he saw the angel?"

III After You Read the Story

ANSWER KEY

Before You Read the Story

1. a. foot	2. a. acting	3. a. foot
b. narrow	b. further	b. crushed
c. flat	c. crushed	c. acting
d. further	d. ridden	d. imagine
e. crushed	e. imagine	e. further

4. a. rode
   b. ride
   c. ridden
   d. act
   e. acting
   f. acts

5. (Individual answers)

6. a. narrow
   b. flat
   c. foot
   d. further

After You Read the Story

A. 1. angel
   2. sword
   3. field
   4. hit
   5. wall

6. crushed
7. hit
8. fell down to the ground
9. stick
10. talked

B. 1. c
   2. c
   3. a
   4. b
   5. c
   6. a

C. 1. angry
   2. a. bowl
      b. perfume
   3. a. leave
      b. destroy
   4. clothes

LESSON 6
Moses Sees the Promised Land

I. Before You Read the Story

A. Reading Incentive

   "Do you like to get new shoes? Do you like to get new shirts or dresses? Sometimes you cannot wear the same clothes any more because you grow too big for them. Did you ever have to stop wearing something because it was worn out and could not be used any more? How long do you think your clothes would last if you could keep on wearing the same size? How long were the children of Israel traveling in the wilderness? What do you think they did about new clothes?"

B. Pointer Questions

   1. Who was to be the leader to go into the land of Canaan?
   2. What did Moses do before he died?
   3. What were the children of Israel to do in the land of Canaan?

II. Reader

   "Why do you think God chose Joshua to be the new leader for His people? What do you remember about Joshua from the other stories?"

   Locate Mt. Nebo on the workbook map.

III. After You Read the Story

ANSWER KEY

Before You Read the Story

1. a. valley
   b. disobeyed
   c. nobody

2. a. wear
   b. wear
   c. wear

Crossword Puzzle

Across

3. wear
4. disobeyed

Down

1. valley
2. nobody

After You Read the Story

A.
1. forty
2. clothes
3. Joshua
4. Moses
5. hit
6. ask
7. see
8. died
9. grave
10. strong

B.
1. b
2. d
3. c
4. a
5. g
6. e
7. f
8. h

C.
1. b
2. c
3. a
4. a
5. b

D. <u>He told them if they would obey God, God would be with them and help them.</u>

But if they would not obey God, God would make it hard for them.

E. Blessed is every one that feareth the LORD. Psalm 128:1

Gradebook: 37 points for the entire lesson counting one point for correctly printing the memory verse

EXTRA ACTIVITY

Have the children print several sentences describing what they imagine Moses could see from the mountain.

LESSON 7
The People Get Ready to Go Into the Good Land

I. Before You Read the Story

A. Reading Incentive

"What is the title of your story? Do you think the children of Israel were excited about going into the land? See what it says in the paragraph at the bottom of the first page. There must have been an eager hustle and bustle in camp those days.

"How soon were they going to enter the land? What did they have to do to get ready?"

B. Pointer Questions

1. What were the two men supposed to do in the land?
2. What did Rahab do for the men?

II. Reader

"Why did God tell Joshua that Moses was dead? Did Joshua not know that? Where did Moses die? Was anyone with him? Had Moses gone up on a mountain before this time? How long had he been gone when he came back again?

"What did God mean when He said, 'Every place you walk, that land will be yours'? [God was going to give them all the land wherever they went.]"

Locate Jericho on the workbook map.

"The two men were not to let the people of the land see them. Do you know of any who did? [Rahab and others who reported to the king.] What did the people do who saw them?

"What do you think it was like on the top of Rahab's house? Houses in those days had flat roofs. People could keep things on the top of the house, and they could go up there to do things like you might do things on the porch of your house. What did Rahab have on the roof of her house? Do you know what flax is? It is a plant that has long strands of fibers. People use it to make linen cloth. What did the men on the roof use her flax for?"

III. After You Read the Story

Workbook Exercises

The questions in Part B do not have answers stated in the reader. You may want to do them together unless you have discussed those questions in the story discussion.

ANSWER KEY

Before You Read the Story

1. Jordan

2. Jericho

3. 2, long, short, Rahab

4. within

5. a. Jordan
   b. Jericho
   c. Rahab

6. a. within
   b. Jericho
   c. Rahab
   d. Jordan

7. a. Caleb (All others are cities.)
   b. Jordan (All others are men.)
   c. Aaron (All others name women.)
   d. leader (All the others state position.)

After You Read the Story

A. 1. Jordan
   2. walk
   3. two
   4. Jericho
   5. house
   6. flax
   7. find

B. 1. a   4. b
   2. c   5. b
   3. b   6. c

C. 1. God 6. Joshua
2. God 7. Joshua
3. God 8. the king
4. Joshua 9. Rahab
5. all Israel 10. Rahab

D. a. 6
b. 3
c. 1
d. 4
e. 7

E. Blessed is every one that feareth the LORD. Psalm 128:1

EXTRA ACTIVITY

Give the children graph paper and let them try making a crossword arrangement with words from a given page in the reader.

LESSON 8
Rahab's Kindness

I. Before You Read the Story

A. Reading Incentive

"What was going on in the camp of Israel? [They were getting ready to enter Canaan.] Were all the people of Israel in camp getting ready? Where were two of the men? In what danger were they? How could they get away without being caught? What do you think the men could have been thinking as they hid in the flax on the roof? Could you think of a safe way for them to get back to their camp?"

B. Pointer Questions

1. What did Rahab say about the people of her land?
2. What were three things in the instructions to Rahab?
3. What news did the two men have for Joshua?

II. Reader

"What was all around the city of Jericho? How did people usually get in and out of the city? What would happen if these men went out the gate?

"What was so important about Rahab's rope? [That rope could make the difference between life or death.] How could it mean life for Rahab and her family? How could it bring death to them?"

III. After You Read the Story

ANSWER KEY

Before You Read the Story

1. a. rope
   b. rope

2. a. business
   b. business
   c. business

3. a. dried
   b. dried

4. (Individual work)

After You Read the Story

A.
1. yes
2. yes
3. yes
4. no
5. no
6. yes
7. no
8. no
9. yes
10. no
11. yes
12. no

B.
1. dried up
2. heaven, earth
3. father, mother, brothers, sisters
4. Rahab
5. Egypt
6. Red Sea
7. Lord, God
8. high, thick
9. two, three
10. (any two) let, get, seeing, told, go, hide, look
11. window
12. afraid
13. mountains

C. "I know that the Lord has given you this land."

D.
a. Put the rope in the window.
b. Stay in the house.
c. Keep quiet about the business.

E.
1. They would save her when they came into the land.
2. Rahab's house was on the wall.
3. The rope was red.
4. They hid until the men who were looking for them came back again.

F.
3   8
1   6
4   9
2   7
5

G. (A picture of a red rope in a window)

H. Blessed is every one that feareth the LORD. Psalm 128:1

I.
1. Lord
2. blessed

LESSON 9
Going Over Jordan

I. Before You Read the Story

A. Reading Incentive

Locate Israel's position on the workbook map.

"The children of Israel were almost in the land of Canaan. There was only a river between them and the land where they would live. All they had to do was cross the river and they would be there. How do you think they would get across? Would they build a bridge? Would they use boats? They had to carry all their tents and the tabernacle, and take all their animals somehow.

"What did God do at the Red Sea for His people to get across the water?

Do you remember what He told Moses to do before the waters went apart? [hold out his rod over the sea]

"Find out what the directions were for the people at the Jordan River and what happened."

B. Pointer Questions

1. Who was to go first?
2. Who was last to get across the river?
3. Why did God stop sending manna?

II. Reader

"Pretend that you are one of the people of Israel and a child came to you and asked why those twelve stones are piled near the river. How would you answer?

"Why should the people of Canaan be afraid of the great God? [They worshiped idols and God would punish them for it. And their idols could not help them.]

"What question did Joshua ask the man who met him? What was his answer? Did that mean he had come to help them fight, or was he their enemy?"

III. After You Read the Story

ANSWER KEY

Before You Read the Story

(Individual sentences)

Crossword Puzzle

Across	Down
3. enemy	1. heard
4. idols	2. valley
6. priests	5. dried
8. business	7. sword
9. promised	10. meant
11. captain	
12. whether	

After You Read the Story

A. 1. The priests
2. priests
3. stepped
4. dry ground
5. middle
6. twelve stones
7. fruit
8. idols
9. from God
10. shoe

B. 1. The waters parted when the priests' feet stepped into the water.
2. They came back when everyone was on the other side of the river.
3. God stopped sending manna soon after they were in the good land.
4. God's captain came to Joshua.

C. "When we came into this land, we came across the river here. God made the waters part and stand up, and we came across on dry ground."

D. 1. a. wisely
   b. wanted
   c. worshipful
   d. showed
   e. stopped
   f. served
2. fright (circled in verse 1)
3. (verse 2 circled)
4. (second line in verse 1 and last line in verse 3 underlined)

5. With worshipful fear.
6. Blessed is every one that feareth the LORD. Psalm 128:1

EXTRA PRACTICE

Draw a picture of the stones Israel set up for a memorial. The space at the end of the lesson could be used for this drawing.

LESSON 10
How Jericho Was Destroyed

I. Before You Read the Story

A. Reading Incentive

"What was right across the Jordan River when the children of Israel got there? [the city of Jericho] Do you remember what was all around the city? How do you think the children of Israel will go about it to destroy the city and the enemies in it? What kind of things do you think people would try when they want to break down a wall? What kind of directions did God give for them to do?"

B. Pointer Questions
1. Who was supposed to march around the city?
2. What did they do differently on the seventh day?
3. Who were the only people in Jericho who were not killed?

II. Reader

"Who besides the men of war would be going around the city? [priests] What were they to carry? Do you think you would have heard laughing, talking, and shouting as they went around the city if you had been there? What could you have heard? [tramping feet and trumpets]

"Does shouting make walls fall down? What made those walls fall down? [God did it to show His power. It was not the children of Israel that made them fall.]"

III. After You Read the Story

ANSWER KEY
Before You Read the Story

1. marched

2. shout

3. *marched*—mar, march, arch, (or) arched

   shout—out

4. shout

5. marched

After You Read the Story

A. *Numbers that should have X's:*
   1, 3, 5, 7, 9, 11

B. 1. a, c, e
   2. a, c, e
   3. a, c, e
   4. a, c, e
   5. a, c, e
   6. a, c, e
   7. b, c, d, e, f

C. 1. Rahab lived with the children of Israel.
   2. One man kept some gold and silver for himself.

D. a. day
   (Answers interchangeable for b-d)
   b. times
   c. priests
   d. trumpets

E. 1. Moses   7. Rahab
   2. Joshua   8. The priests
   3. God   9. God
   4. Joshua   10. Joshua
   5. Rahab   11. The priests
   6. Rahab   12. Rahab

F. 1. become
   2. look over secretly
   3. a. here
      b. where
   4. carrying
   5. go around

Gradebook: 64 points for all written work counting two points for each sentence in Part C

LESSON 11
Why Israel Lost a Battle

I. Before You Read the Story

A. Reading Incentive

"What wonderful thing had God done for the children of Israel? Was that all the enemies they would need to fight? No, there were many cities in the land with wicked people in them, whom God wanted Israel to destroy. So they would have many more battles to fight. Do you think they would need to be afraid? Remember the sentence from yesterday's lesson that said, 'God helped the children of Israel in wonderful ways when they obeyed Him.'

"Look at the title for the new story. Do you have any idea why they might have lost a battle? Do you know of anything in which they did not obey God? Find out what happened at the battle and why it went that way."

B. Pointer Questions

1. How many men went to fight Ai?
2. Why did God not help Israel?

II. Reader

"Had God brought them over the Jordan River to destroy them? What would it do to God's great Name if the enemies did destroy Israel? [The people of the land heard what a great God Israel had. Now if they could kill Israel, what would they say about God?]

"How had Achan troubled Israel? [Because he disobeyed, they had the trouble at Ai.]"

III. After You Read the Story

ANSWER KEY

Before You Read the Story

1. Achan, Ai, chased

2. battle

3. tore

4. Ai

5. Achan

6. a. chased
   b. tore
   c. battle

7. a. battle
   b. Ai
   c. chased
   d. Achan
   e. tore

8. a. tear
   b. tore
   c. torn
   d. stole
   e. stolen
   f. steal
   g. hid
   h. hide
   i. hidden
   j. taken
   k. took
   l. take

After You Read the Story

A. 1. small
   2. thousand
   3. Israel
   4. afraid
   5. earth
   6. gold and silver
   7. find
   8. stoned

B. 1. a   5. a
   2. c   6. a
   3. b   7. c
   4. a   8. a

C. (Everything should be underlined.)

D. 1. He got them at Jericho.
   2. They burned Achan's things.

E. 1. yes
   2. no
   3. no

F. Blessed are they that hear the word of God, and keep it. Luke 11:28

EXTRA ACTIVITY

Find and print all the words in the story that have capital letters but are not at the beginning of sentences.

Later discuss the lists the children have found and classify the words as people's names, words that refer to God, names of cities, a river, and a nation.

LESSON 12
God Helps Israel Fight Ai

I. Before You Read the Story

A. Reading Incentive

"What was the first city God gave Israel in the land of Canaan? What was the next city He wanted to give them? Why didn't they get that city? Was the sin taken care of? Could they depend on God's help again? What did God tell them to do to get Ai? Were they to march around the wall again? What were the directions?"

B. Pointer Questions

1. How many groups of men did Joshua make?
2. What sign did Joshua give his men who were hiding?

II. Reader

III. After You Read the Story

Workbook Exercises

You may want to discuss the new phrase exercise with the class (Part B).

For Part D do not confuse Joshua's instructions in paragraph 2 with the action of the story.

ANSWER KEY

Before you Read the Story

1. ing

2. running, winning

3. chasing, hiding

4. run, win

    chase, hide

5. (Individual sentences)

6. spear

Crossword Puzzle

Across	Down
1. spear	2. running
3. chasing	4. hiding
5. winning	

After You Read the Story

A. 1. all
   2. people
   3. themselves
   4. two
   5. behind
   6. gates
   7. pretended
   8. spear
   9. city
   10. read

B. 1. to the city
   2. toward Ai
   4. not very far away
   6. after them
   7. behind them
   8. away from their enemies
   9. away from them
   12. in front of them
   14. out of the city
   17. behind the city

C. 3	6	9	D. a. 4
1	8	10	b. 5
2	5	12	c. 3
4	7	11	d. 6

E. Blessed are they that hear the word of God, and keep it. Luke 11:28

LESSON 13
Tricky People Trick Israel

Be Prepared

Bring a piece of animal skin such as a chamois, or gloves made from some kind of skin.

I. Before You Read the Story

A. Reading Incentive

"So far Israel took two cities in the new land. Which cities were they? The people in the other cities saw what God was doing for Israel, and they were afraid. Would they be the next ones to be killed? There was a town named Gibeon not far away from where Israel was, and the people in Gibeon were afraid. [Locate Gibeon on the workbook map.] They decided to do something so that Israel would not kill them. Can you think of a plan that might have worked for them? What did they decide to do?"

B. Pointer Questions

1. What did the men of Gibeon do to make it look like they came a long way?
2. What did Joshua promise them?
3. What work did the Gibeonites have to do for Israel?

II. Reader

"Why did the men of Gibeon want Israel to think they came from far-away? [Israel knew they were supposed to kill everybody in the land.]

"What was the answer the Gibeonites gave to each of Israel's questions? Which question did they not answer? [Who are you?]

"How can bottles tear? [Discuss the type of bottles described in the workbook, and show the children a piece of animal skin, such as a chamois.]

"Was there any way they could have kept from being tricked? [God knew what was going on. If they had asked God, He would have told them what to do.]"

III. After You Read the Story

Workbook Exercises

The answers to exercise B are not directly stated in the reader. You may want to be sure that class discussion covers those thoughts.

ANSWER KEY

Before You Read the Story

1. cracked, crack
   patched, patch

2. moldy, mold
   tricky, trick

3. join

4. message

5. Gibeon

6. a. split
   b. patched
   c. cracked
   d. moldy
   e. Gibeon
   f. message
   g. tricky
   h. journey
   i. join

After You Read the Story

A. *Numbers that should have X's:*
   1, 2, 5, 6, 7

B. 1. a
   2. c
   3. b
   4. c
   5. a

C. 1. Now let us join you.
   2. We will be your servants.
   3. He promised that he would
      never kill them.

D. 1. Gibeon, Jericho, Ai
   2. bread
   3. plan
   4. message
   5. a. far
      b. old
      c. old / cracked / patched
      d. old
      e. old
      f. dry / moldy
   6. a. heard
      b. things
      c. join
      d. bread
      e. long
      f. they
   7. a. later
      b. close
      c. town
      d. servants
   8. a. living
      b. right
      c. careful
      d. more

E. (The fourth pictures should be circled.)

F. Blessed are they that hear the word of God, and keep it. Luke 11:28

LESSON 14
Israel Helps Gibeon

I. Before You Read the Story

A. Reading Incentive

"Do you think there were more cities and kings in the land of Canaan for Israel to overcome? There were many, many more! These other kings heard the news about Jericho and Ai too. And now one of the kings heard how the people of Gibeon went and joined with Israel. Now Israel would have more help and be even stronger. This king was very much afraid. What plan do you think he had? Did his plans work out? What interesting things did God do in the battle?"

B. Pointer Questions

1. How many kings got together to fight Gibeon?
2. How did Joshua's men trap the kings?

II. Reader

"Why do you think the kings decided to fight Gibeon instead of fighting Israel? They probably knew Israel's God was too great for them to fight. If they could destroy Gibeon, they would keep Israel from being quite so strong.

"Why could they not finish fighting if the sun went down? [They would not be able to fight in the dark.]"

Point out the five circles on the workbook map as the cities of the five kings who attacked Gibeon. "There were five cities that Israel did not need to attack one at a time as they had the other cities. These kings and their armies came to fight and were all beaten at once.

"What are some of the other good things you think God may have been doing for His people? [He made their crops grow. He gave them good health. He made them rich with animals. He kept their enemies from bothering them.]"

III. After You Read the Story

Workbook Exercises

You may want to discuss homophones and do some of the items in exercise D with the class.

ANSWER KEY

Before You Read the Story

1. a. Gibeonites
   b. settled
   c. cave
   d. fought
   e. hailstones

2. hailstones

3. a. fought
   b. fight
   c. fought

4. a. fought
   b. settled

c. cave
d. Gibeonites
e. hailstones

Acrostic Puzzle

1. hailstones
2. fought
3. Gibeonites
4. settled
5. cave

After You Read the Story

A. 1. five   3. hailstones
   2. Joshua   4. in a cave

B. 1. they had joined themselves to Israel.
2. The hailstones killed most of them.
3. He asked God to let the sun and moon stand still.
4. They put big stones at the mouth of the cave.

C. 1. c
2. e
3. a
4. d
5. b
6. f

D. 1. four
2. knew
3. been
4. whole
5. there
6. to

E. 1. in the cities
4. against Gibeon
5. out of heaven
8. by the cave
10. away from them
12. in a cave
13. upon them
15. at the mouth
16. out of the cave
18. in this new land

F. 1. land
2. fight
3. more
4. done
5. praise

G. Blessed are they that hear the word of God, and keep it. Luke 11:28

LESSON 15
Living in the New Land

I. Before You Read the Story

A. Reading Incentive
"The children of Israel settled in their new land in an orderly way. They divided the land into sections and gave the sections to the different tribes. But one tribe did not get any land. Why did they not get any? What was special about them? What were they supposed to do? Where would they live?"

B. Pointer Questions
1. What was the special work of the Levites?
2. Why do you think Joshua wanted to talk to the older men and leaders?

II. Reader
"How many sons did Jacob have?" Print the names of the twelve sons on the board.

1. Reuben
2. Simeon
3. Levi
4. Judah
5. Dan
6. Naphtali
7. Gad
8. Asher
9. Issachar
10. Zebulun
11. Joseph
12. Benjamin

"Israel divided the land of Canaan into twelve sections. What did they call the family group of each of Jacob's sons? Instead of Joseph being the leader of a tribe, each of his sons was the leader of a tribe. That made two tribes in Joseph's family. How many tribes were there then? [Erase Joseph's name in the list and print Ephraim and Manasseh in its place.] That makes thirteen tribes and only twelve sections of land. Which tribe would not get any land?

"What does one of the Ten Commandments say about killing? [God's law was that if someone killed another person, he would have to die.] What if someone happened to kill a person by accident? Where could he run to be safe? *Refuge* means 'safety.' He would not need to die for his accident. Could he ever come out of that city and live in his own home again? [yes, after the high priest died]"

III. After You Read the Story

Workbook Exercises

Part E does not directly relate to this lesson story but reviews word meanings taught in workbook Lessons 5 and 10. Let the children turn back for help.

ANSWER KEY

Before You Read the Story

1. Levites
2. certain
3. remained
4. refuge
5. courage
6. separate
7. amount
8. according
9. a. certain
   b. amount
   c. Levites
   d. refuge
   e. courage
   f. separate
   g. according
   h. remained

After You Read the Story

A. 1. Levi
2. drive out
3. tribe
4. cities
5. happened to kill
6. until the high priest died

B. *Numbers that should have X's:*
2, 3, 5, 7, 8

C. 1. b
2. b
3. a
4. b
5. c

D.		
1. no		7. yes
2. no		8. yes
3. yes		9. no
4. no		10. yes
5. no		11. no
6. no		12. yes

E. 1. e   7. h
2. d   8. l
3. b   9. j
4. f   10. g
5. c   11. i
6. a   12. k

Gradebook: 59 points for all written work

LESSON 16
After the Death of Joshua

I. Before You Read the Story

A. Reading Incentive

"You will read about a very strange punishment in this lesson. What was the punishment, and why was the person punished this way?"

B. Pointer Questions

1. What helped Israel to keep on obeying God after Joshua died?
2. What happened when Israel did not obey God?
3. When did God help Israel?

II. Reader

"Where was Joseph when he died?

"Why did Israel start to worship gods and idols? [They were letting their enemies who did not love God live with them.]"

III. After You Read the Story

Workbook Exercises

Discuss phrases that tell *when.* You may want to do exercise B in the workbook orally before the children do the lesson.

ANSWER KEY

Before You Read the Story

1. a. deserve
   b. thumbs
   c. deserve
   d. toes, thumbs
2. a. thumbs, toes
   b. table
3. a. table
   b. thumbs, toes
   c. deserve

Acrostic Puzzle

1. thumbs
2. table
3. deserve

After You Read the Story

A. one hundred ten
    forty, one, seventy

B. 1. when he was one hundred ten years old
3. all the time that Joshua lived
5. a while after Joshua died
8. all the time they were in the wilderness
9. for forty years
10. after this
13. when they cried to the Lord for help

C. 1. Joshua was one hundred ten years old.
2. They carried Joseph's bones.
3. They cut off his thumbs and his big toes.
4. He had done that to other people.
5. Israel began to worship gods and idols.

D.
1. sad
2. enemies
3. live
4. gods / idols
5. hard
6. destroy
7. follow
8. cried

E. *The words in bold print should be circled.*

A **nation is** a group of people who live in **the** same land and have **the** same ruler. Israel was a **nation**. When they served **the Lord**, **God blessed** their **nation**.

Israel was not **the** only **nation** in Canaan. Every **nation** that had another **god*** instead of **the Lord**, was their enemy. Those nations were not **blessed**, because **God** helped Israel to drive them out.

Sometimes **the nation** of Israel stopped serving **the Lord**. In these times they were not **blessed**, but **God** made things hard for them.

*(You may want to accept the word *god* as correct uncircled.)

F. Blessed is the nation whose God is the LORD. Psalm 33:12

EXTRA ACTIVITY
"Print sentences to tell what you imagine the enemies did to make life hard for Israel."

LESSON 17
Ehud Helps Israel

I. Before You Read the Story

A. Reading Incentive
"Did you ever have a secret to tell someone? Someone in our story had a secret. Neither you nor I ever had a secret like that one. It was a very dangerous secret. It began when Israel was having a hard time and they called to God for help. See if you can figure out what the secret was."

B. Pointer Questions
1. Who was a left-handed man?
2. Who was a fat man?
3. Why did no one catch Ehud when he killed their king?

II. Reader

"Where did King Eglon live? [Locate Moab on the workbook map.] Do you know what another king from Moab did once before? [It was a king of Moab who wanted Balaam to curse Israel.]

"Why did God help Moab instead of helping Israel? [Israel had sinned and God made their enemies strong to punish them.]

"Why do you think Ehud took a dagger and a present? [He wanted to kill the king, but he wanted the king to think he was friendly.]

"What do you think Ehud's message was? [He did not say words, but his actions meant, "God wants you to die." God had helped Eglon to be strong at one time, but Eglon did not worship God, and he needed to be punished too.]"

Avoid dwelling on the details of the killing or emphasizing the horror of it. If a sensitive child seems to be upset by it, explain that God allowed and directed such things in the Old Testament to punish the wicked.

III. After You Read the Story

Workbook Exercises

Part B again includes inference questions.

A clue for number 2 in Part C is that the rhyming words appear in the paragraph in the order given in the exercise.

ANSWER KEY

Before You Read the Story

1. Eglon, Ehud, Moab
   a. Ehud
   b. Eglon
   c. Moab

2. key, locked, unlocked

3. eighteen

4. left-handed

5. unlocked

6. stuck

7. a. left-handed
   b. locked
   c. unlocked, key
   d. Ehud, Eglon
   e. secret
   f. eighteen
   g. stuck
   h. Moab
   i. seat
   j. dagger

After You Read the Story

A. 1. left-handed (line through)
   2. fat (circled)
   3. eighteen (an X after)
   4. present (underlined)
   5. secret (two X's before)
   6. dagger (box around)
   7. Ehud (two lines under)
   8. servants (line above)

B. 1. c
   2. b
   3. a
   4. b
   5. b

C. 1. a. present
    b. king
    c. tell
    d. secret
    e. men
  2. a. while
    b. king
    c. far
    d. went

    e. back
    f. told
    g. was
    h. they
    i. long
    j. time
  3. Israel (circled), Moab

D. Blessed is the nation whose God is the LORD. Psalm 33:12

LESSON 18
How a Woman Helped

I. Before You Read the Story

A. Reading Incentive

"What did Ehud do for the children of Israel? What did he do after he killed King Eglon? [He was the leader in Israel for a long time.] What happened after Ehud died? When Israel cried to God for help, God always was ready to help them. One time God chose to use a woman to help them. Your story tells about two women. Find out what they did to help."

B. Pointer Questions
1. Whom did God show what Israel should do?
2. On what condition would Barak go to battle?

II. Reader

Point out Hazor on the workbook map and tell the children that is where the king lived whose captain fought Israel and died in Jael's tent. The captain lived at Harosheth, and Israel gathered to battle on Mount Tabor.

Again, avoid dwelling on the visualization of the violence in the story.

III. After You Read the Story

Workbook Exercises

The last two questions in exercise C are of a general nature. Discuss them with the children and relate them to the Bible memory verse.

Encourage the children to use a different word for each answer in the acrostic puzzle.

ANSWER KEY

Before You Read the Story

1. army, hammer, thirsty (accept *iron* also)

2. milk, nail, nine

3. Barak, Jael

4. a. thirsty, milk
   b. Barak, Jael
   c. army
   d. nine, iron
   e. pounded, hammer

Acrostic Puzzle

1. ha *M* mer

2. po *U* nded

3. *N* ail (or) *N* ine

4. *T* hirsty

5. J *A* el (or) n *A* il

6. *B* arak

7. ir *O* n

8. a *R* my (or) i *R* on

After You Read the Story

A. 1. Israel
   2. Israel's enemies
   3. a woman
   4. Barak
   5. the captain
   6. Jael / a woman
   7. God
   8. the captain
   9. Barak
   10. Jael / a woman

B. 2   5   12   15
     1   6   10   16
     4   7   9   14
     3   8   11   13

C. 1. Barak gathered ten thousand men.
   2. They had nine hundred chariots of iron.
   3. They got along well for forty years.
   4. God let their enemies rule over them.
   5. God helped them to overcome their enemies.

D. Blessed is the nation whose God is the LORD. Psalm 33:12

Gradebook: 57 points for the entire lesson counting two points for each sentence in Part C and only one for the memory verse

EXTRA ACTIVITY

Let the children look in Judges 4 and see if they can find out the name of the woman of Israel who told Barak what to do.

LESSON 19
An Angel Speaks to Gideon

I. Before You Read the Story

A. Reading Incentive

"Where do you live? [in a house] In this story the people of Israel lived in some unusual places. Find out where they were living and why they lived in such places."

B. Pointer Questions

1. What did the angel call Gideon?
2. What did Gibeon fix for the angel?
3. What did the angel do with it?

II. Reader

"Who were the Midianites? Do you know where the land of Midian was? [You may want to show a copy of the workbook map for Unit 2.] Do you remember anything else about the land of Midian? [Moses went there and his wife was a Midianite.]

"Why was Gideon trying to hide his wheat from the Midianites? [They would take it away.]

"How did Gideon know the man was an angel? [A man could not make fire come out of a rock, or disappear the way the angel did.]"

III. After You Read the Story

Workbook Exercises

Discuss the phrase exercise in Part D and do a few samples in class.

ANSWER KEY

Before You Read the Story

1. a. *Gideon*, Gideon
   b. nation, Midianites
   c. Threshing, wheat
   d. staff
   e. Broth
   f. dens

2. a. cakes
   b. dens
   c. Gideon / nation
   d. meal
   e. Midianites
   f. threshing
   g. wheat

3. a. meal
   b. broth
   c. cakes
   d. job
   e. pour
   f. Midianites
   g. Gideon
   h. threshing, wheat
   i. staff
   j. nation
   k. dens

4. a. bread (The others are liquid.)
   b. sleep (The others are done with liquid.)
   c. Eglon (The others were Israelites.)
   d. meal (The others are sticks.)
   e. cakes (The others are openings.)
   f. nation (The others name nations.)

After You Read the Story

A. 1. b
   2. d
   3. e
   4. a
   5. c

B. 1. Israel began worshiping idols again.
   2. He let a wicked nation rule over them.
   3. He was threshing wheat.
   4. The food was burned up.

C. 1. Gideon
   2. the angel
   3. the angel
   4. Gideon
   5. Gideon
   6. the angel
   7. the angel

D. grave, fight

E.
1. when
2. when
3. where
4. when
5. where
6. where
7. where
8. when
9. where
10. where
11. when
12. where

F. Blessed is the nation whose God

is the LORD. Psalm 33:12

EXTRA ACTIVITIES
1. Have the children number in order of the story the quotations given in exercise C.
2. Let the children build crossword arrangements with the new words on graph paper.

LESSON 20
Gideon Destroys Idols

I. Before You Read the Story

A. Reading Incentive

"Who was the man to whom an angel came and talked? What was God planning for that man to do? Do you know the reason the Midianites were making trouble for Israel? [They worshiped idols, and God let this happen to punish them.] What do you think Gideon's first job was to save Israel? Was it to kill the Midianites?"

B. Pointer Questions

1. Did Gideon do the work by himself?
2. What did Gideon do to be sure God would help him?

II. Reader

"An altar was usually a big thing made of stone. How could Gideon throw down the altar of Baal? [by using the ox] An ox is a strong animal. Gideon could hitch the ox to the altar and let the animal pull it over. What else was he supposed to do with the ox?

"Why did the men of the city think Gideon should die? [They probably worshiped Baal, and they did not like to have someone do such things against their god.] Was Baal angry with Gideon? [No, because Baal was just an idol, and idols cannot talk or think or even know what happens to them.]

"Why did Gideon do these things before he went to fight the Midianites? [God wanted Israel to get rid of their idols and worship Him so He could help them.]"

Locate the Valley of Jezreel on the workbook map as the place where the Midianite army camped.

III. After You Read the Story

Workbook Exercises

Have the children read the directions, then tell you what they understand that they are to do especially for Parts A and B.

ANSWER KEY

Before You Read the Story

1. floor
2. Baal
3. wet, dew
4. bowl
5. satisfied
6. grove
7. fleece
8. Wool
9. ox

Crossword Puzzle

Across	Down
4. satisfied	1. Baal
5. wet	2. dew
6. fleece	3. bowl
7. wool	6. floor
9. grove	8. ox

After You Read the Story

A. 1. (b) because God did not want His people to worship idols
   2. (f) because they were afraid to have other people see them do it
   3. (a) because he cut down the grove and threw down the altar of Baal

4. (c) because Baal could not talk
5. (e) because he wanted to be very sure God would help him
6. (d) because he still was not satisfied and wanted to be sure once more

B.
1. G	7. E
2. E	8. G
3. B	9. G
4. E	10. B
5. G	11. E
6. B	12. G

C. *Underline:* Midian, Egypt, Israel, Moab
Circle: Israel

D. 1. short sword
2. fastened
3. clothes
4. the upper part of the leg

EXTRA ACTIVITY

Have the children find words in Part C to print under the headings *Kings, Women, Men of Israel.*

LESSON 21
A Strange Dream

Be Prepared

As a visual aid to Gideon's numbers mark 320 strokes on the blackboard. Put 20 strokes in each row, and make a column of 16 rows. Each stroke represents 100 men.

I. Before You Read the Story

A. Reading Incentive

"Who would help Gideon and his men to win the battle against the Midianites? What did God do in the last lesson to help Gideon to trust Him for His help? In this lesson God does some more things to help Gideon to completely trust Him. For one thing, God told Gideon to send most of his men home and not to have them help in the battle. Why do you think He did that? How could they win the war without a lot of people to fight? The only way would be for God to help them in a special way. Gideon would not go to battle like that unless he really did believe that God was going to help them. Find out what else God did to help Gideon to not be afraid."

B. Pointer Questions

1. Which men were supposed to leave Gideon's army?
2. What did a Midianite man dream?

II. Reader

Refer to the marks on the board and explain that every mark stands for 100 men to show how many men were ready to help Gideon with the battle.

Erase or cross out the first mark and say, "One hundred men were afraid, so they left. One hundred more men were afraid and left. [Remove the next mark.] Then one hundred more left, and more, and more, and more! [Remove eleven rows of strokes and emphasize that each stroke represents 100 men.] How many men were left?

"How many of the men lapped with their tongues to drink water? [Circle three strokes on the board.] Each stroke stands for 100 men so this would be 300 men. All the other men got down on their knees to drink, and those are the ones Gideon told to go home. [Cross out or erase the rest of the row and the four remaining rows.] Three hundred men would seem like a large crowd to us, but it was not very many at all compared with what Gideon had in the beginning, and it would not seem like nearly enough to fight the great army of the Midianites.

"What do you think the little bun in the dream stood for? [Gideon's little army] What do you think the big tent stood for? [the big Midianite army] What was the meaning of the little bun knocking over the big tent?"

III. After You Read the Story

Workbook Exercises

The first question in exercise A will be answered by arithmetic or by elimination of the other answers.

ANSWER KEY

Before You Read the Story

1. bun, won

2. knees, knock

3. counted, count
   knees, knee
   lapped, lap
   lapping, lap

4. twenty-two

5. (Picture of a dog)

6. a. knees
   b. knock
   c. bun
   d. counted
   e. Twenty-two
   f. won
   g. dog

7. a. lapping
   b. lap
   c. lapped
   d. lapped

After You Read the Story

A. 1. thirty-two thousand
   2. twenty-two thousand
   3. ten thousand
   4. three hundred

B. A cake of barley bread rolled down into the camp. It came to a tent, and the tent fell over.

C. Even though there were only three hundred men in Gideon's army, yet God was going to destroy the big army of the Midianites.

D. 1. c   7. j
   2. d   8. k
   3. e   9. i
   4. b   10. g
   5. f   11. h
   6. a

E. 1. e   6. i
   2. d   7. g
   3. b   8. j
   4. a   9. h
   5. c   10. f

F. Blessed is that man that maketh the LORD his trust. Psalm 40:4

EXTRA ACTIVITY

Print these numbers on the board. Have the children copy them and print number words from the story to match each one.

22,000   10,000   300   1

LESSON 22
God Helps Israel

I. Before You Read the Story

A. Reading Incentive

"It was nighttime when Gideon told his men to get up to go to the battle. How do you think 300 men would go about fighting the thousands of the Midianites in the night? Gideon gave three things to each of his men. Find out what each man had and what they did with them."

B. Pointer Questions

1. What did the men of Ephraim do to help?
2. Why did Gideon ask for bread along the way?

II. Reader

"Where were the lamps the men held? Could you see a lamp inside an earthen pitcher? What would have happened when all the pitchers were broken? [The lamps would have shone out all around the Midianite camp.]

"How do you think Gideon and his men could catch the kings they were chasing if his men were tired and hungry? [God gave special help. Gideon said to some men, "After God gives us the kings . . ."]

"What time of day did all these things happen? [They happened at night-time, because Gideon started back before the sun was up.]"

III. After You Read the Story

ANSWER KEY

Before You Read the Story

1. a. fifteen
   b. lamp
   c. pitcher
   d. scared

2. a. lamp
   b. flesh
   c. pitcher
   d. Ephraim

3. fifteen

4. scared

5. tear

6. a. fifteen
   b. lamp
   c. tear
   d. pitcher
   e. Ephraim
   f. scared
   g. Flesh

Acrostic Puzzle

1. *P* itcher
2. fles *H*
3. tea *R*
4. sc *A* red
5. f *I* fteen (or) p *I* tcher
6. la *M* p

After You Read the Story

A. 1. three

2. trumpet, pitcher, lamp
3. Ephraim
4. two
5. tired, hungry
6. eat
7. tear, thorns

B. 1. They were not pleased that Gideon had not called them to come and help sooner.
2. Gideon told them that what they did was even greater than what he did because they had killed two great men.
3. The men who were with him were tired and hungry.
4. He told his oldest son to kill them, but he was afraid to do it because he was still a boy.

C. lamp, pitcher, trumpet, (pictures for pitcher and trumpet)

D. 1. two   6. eat
   2. kings   7. give
   3. men   8. thorns
   4. were   9. place
   5. bread   10. break

E. Blessed is that man that maketh the LORD his trust. Psalm 40:4

Gradebook: 55 points for the entire lesson counting only one point for each sentence in Part B

EXTRA ACTIVITY
Have the children print all the phrases they can find in the story beginning with *of*. Sometimes there will need to be only one word after *of*, sometimes there will be several. See if the children recognize the noun that ends the phrase.

LESSON 23
Abimelech and Jephthah

I. Before You Read the Story

A. Reading Incentive
"How many children do your parents have? How many children do you think Gideon had? He had a very big family. Your story will tell you how many children he had and what happened to most of them."

B. Pointer Questions
1. Which of Gideon's sons wanted to be the ruler?
2. How did God punish Abimelech?
3. What did Jephthah promise to God?

II. Reader
"Why did Abimelech kill his brothers? [He wanted to make sure they would not be rulers instead of him.]

"Did anybody want Abimelech for a king? [Yes, some men got together and made him king.]"

III. After You Read the Story

Workbook Exercises
You may want to make sure that the children understand the directions for exercise B.

Exercise C includes some inference questions.

ANSWER KEY

Before You Read the Story
1. Abimelech
2. Jephthah
3. k
4. f

After You Read the Story
A.
1. Jephthah   8. Abimelech
2. Abimelech   9. Abimelech
3. Jephthah   10. Jephthah
4. Abimelech 11. Jephthah
5. Abimelech
6. Jephthah
7. Jephthah

B. 1. d
   2. a
   3. c
   4. b

5. f
6. g
7. e
8. h

C. 1. c
   2. c
   3. a
   4. a
   5. b

D. 3
   1
   5
   2
   4
   6

E. 1. seventy
   2. youngest
   3. strong
   4. big
   5. young
   6. wicked
   7. badly
   8. burnt
   9. poor
  10. only

F. Blessed is that man that maketh the LORD his trust. Psalm 40:4

LESSON 24
A Son Promised

I. Before You Read the Story

A. Reading Incentive

"How many children did Gideon have? How many children did Jephthah have? Today we will read about another man and his wife. Would you like to guess how many children they had? You will find out when you read the story."

B. Pointer Questions

1. How long did Israel serve the Philistines?
2. What instructions did the angel give the woman?

II. Reader

"What was one wonderful thing the man and woman saw the angel do? [He went up to heaven in the flame of fire.] Why were they afraid? [They knew that no one can see God and live because He is so holy. They were probably afraid that the angel was so holy that something would happen to them because they had seen him.]"

Locate Zorah on the map as the home of Samson's parents.

III. After You Read the Story

ANSWER KEY

Before You Read the Story

2. a. Philistines
   b. flame

3. a. years (The rest name people.)
   b. angel (The rest are human.)
   c. Abimelech (The rest are nations.)
   d. children (The rest are singular.)
   e. heaven (The rest are verbs.)
   f. secret (The rest are verbs.)

After You Read the Story

A. 1. forty   6. kid
     2. children   7. his name
     3. son   8. flame
     4. hair   9. fell
     5. field   10. much afraid

B. 1. woman   4. angel
     2. man   5. man
     3. woman   6. angel

C. *Possible sentence:* The man and his wife offered the kid as an offering to the Lord, and the angel did some wonderful things.

D. 1. They had to serve the Philistines because they sinned.
2. He would start to help Israel so they would not need to serve the Philistines.
3. He wanted him to teach them what to do to the child.
4. The angel said his name was a secret.

E. 4   8   10
    3   5   9
    2   7   12
    1   6   11

F. Blessed is that man that maketh the LORD his trust. Psalm 40:4

EXTRA ACTIVITY

Have the children print numbers after the quotations in exercise B to show the order in which they appear in the story.

LESSON 25
Samson, a Strong Man

I. Before You Read the Story

A. Reading Incentive

"What was the angel's message to the woman that did not have any children? What did he say her son would begin to do? Would you expect that son to make friends with the Philistines? Would you expect him to marry a Philistine woman? What happens when he does?"

B. Pointer Questions

1. What did the man and his wife name the baby God gave them?
2. Whom did Samson's parents think he should marry?
3. What secret did Samson have?

II. Reader

III. After You Read the Story

Workbook Exercises

Make sure the children understand the directions for Part B.

ANSWER KEY

Before You Read the Story

1. a. Samson
   b. lion
   c. bees

2. roared

3. bees, roared

4. a. Samson
   b. bees
   c. roared
   d. lion / Samson

5. a. Samson
   b. lion, roared
   c. bees

6. (Individual work)

After You Read the Story

A. 1. son
   2. angel
   3. man
   4. swarm
   5. offering
   6. name
      Samson, Sam, son

B. 1. yet
   2. quiet
   3. take in your hands
   4. keep the same
   5. the same
   6. fair
   7. at the same time
   8. opposite of left
   9. opposite of wrong
   10. still there
   11. opposite of right
   12. went away

C. 1. promise
   2. a. every year
      b. cry
   3. a. be careful
      b. do
   4. dead body

D. 1. no   6. no
   2. no   7. yes
   3. no   8. yes
   4. no   9. yes
   5. no   10. no

LESSON 26
Samson's Riddle

I. Before You Read the Story

A. Reading Incentive

"Samson was begging his parents for what? Why did they not want him to marry the Philistine woman? He went ahead and married her anyway. Think about what he did. He went against what his parents said. He married someone who did not love God. In the end do you think he will be glad or sad?

"Samson made a great feast for his wedding. At the feast he asked a hard riddle. This was his riddle: 'Out of the eater came forth meat, and out of the strong came forth sweetness.' Do you think you know what he might have been talking about? You can find out when you read the story."

B. Pointer Questions
1. What would Samson give his friends if they guessed his riddle?
2. How did the men get the answer?

II. Reader
"What two words in the riddle mean the lion? [*eater* and *strong*] What two words in the riddle mean the honey? [*meat* and *sweetness*] In those days, the word *meat* meant anything to eat, not only animal flesh."

III. After You Read the Story

ANSWER KEY

Before You Read the Story

1. a. begging
   b. sweetness
   c. riddle
   d. eater

2. a. eater
   b. sweetness
   c. clothing
   d. begging
   e. riddle

C.
1. where	7. where
2. when	8. where
3. where	9. when
4. where	10. when
5. when	11. when
6. when	12. where

D. 1. meat
2. honey
3. wife
4. fire

E. 2
5
4
1
3

Crossword Puzzle

Across
4. sweetness
5. begging

Down
1. riddle
2. clothing
3. eater

After You Read the Story

A. *Answers may vary unless they are specified to come from the reader.*
1. sweet
2. hard
3. great
4. last
5. young
6. strong

B. 1. feast
2. thirty
3. riddle
4. seven
5. clothing
6. lion, honey
7. wife
8. burn
9. cried
10. people

F. *Words in bold print should be circled.*

Mercy is kindness to someone who does not deserve kindness. **Merciful** people show kindness and **mercy** to others. That makes others like them, and **they obtain mercy** from others. That means **they** get **mercy** shown to themselves.

G. Blessed are the merciful: for they shall obtain mercy. Matthew 5:7

Gradebook: 60 points for the entire lesson

LESSON 27
How Samson Treated the Philistines

I. Before You Read the Story

A. Reading Incentive

"What was going on when Samson asked some men a riddle? [marriage feast] What did Samson say he would give the men if they answered his riddle? What would the men have to give Samson if they could not guess the riddle? Who will have to give the clothes? Where do you think Samson would get clothes for thirty men? Would his mother make them? Would he buy them?"

B. Pointer Questions
1. What happened to Samson's wife?
2. What did Samson do with 300 foxes?

II. Reader

"Whose house did the Philistines burn? Why do you think they would do something mean to one of their own people? [This man had made Samson angry by giving Samson's wife to someone else. If they punished him, maybe Samson would be satisfied and not do more mean things to them.] Was Samson satisfied after his wife's father was punished? Was Samson merciful to the Philistines? Do you think the Philistines will be merciful to Samson?"

III. After You Read the Story

Workbook Exercises

The questions in Part C are inference questions. Be sure to cover those points in discussion before expecting the children to produce answers.

ANSWER KEY

Before You Read the Story

1. foxes

2. prettier

3. tied

4. a. pretty
   b. prettier
   c. prettiest

d. tie
e. tied
f. foxes
g. fox

5. a. holes
   b. meat

After You Read the Story

A. 1. yes   6. no
2. yes   7. yes
3. no   8. yes
4. yes   9. no
5. no   10. no

B. 1. b
2. c
3. d
4. a

C. 1. Samson burned their crops because he could not have the wife he wanted.
2. They did it to punish him for making Samson angry.

D. a. 1   g. 4
b. 4   h. 4
c. 1   i. 1
d. 6   j. 2
e. 2
f. 2

E. 1. angry   5. hated
2. wife   6. younger
3. off   7. sister
4. father   8. after

F. Blessed are the merciful: for they shall obtain mercy. Matthew 5:7

LESSON 28
How God Helped Samson

I. Before You Read the Story

A. Reading Incentive

"Do you remember the things that happened between Samson and the Philistines up to this time? Where did the mean things start? [with the riddle] What did Samson do because he was angry about the way the Philistines got the answer to his riddle? [He killed thirty men and left his wife.] Then what did his wife's father do that was not nice? What did Samson do because he was angry that he could not have his wife? What did the Philistines do next? [They burned her father's house.] Then Samson did something else mean. What was it? [He killed many more Philistines.]

By this time each side thinks that the other has done more bad things to them than they have done. In our new lesson the fight goes on. As you read how it goes back and forth, think about what the angel said Samson would begin to do. What was it? [to deliver Israel from the Philistines]"

B. Pointer Questions

1. What two things did Samson do with a bone?
2. Why did the Philistines shout?

II. Reader

"What did the Philistines say when Israel asked what they want? What did Samson say when the men of Israel asked what he had done? Does that sound like something you ever heard? When people think about what happened to them and they want to get even with somebody, the fight just keeps going back and forth and getting worse and worse. It does not help anything if you want to do something mean to someone because they were mean to you. What happens instead when you are merciful to people who are not nice? [They usually start to be merciful to you too. You obtain mercy.]

"Why would it be a victory for the Philistines if Samson died of thirst? [They would be glad Samson was dead even if they did not kill him.]"

III. After You Read the Story

Workbook Exercises

Discuss exercise A with the children to be sure they understand where to get their answers. The first two questions have the answer choices underlined in the questions. If the children have trouble, you could direct them to find the *or* in the question and underline a choice on either side of the *or*, to find the possible answers.

You may want to have oral discussion on the questions in exercise D.

ANSWER KEY

Before You Read the Story

1. a. tie
   b. ruling
   c. hollow
   d. afterward
   e. strength
   f. victory

2. a. tie
   b. hollow
   c. strength
   d. afterward
   e. victory

3. a. ruled
   b. rules
   c. ruler
   d. rule
   e. ruling

After You Read the Story

A. 1. Israel
   2. tie
   3. men of Israel
   4. men of Israel
   5. new

6. the ropes
7. one thousand
8. bone
9. thirsty
10. bone

B. 1. They tied Samson with new ropes.
   2. God made a hollow place in the bone.
   3. Water came out of the hollow place.
   4. Samson came to the gates at midnight.
   5. God gave Samson strength to carry the gates away.
   6. Samson killed a thousand Philistines and got water.

C. 4   5
   2   6
   1   8
   3   7

D. 1. no
   2. no

E. 1. God

2. *verse 1* The ropes fell apart.

verse 2 Samson killed a thousand men with a bone.

verse 3 Water came from a bone.

verse 4 Samson carried the gates away.

F. Blessed are the merciful: for they shall obtain mercy. Matthew 5:7

LESSON 29
Samson and Delilah

I. Before You Read the Story

A. Reading Incentive

"Why could Samson do all the unusual things he was doing to the Philistines? What made him so strong? Why do you think they wanted to know, and what do you think they found out?"

B. Pointer Questions

1. What would the Philistines give Delilah if she found out why Samson was so strong?
2. Do you think Delilah loved Samson?

II. Reader

"Did the Philistines try what Samson told them the third time? Did it work? Do you wonder what he told them that time? He said if she fastened his hair in with the threads of the weaving it would make him weak. Weaving was done on a big frame fastened in the ground. While he was sleeping, Delilah fastened his hair in with the weaving threads, but he just got up and took the whole frame along with his hair.

"Why would cutting his hair make Samson weak? Do you get weak if your hair is cut? [Samson's hair was not cut because the angel had said it should not be. His strength came from God because God wanted him to begin to deliver Israel from the Philistines. If Samson's hair was cut, he would be disobeying God, and God would no longer bless him with strength.]"

III. After You Read the Story

Workbook Exercises

Parts B and C involve inference reasoning.

Make sure the children understand what to do with the words in exercise D.

Many of the sentences in exercise F may be correctly completed with either word. Accept either unless you specify that you want the children to give the words used in the sentences in the reader.

ANSWER KEY

Before You Read the Story

1. a. Delilah
   b. razor
   c. twigs
   d. thread

2. figure

3. twigs

4. a. Delilah
   b. figure
   c. razor
   d. Twigs
   e. thread

5. a. twig (The rest are cords.)
   b. sing (The rest are mental activities.)
   c. staff (The rest can cut.)
   d. Barak (The rest are women.)

After You Read the Story

A. 1. Delilah
   2. money
   3. green twigs
   4. new ropes
   5. lie
   6. razor
   7. strength

B. 1. b   3. c
   2. a   4. b

C. 1. no (She loved money more, and was willing to see him defeated to get what was promised her.)
   2. no (She had always tried everything that he said would make him weak.)

D. 1. Please tell me how you can be tied.
   2. There has never been a razor on my head.

E. 1. figure   5. seven
   2. money   6. green
   3. strong   7. weak
   4. twigs   8. never

F. 1. not   4. never
   2. never   5. not
   3. not   6. never

G. Blessed are the merciful: for they shall obtain mercy. Matthew 5:7

EXTRA ACTIVITY

"Print some sentences telling about some very hard things that you think would have been easy for Samson to do."

LESSON 30
A Sad End

I. Before You Read the Story

A. Reading Incentive

"Remember what Samson's parents said when Samson wanted to marry a Philistine woman? Samson went ahead and married her anyway, but he could not have her after all. Then he loved another ungodly woman. Do things seem to be working out for Samson the way he would like? Look at the title of your story. The end is always sad for those who go against God and their parents. What did Delilah just find out at the end of the last lesson? Could the Philistines really make Samson weak? What did they do to him? How did he die?"

B. Pointer Questions

1. Why was Samson blind?
2. Against what did Samson want to lean?
3. Who buried Samson and where?

II. Reader

"Did the men believe that it would really work when Delilah called them this time? How do you know? [They brought the money they had promised.] Why do you think Delilah made Samson go to sleep? [So he would not know they were cutting off his hair.]

"Why was the Lord not with Samson when he woke up? [Samson no longer had the mark that he obeyed God, so God did not help him.]

"Why was Samson at the gathering for idol worship? Did he worship their idol too? [The Philistines brought him there so they could laugh at him.]"

III. After You Read the Story

ANSWER KEY

Before You Read the Story

1. a. shaved   c. fooled
   b. lean   d. useless

2. a. useless
   b. lean
   c. fooled
   d. shaved

3. a. shaved
   b. fooled
   c. lean
   d. useless

After You Read the Story

A. a. 2   e. 3
   b. 4   f. 5
   c. 2   g. 6
   d. 6   h. 7

B. 1. money
   2. He did not know that the Lord was not with him and would not help him.
   3. They said their god had given Samson to them.
   4. Samson killed more Philistines when he died than he did all the time that he was alive.

C. 1. Ehud   9. Joshua
   2. Balaam   10. Moses
   3. Eglon   11. Barak
   4. Samson   12. Jael
   5. Achan   13. Gideon
   6. Miriam   14. Jephthah
   7. Rahab   15. Abimelech
   8. Aaron

D. 1. c
   2. e
   3. a
   4. f
   5. b
   6. d

E. 1. c
   2. b
   3. a
   4. d

EXTRA ACTIVITY

Have the children turn to the table of contents and read the lesson titles for the unit, then print a sentence or so to tell which story they liked best and why.

Reading Test   Unit 3

ANSWER KEY

A. 1. The earth
   2. rod
   3. a rock
   4. hit
   5. Snakes
   6. Balaam
   7. A donkey
   8. blessed
   9. a mountain
  10. Joshua

B. 1. b
   2. d
   3. f
   4. a
   5. e
   6. c
   7. g
   8. j
   9. i
  10. h
  11. l
  12. k

C. 1. Samson
   2. Abimelech
   3. Eglon
   4. Achan
   5. Rahab
   6. Jael
   7. Ehud
   8. Jephthah
   9. Gideon
  10. Joshua

D. 1. They set up twelve stones at the place they crossed the river.
   2. The walls fell down flat.
   3. They tricked Israel into believing that they had come from far away.
   4. They cut off Samson's hair.

Gradebook: 40 test points counting two points for each sentence in Part D

Unit 4

UNIT 4
General Plan

Reader

The reading stories of this unit are from the books of Ruth and 1 Samuel. Bible memory work is again a passage—Psalm 23. Keep reviewing the preceding verses in daily oral recitation as you add a new verse each week.

Workbook

Remove and file the unit tests before distributing the books.

Teacher's Manual

I. Before You Read the Story

As in Unit 3, the daily lesson plans include some reading incentive discussion and pointer questions which may be printed on the board for the children to find answers.

II. Reader

Discussion questions given in the manual are the type to challenge independent thinking. Use these even if the children do not have ready answers. They will learn by hearing you explain the thinking involved. Discuss any pointer questions you have assigned. Also continue to exercise their memory and understanding with questions which are directly answered in the story.

III. After You Read the Story

Any workbook explanations and the answer key are given in this section.

Reading Lessons   Unit 4

LESSON 1
The Story of Ruth

I. Before You Read the Story

A. Reading Incentive

"Do you know what your name means? Most names have a meaning. The name *Ruth* means 'companion.' Your story tells the meaning of another name."

B. Pointer Questions

1. Why did Elimelech's family move to Moab?
2. What was not pleasant about Naomi's life?

II. Reader

"What do you think people could do for food if they cannot get crops to grow? [Work for wages to buy food; move to a place where food will grow.]

"Why do you think Naomi wanted to go back to the land of Canaan? It must have been more than a matter of having food to eat. [Family ties, worship practices, and old friends may have made her want to return.] Who was going to go with her? Did Naomi think they should go along? Which one decided to stay in the land of Moab? She would have been leaving family ties, worship practices, and old friends if she went to the land of Canaan which would have been strange to her. Which one was willing to leave her friends and gods to go with Naomi? What did she say that tells us she did not believe in idols?

"What would we call the relation between Naomi and the girls whom her sons had married? [mother-in-law and daughters-in-law]"

III. After You Read the Story

Workbook Notes

Trace the move from Bethlehem to Moab and back again on the workbook map.

Relate the Bible memory verse to the provisions with which our lives have been blessed. "Have you ever been without food because of a famine? Have you ever been in want? It is our Good Shepherd who has given us all the blessings that we have."

ANSWER KEY

Before You Read the Story

1. *Circled names:* Elimelech, Naomi, Orpah, Ruth
   Other names: grandmother, widows

a. grandmother
b. widows
c. Elimelech
d. Naomi
e. Ruth, Orpah

2. harvest
grain
cutting
glean
grain

3. a. pasture
   b. excitement
   c. pleasant

4. a. widows
   b. harvest
   c. pasture
   d. excitement
   e. pleasant
   f. grain
   g. glean
   h. cutting

5. 7

6. 3

After You Read the Story

A. 1. Bethlehem
   2. Moab
   3. the two sons, Elimelech
   4. Ruth
   5. pleasant
   6. cutting grain
   7. kind, good, worker
   8. the poor
   9. gleaning

B. 1. there is not enough food or pasture.
   2. city.
   3. Naomi was the mother of their husbands.
   4. dead.
   5. gather crops.

C. 2 8 14
   4 7 12
   5 6 15
   3 9 11
   1 10 13

D. 1. shepherd
   2. The Lord
   3. want, not
   4. not want
   5. the Lord, shepherd

E. The LORD is my shepherd; I shall not want. Psalm 23:1

EXTRA ACTIVITY

Spend some time helping the children become acquainted with the table of contents, or have an older student conduct the exercise. Say lesson titles for the children to find in the list of titles and respond with the number of the page on which the lesson begins. After some practice have them turn to the page and find the lesson named rather than just saying the number.

LESSON 2
Ruth and Boaz

I. Before You Read the Story

A. Reading Incentive

"Were you ever a stranger? What is a stranger? What does it feel like to be a stranger? One thing a stranger likes is a friend. Who is a stranger in this story? Who is a friend? What finally happened to the stranger and the friend?"

B. Pointer Questions

1. Who was Boaz?
2. What good things had Boaz heard about Ruth?

II. Reader

"When you meet someone, what do you often say first of all? [hello, good morning, or similar greetings] What did Boaz say when he met his helpers? What kind of man was Boaz? [a godly man]

"Why did Ruth beat her grain before she took it home? [That made the grain come out of the little shells that were around it.]

"How many ways can you think of in which Ruth was a good example to us? [She did as she was told. She worked faithfully until the end of harvest. She appreciated the kindness of others. She chose to leave her idols to serve the true God. She was willing to go to a strange land with her mother-in-law.]

"What do you think Naomi might have wanted Ruth to talk to Boaz about? [The land that was for sale belonged in their family.] Did Boaz appreciate what Ruth said?"

III. After You Read the Story

ANSWER KEY

Before You Read the Story

1. *Circled names:* Boaz, David
   Other names: mother-in-law, reapers, relatives, shepherd
   a. Boaz, David
   b. mother-in-law
   c. shepherd
   d. Reapers
   e. relatives

2. a. notice
   b. pick
   c. dressed
   d. bought

3. closely, purposely

4. mother-in-law, mealtime

5. bought, sale

6. a. relatives
   b. related
   c. relation
   d. reap
   e. reaping

f. reapers
g. bought
h. buy
i. buying

After You Read the Story

A. 1. Boaz
   2. reapers
   3. noticed
   4. purposely
   5. mealtime
   6. glad
   7. relation / relatives
   8. could not
   9. bought
   10. David's

B. 1. no   7. yes
   2. yes   8. yes
   3. no   9. no
   4. yes   10. no
   5. no   11. yes
   6. yes   12. yes

C. 1. Boaz said, "The Lord be with you."

2. They answered, "The Lord bless you."

3. a. She had been kind to her mother-in-law.

b. She had been willing to leave her own land.

c. She loved and trusted God.

4. a. He saw to it that she had plenty to eat.

b. He told his helpers to let grain fall for her.

5. He gave his relative first chance to buy the land.

D. 1. c
2. e
3. b
4. a
5. d

E. The LORD is my shepherd; I shall not want. Psalm 23:1

EXTRA ACTIVITY

Have the children print in their own words the story of Ruth without referring to their readers.

LESSON 3
The Story of Samuel

I. Before You Read the Story

A. Reading Incentive

"Did you ever wish for something very much? Someone in our story wanted something very much. What did she do to get it? Did she keep it when she got it?"

B. Pointer Questions

1. Whom did Hannah ask for what she wanted?
2. What did she say she would do with her son?
3. What does the name *Samuel* mean?

II. Reader

"What did Hannah have that she could be happy about? Why was she not happy? Why was Elkanah sad? Did you ever realize that your happiness or sadness makes other people feel that way too?

"How did Hannah give her son to the Lord?

"How often did Samuel see his mother? Can you imagine what it would be like to see your mother only once a year? Remember how much Hannah wanted a son. I am sure she loved Samuel very much and wanted to be with him, but she loved God more, and she was not selfish."

III. After You Read the Story

Workbook Notes

On the workbook map, find Ramah (Elkanah and Hannah's home) and Shiloh (the place where they went to worship every year).

ANSWER KEY

Before You Read the Story

1. Eli, Elkanah, Hannah, Samuel, Shiloh
   a. Shiloh
   b. Eli
   c. Hannah
   d. Elkanah
   e. Samuel

2. h

3. a. forget
   b. begins

4. prayer

5. temple

6. a. donkey (The rest are buildings.)
   b. Pharaoh (The rest were men of God.)
   c. Naomi (The rest are cities.)
   d. Hannah (The rest were men.)
   e. begin (The rest speak of completion.)
   f. fight (The rest are reverent acts.)

After You Read the Story

A. 1. sad
   2. every year
   3. son
   4. a priest

5. asked of God
6. the temple
7. a coat
8. five

B. 1. She promised to give him to the Lord.
   2. She named him Samuel because she asked God for him.
   3. Hannah took Samuel to the temple to stay there and help.

C. 1. when   6. when
   2. where   7. where
   3. when   8. when
   4. when   9. where
   5. where   10. when
                11. when
                12. where

D. 1. no   5. not
   2. not   6. don't
   3. None   7. Don't
   4. not   8. never

E. The LORD is my shepherd; I shall not want. Psalm 23:1

Gradebook: 56 points for the whole lesson counting two points for each sentence in Part B

LESSON 4
God Talks to Samuel

I. Before You Read the Story

A. Reading Incentive

"How quick are you to crawl out of bed when someone calls you? Is Samuel a good example or a bad example in this story?"

B. Pointer Questions
1. With whom was God displeased in the story?
2. With whom was He pleased?

II. Reader

"How many times did Samuel run to Eli thinking Eli had called him? What does that tell us about the kind of boy Samuel was? Would you run to answer someone you thought called you three times in a row if they kept saying they had not called you? Who finally figured out where the call was coming from? What did he tell Samuel to do?

"Why do you think Samuel was afraid to tell Eli what God had said? [Eli would not enjoy hearing such a message.]

"How did the people know that Samuel was a man of God? What is a man called who tells the people what God says?"

III. After You Read the Story

Workbook Notes

You may want to give extra explanation on using quotation marks in Part E.

ANSWER KEY

Before You Read the Story

1. bedside

2. cheated

3. cheated

4. a. bedside
   b. cheated

5. (Individual sentences)

6. a. lie
   b. lay
   c. lay
   d. lie

After You Read the Story

A. 1. in bed
2. Eli
3. God
4. Eli, his sons
5. no
6. yes

B. 1. still
2. voice

3. quickly
4. because
5. answered
6. thought
7. if
8. When
9. important
10. punish

C. 1. a   3. c
2. b   4. a

D. 2. *"Here I am."*
3. *"I did not call you. Go and lie down again."*
4. *"Samuel."*
5. *"Speak, Lord, for I will listen."*
6. *"Samuel, my son."*
7. *"It is the Lord. He will do what is right."*

E. 1. c   4. a
2. b   5. d
3. e

F. 1. still, will
   2. knew, too

G. The LORD is my shepherd; I shall not want. Psalm 23:1

EXTRA ACTIVITY

Have the children print in their own words the story of Samuel's call in the night, without referring to the reader.

LESSON 5
God's Word Is Truth

I. Before You Read the Story

A. Reading Incentive

Print the word *ark* on the board. "Of what does that word make you think? [Noah and the flood] There is an ark in this story, but it is not a boat. It was a wooden box covered with gold. The Israelites thought the ark could help them one time when they were in trouble. What did they do with the ark? What happened?"

B. Pointer Questions

1. What was the ark?
2. What made the Philistines afraid?

II. Reader

"Why was God going to punish Eli and his sons? What kind of punishment did He send?

"Why did the Philistines talk about the mighty Gods of Israel when He is just one God? [They were used to thinking of many gods because they worshiped idols.]

"How did Priest Eli feel about taking the ark to the battle?"

III. After You Read the Story

Workbook Notes

Encourage the children to practice their Bible memory verse so they can say it well.

ANSWER KEY

Before You Read the Story

1. a. sang
   b. check
   c. dressed
   d. rocking
   e. packed
   f. row

2. d
   c
   b
   e
   f
   a

3. backward

4. a. chest
   b. chest

5. a. mention
   b. mentioning
   c. mentioned
   d. shocked
   e. shocking
   f. shock

After You Read the Story

A. 1. God was not with them.
   2. no
   3. a chest
   4. glad
   5. afraid
   6. took it
   7. 98
   8. sad
   9. The ark of God was taken.
   10. yes

B. 1. b
   2. a
   3. b
   4. c
   5. c

C. 1. Elimelech
   2. Naomi
   3. Orpah
   4. Ruth
   5. Ruth
   6. Boaz
   7. Boaz
   8. Hannah
   9. Samuel
   10. Elkanah
   11. Eli
   12. Samuel

D. 1. relative
   2. girl
   3. girl servant
   4. a. Hebrews
      b. Israelites

EXTRA ACTIVITY

The Philistines said, "These are the Gods that brought all those bad things on the people of Egypt." Have the children print all the things they can remember that God brought on Egypt.

LESSON 6
The Ark in a Strange Land

I. Before You Read the Story

A. Reading Incentive

"The enemies of Israel had something that did not belong to them. What was it? Where did the ark belong? How did the Philistines get it?

"The Philistines put the ark in the house where they kept their idol, Dagon. Perhaps they thought the ark was an idol too. What happened when the Philistines had the ark?"

B. Pointer Questions

1. What happened to Dagon when the ark was there?
2. Why did the Philistines become sick?

II. Reader

"Just think how unworthy Dagon was of the worship of the Philistines. What would you think of a god that could not even pick itself up when it fell down?

"What did the Philistines plan as a sign to tell them whether their trouble really was God punishing them?"

III. After You Read the Story

Workbook Notes

On the workbook map, locate Ashdod, where the Philistines put the ark with Dagon. From there it was sent to Gath, then to Ekron.

ANSWER KEY

Before You Read the Story

1. Dagon, Gath
   a. Dagon
   b. Gath

2. calves

3. cart

4. hitch

5. calves, hitch

6. Gath, hitch

7. a. Gath
   b. calves
   c. Dagon
   d. cart
   e. box
   f. hitch

After You Read the Story

A. 1. their god's house
   2. Dagon
   3. fell down
   4. punished
   5. sick and died
   6. seven
   7. an offering
   8. a new cart
   9. cows

B. 1. a new cart (underlined)
   2. Dagon (cross under)
   3. an offering (circled)
   4. the ark of God (two lines under)
   5. two cows (cross on)
   6. the calves (three lines under)

C. 1. I
   2. P
   3. I
   4. I
   5. P
   6. I
   7. P
   8. P

D. a. 2
   b. 3

E. 1. green
   2. in green pastures
   3. still
   4. beside the still waters

F. He maketh me to lie down in green pastures: he leadeth me beside the still waters. Psalm 23:2

Gradebook: 47 points for the whole lesson

EXTRA ACTIVITY

Have the children print sentences telling things that an idol cannot do that God can.

LESSON 7
The Ark Goes Home

I. Before You Read the Story

A. Reading Incentive
"The ark was on its way back to Israel, and the Philistines were glad. Why do you think they were glad when they were the ones to take it in the first place? How were they sending it? What would be a sign to them that their troubles were punishment from God?

"Did the cows know what was on their cart? Did they know where it belonged? Would they go back to Israel with it, or would it get lost somewhere in the wilderness?

"What became of the ark, and what became of the cows?"

B. Pointer Questions
1. What did the Israelites do with the cart and the cows?
2. What did Samuel do after the battle so they would remember God's help?

II. Reader
"What would you have heard if you had been there when the Philistines let the cows go? [cows lowing, cart wheels on the road, perhaps the cart or the ark rattling] The people were probably silent in awe as they saw the proof that it was God who had done all those things to them.

"How did the cattle know where to go? [God made them go that way.]"

III. After You Read the Story

Workbook Notes
Follow the travels of the ark to Beth-shemesh (Joshua's home), then to Kirjath-jearim where it stayed twenty years.

You may want to give extra explanation for Part C or do part of the exercise as a class activity.

ANSWER KEY

Before You Read the Story
1. highway, straight
2. free, highway, lowing, straight
3. highway
4. a. border
   b. highway
5. a. confessed
   b. lowing
6. a. straight
   b. free
7. a. highway
   b. border
   c. free
   d. straight
   e. confessed
   f. lowing

After You Read the Story

A. 1. no
2. no
3. yes
4. yes
5. no
6. yes
7. no
8. yes
9. yes
10. yes

B. 1. The cows took the ark to the land of Israel.
2. The people were harvesting wheat.
3. The men of Levi took care of the ark.
4. Some men looked in the ark.
5. The Lord killed many of them.
6. They had to put away their idols.
7. Samuel prayed for the people.

C. a. 6 (Come back to the Lord, put away the idols, and serve only the Lord.)
b. 10 ("Till now the Lord has helped us.")
c. 7 (Yes)
d. 2 (Joshua's field)
e. 8 (Do not stop praying to God for us.)
f. 4 (They were very much afraid.)
g. 9 (A great thunder)
h. 1 (On the cart beside the ark)
i. 5 (They were still under the rule of their enemies.)
j. 3 (Over fifty thousand)

D. 1. to
2. right
3. their
4. wood
5. for
6. not

E. He maketh me to lie down in green pastures: he leadeth me beside the still waters. Psalm 23:2

EXTRA ACTIVITY

Print these review words on the board and have the children print pronunciations for them, marking short vowels with breves and using the schwa in unaccented syllables. Allow them to find the pronunciations in the workbook for help.

harvest	reapers
notice	backward
temple	David
border	shepherd
pleasant	Dagon

LESSON 8
Israel Wants a King

I. Before You Read the Story

A. Reading Incentive

"Did you ever ask for something that your parents said was best for you not to have? Someone in this story asked for something that was not good for them. What did they want and what was wrong with it?"

B. Pointer Questions
1. Who was the ruler in Israel?
2. What was wrong with having Samuel's sons rule?
3. What would a king do with the sons of the people of Israel?

II. Reader

"Whom did the people of Israel want to be like? The Egyptians had a king. The Philistines had a king. Were they good examples to follow? [No, they worshiped false gods.]

"Do you think the people understood how it would be better for them to have God for their ruler than to have a king? Do you think they were satisfied with the better way?"

III. After You Read the Story

ANSWER KEY

Before You Read the Story

1. a. oliveyards
   b. vineyards
   c. horsemen
   d. cooks
   e. tools

2. horsemen, horse, men
   oliveyards, olive, yards
   vineyards, vine, yards

3. vineyards

4. cooks, tools

5. horsemen, oliveyards, vineyards

After You Read the Story

A. 1. Samuel   5. God
   2. not good   6. listen
   3. Samuel   7. take
   4. king   8. hear

B. a. 4
   b. 6
   c. 1
   d. 7
   e. 3
   f. 5
   g. 2

C. fields   servants
   oliveyards   daughters
   sons   donkeys
   vineyards

D. *Any of these phrases:*
   All the time
   All the time that Samuel lived
   Each year
   Finally

E. *Any of these phrases:*
   to the different cities
   At this place

F. 1. 6, 7
   2. 1, 2
   3. 2
   4. 4, 5
   5. 8

G. He maketh me to lie down in green pastures: he leadeth me beside the still waters. Psalm 23:3

LESSON 9
Saul Looks for Lost Donkeys

I. Before You Read the Story

A. Reading Incentive

"Everyone sometimes thinks of things they want that are not the best for them. When we understand that what we wanted is not the best for us, it is wise to be satisfied not to have it. Did you ever hear anybody keep on begging for something they were told they should not have? What do we think of such people? They are like spoiled children. Did the people of Israel act like spoiled children, or were they wise?"

B. Pointer Questions

1. Who was a very tall man?
2. Was Saul an obedient son?
3. Why did Saul think they should go home before they found the donkeys?

II. Reader

"Why did God let Israel have a king if it was not good for them? [God does not force people to obey Him. He wants them to willingly obey.]

"What was the servant's idea when Saul suggested going home? What did the servant think the man of God might tell them? Can you think of an example of a time when a man of God said something would happen and it did happen? [Samuel told of the punishment God would bring on Eli and his sons, which came to pass.] Who do you think this man of God might be?"

III. After You Read the Story

Workbook Notes

Introduce the term *compound sentence* and explain the likeness in principle to compound words. Teach the children to recognize *and* as a link that is not part of either sentence. You may have them locate and circle the *and* in each of the sentences in Part D, then let different children read the two sentences within the compound sentence. Remind them to use correct capitalization and punctuation for both of the short sentences.

Review the negative words and tell the children that the words for the sentences in Part E can be found by looking in the reader.

ANSWER KEY

Before You Read the Story

1. powerful, shoulders, unhappiness, worrying

2. unhappiness (with *un* and *ness* circled), happy

3. a. Kish
   b. Saul

4. a. shoulders
   b. unhappiness

5. powerful

6. worrying

7. a. Kish
   b. Saul
   c. powerful
   d. worrying
   e. shoulders
   f. unhappiness

After You Read the Story

A.
3	5	12
1	7	11
2	8	10
4	6	9

B. 1. Kish was Saul's father.
   2. Saul and a servant were looking for lost donkeys.
   3. He thought his father would worry about them.
   4. They decided to see the man of God.
   5. They had some money for a present.
   6. Samuel was in the city.

C. 1. ahead
   2. over
   3. after
   4. best
   5. always
   6. unhappiness

7. powerful
8. tall
9. lost
10. servant
11. stop
12. different
13. bless
14. young
15. hurry

D. 2. We want a king to rule over us. We want him to fight our battles for us.
   3. The Lord talked to Samuel. He told him to make Israel a king.
   4. Kish was a great man. Saul was also a tall man.
   5. All our bread is gone. We do not have a present to give him.
   6. He blesses the sacrifice. Then the people eat.

E. 1. No
   2. none
   3. not

F. He maketh me to lie down in green pastures: he leadeth me beside the still waters. Psalm 23:2

LESSON 10
Saul and Samuel

I. Before You Read the Story

A. Reading Incentive

"Did Israel have their king yet? Were they going to have a king? Who do you think would decide who should be the king? [God] Who do you think might become the new king?"

B. Pointer Questions

1. How did Samuel know Saul when he came?
2. What did Samuel do to Saul the next morning?

II. Reader

"Did Saul know Samuel when he saw him? What do you think might have surprised Saul? [Samuel told them about the donkeys before they asked. Samuel talked about Israel wanting Saul. Samuel gave them the best seats above thirty other people who were invited.]

"Which was the smallest tribe of Israel? Did Saul think he was a great man?

"How could Samuel and Saul talk on the top of the house? [Their houses were made with flat roofs, and the people often went to the roof of the house to do things.]

"What did Samuel mean when he said Saul would be turned into another man? Would he no longer be Saul? [The change would be inside him. Other people would still think he was the same man.]"

III. After You Read the Story

Workbook Notes

Call attention to the word *anointed* in question 5 of exercise A. You may want to explain the word as naming the act of pouring oil.

Have the children say the first two verses of Psalm 23.

ANSWER KEY

Before You Read the Story

1. Gilgal
2. oil
3. a. prophets
   b. prophesy
4. worried
5. a. greet
   b. wine
6. a. wine
   b. prophets
   c. oil
   d. Gilgal
7. a. prophesy
   b. worried
   c. greet
8. smallest

After You Read the Story

A. 1. from which land he would come
2. no
3. three days
4. on the top of Samuel's house
5. no
6. what had happened to his son
7. seven
8. what to do
9. the Spirit of God
10. at Gilgal

B. 1. Benjamin
2. found
3. oil
4. smallest
5. men
6. kids, loaves, bread, wine
7. prophets

C. 1. yes

2. no
3. no
4. no
5. no
6. yes
7. no

8. yes
9. no
10. no
11. no
12. no
13. yes
14. yes

D. 1. a. stay

b. stayed

2. got rid of

3. girls
4. pour oil on the head

Gradebook: 54 points for all written work

EXTRA ACTIVITY

Have the children draw a picture to show what the three men who met Saul were carrying.

LESSON 11
Saul Is King

I. Before You Read the Story

A. Reading Incentive

"What are the things Samuel had prophesied would happen to Saul on the way home? Why do you think Samuel had told Saul on ahead that these things would happen? [Perhaps to help Saul believe for sure that the things he said about the kingdom were true.]

"Up to this time nobody except Samuel and Saul knew who was to be the king. How did the people of Israel find out?"

B. Pointer Questions

1. Why could the people not find Saul when they knew he was to be the king?
2. What did the people shout when they found Saul?

II. Reader

Explain the process of the lot as God's way of showing who was to be the king. That eliminated all possibility of man's opinion or preference determining the matter.

"Which tribe was taken by lot? Then they cast the lot again to see from which family in that tribe their king would come. Then they cast the lot to see which man in that family was to be the king. Did it hold out to be Saul? How could it always happen to be the right one chosen? [God was directing, and He made it hold out that way.]"

III. After You Read the Story

Workbook Notes

Follow Saul from Ramah, by Rachel's grave, to his home at Gibeah.

Discuss the rebus in exercise E with the children and explain the parallel between restoring and leading a soul and a sheep.

ANSWER KEY

Before You Read the Story

1. anywhere

2. a. prophesied
   b. despised

3. a. stuff   d. stuff
   b. stuff
   c. stuff

4. d   b   a
   c

5. a. attention
   b. prophesied
   c. anywhere

6. a. attention
   b. plainly
   c. despised
   d. prophesied
   e. stuff
   f. anywhere

After You Read the Story

A.   2   6   9
      4   8   10
      1   7   12
      3   5   11

B. 1. grave   8. tribe
   2. own   9. hearts
   3. donkeys   10. Egypt
   4. stuff   11. Kish
   5. along   12. Israel
   6. very   13. near
   7. edge   14. group

C. God save the king!

D. 1. *"Where did you go?"*
   2. *"He told me plainly that the donkeys had been found."*
   3. *"Look, he has hidden himself among the stuff."*
   4. *"God save the king!"*
   5. *"How shall this man save us?"*

F. He restoreth my soul: he leadeth me in the paths of righteousness for his name's sake. Psalm 23:3

LESSON 12
God Helps Israel

I. Before You Read the Story

A. Reading Incentive

"Israel had wanted a king to fight their battles. When there is trouble, is fighting the only way to settle it? One time when an enemy nation came to fight one of the cities of Israel, the Israelites thought they would rather make an agreement with them than fight them. The enemy said they would make an agreement on one condition. What was the condition they demanded? Did Israel meet the condition?"

B. Pointer Questions

   1. What did Saul send with the messengers that went to call Israel together?

2. How many men came?

3. How would they help the people who were in trouble?

II. Reader

"Why did the people of Saul's town weep? Was the enemy attacking them to fight them or take out their eyes? [They may have felt so sorry for their fellowmen in the other city.]

"When did they attack the enemy? How do you know they were done before dinner time?"

III. After You Read the Story

Workbook Notes

Study exercise E with the children to teach them that *and* is not always an indication of a compound sentence. Have them find the *and* in a sentence, then let two different children read the parts. Are they both sentences?

ANSWER KEY

Before You Read the Story

1. a. weep
   b. condition
   c. altogether
   d. command
   e. agreement
   f. command
   g. agreement
   h. altogether

2. a. coasts
   b. weep
   c. yoke
   d. command
   e. altogether
   f. agreement

3. a. condition
   b. condition

4. a. yoke   c. yoke
   b. yoke   d. yoke

5. a. command
   b. command

6. a. coasts
   b. coasts
   c. coasts

After You Read the Story

A. 1. right eyes
   2. seven
   3. a yoke of oxen
   4. were afraid not to come.
   5. three hundred thirty thousand
   6. three
   7. in the cool of the early morning
   8. yes
   9. Israel
   10. They should be put to death
   11. the Lord
   12. no

B. 1. serve   10. afraid
   2. all   11. counted
   3. pleasant   12. tomorrow
   4. older   13. hot
   5. seven days   14. happy
   6. coasts   15. divided
   7. weep   16. king
   8. began
   9. come after

C. 1. yoke
   2. oxen
   3. us
   4. went
   5. If
   6. land
   7. left
   8. herd
   9. Altogether
   10. very
   11. enemy
   12. hot
   13. enemies
   14. Lord
   15. praise

E. 2. b
   3. a
   4. b
   5. a
   6. b

D. You will have help.

F. He restoreth my soul: he leadeth me in the paths of righteousness for his name's sake. Psalm 23:3

LESSON 13
Israel Confesses Sin

I. Before You Read the Story

A. Reading Incentive
"What is the first thing you remember about Samuel? He was a child when he first served the Lord in the temple. Now he is old and grayheaded. He gathered the people together one more time to talk to them. What do you think he wanted to tell them?"

B. Pointer Questions
1. What would Samuel do if he had done anything wrong?
2. What proved to the people that it was wicked to ask for a king?

II. Reader
"How could Israel have God's blessing now that they had a king? [They could not undo their sin. But the king and all the people should follow God's directions from this time on.]"

III. After You Read the Story

Workbook Notes
Discuss exercise D with the children. Tell them to look over the story for all the occurrences of the word *of*. Each one is part of a phrase. Tell them to include as many of the following words as they need to have a meaningful phrase. They should not repeat any phrases that they find more than once. Quote some examples and let the children also think of some phrases that begin with *of*, for practice. (of you, of me, of corn, of bread, of a storm, of the weather, of the Lord, of the large river)

ANSWER KEY

Before You Read the Story

1. a. judges
   b. unfair
   c. grayheaded
   d. childhood
   e. season
   f. miracle

2. a. judges   d. grayheaded
   b. unfair   e. season
   c. childhood   f. miracle

3. a. season
   b. season

4. a. judges
   b. judges

5. *childhood*—child, hi, (or) hood
   grayheaded—gray, ray, he, head, (or) ad
   season—sea, as, son, (or) on
   unfair—fa, fair (or) air

After You Read the Story

A. 1. b   4. c
   2. e   5. d
   3. a

B. a. 2 (no)
   b. 5 (Moses and Aaron)
   c. 1 (old and grayheaded)
   d. 4 (right and good things the Lord had done for them)
   e. 3 (the Lord and the king)
   f. 7 (keep following the Lord)
   g. 8 (wheat harvest)
   h. 6 (judges)
   i. 10 (Samuel)
   j. 9 (They would die.)
   k. 11 (Samuel)

C. 1. Samuel mentioned Moses and Aaron.
   2. God sent thunder and rain.
   3. It was the season of wheat harvest.

D. of the land
of Egypt
of wheat harvest
of you
of the Lord
of Samuel

E. He restoreth my soul: he leadeth me in the paths of righteousness for his name's sake. Psalm 23:3

EXTRA ACTIVITY

Samuel told the people to stand still so he could talk to them about the Lord and the right and good things He had done for them and their fathers. Let the children see how many things they can list of the good things God did for His people.

LESSON 14
Saul Disobeys God

I. Before You Read the Story

A. Reading Incentive

"Saul had been the king for two years now. Do you remember some of the things Samuel had told the people that their king would do? Saul took men to work for him. He chose three thousand men for his army. And one day the Philistines came to fight again. How did the people feel when the enemy came? What do you think we could do if an enemy came into our land? See if you can find someone in the story who did not seem to be afraid. See if you can find someone who was afraid."

B. Pointer Questions

1. How many men were in the Israelite army?
2. How many were in the Philistine army?
3. How many men were with Saul when Samuel left him?

II. Reader

"Do you have any idea what made the Philistines come to fight Israel? [Jonathan had killed some of them.]

"What do you think Samuel was going to do when he got to Gilgal? [Offer an offering and ask for God's direction] Do you think Saul really wanted to offer the offering? [He said he forced himself.] Why did he offer the offering? [He was afraid the enemy would come upon them before he had prayed.] Was it a good thing to do what he did? What was the punishment for his foolishness?"

III. After You Read the Story

ANSWER KEY

Before You Read the Story

1. forced, scattered

2. forced, forever, scattered

3. Jonathan

4. a. scattered
   b. forever
   c. forced

5. a. Jonathan
   b. scattered
   c. forced
   d. forever

After You Read the Story

A. 1. two years
2. seven days
3. forever
4. three thousand
5. two thousand
6. one thousand
7. many like the sand
8. six hundred
9. it does not matter

B. caves   pits
bushes   high places
rocks   across the river
(Picture of one of these places)

C. 4   7
2   5
3   6
1   8

D. 1. c
2. a
3. e
4. d
5. b

E. 2. Some hid in bushes and some hid in rocks.
3. Samuel did not come and the people were getting scattered.
4. Samuel came and Saul went out to meet him.
5. "I forced myself and I offered a burnt offering."
6. "You have done a foolish thing and you did not obey God."

F. He restoreth my soul: he leadeth me in the paths of righteousness for his name's sake. Psalm 23:3
Saul

Gradebook: 50 points for the
whole lesson

LESSON 15
Jonathan Helps Israel

I. Before You Read the Story

A. Reading Incentive

"What were most of the people of Israel doing? [hiding] Two men were
not hiding. Can you tell me who these brave men were? What was to be
their sign whether they should go to the enemies? What could just two men
do against such a multitude of Philistines? What do you think happened?"

B. Pointer Questions

1. How many Philistines did Jonathan and his helper kill?
2. Who killed the rest of them?
3. Why were the people so hungry?

II. Reader

"Do you think it was a steep place where Jonathan and his helper went
to get to the Philistines? Why?

"Why do you think Saul wanted the ark and the priest? [Perhaps to find
out what the Lord wanted them to do.]

"Did Israel kill all the Philistines? How do you know? [Jonathan thought
they would have been able to kill more if they had eaten.]"

III. After You Read the Story

Workbook Notes

The Philistines camped at Michmash, while Saul and his men were at
Gilgal. Find these places on the map.

ANSWER KEY

Before You Read the Story

1. a. watchmen
   b. woods
   c. earthquake

2. a. disappearing
   b. frightened
   c. climbing

3. frightened

4. a. earthquake
   b. watchmen
   c. disappearing
   d. climbing
   e. frightened
   f. woods

5. a. appear   g. climbing
   b. disappear   h. climb
   c. disappearing i. climbed
   d. frighten
   e. fright
   f. frightened

After You Read the Story

A. 1. hands, feet
2. twenty
3. earthquake
4. eat
5. honey, woods
6. sheep, calves, oxen
7. blood

B. a. 2   g. 3
b. 6   h. 5
c. 1   i. 4
d. 9
e. 7
f. 8

C. 1. see   6. weak
2. There   7. know
3. knew   8. ate
4. for   9. meat
5. not   10. too

D. 1. Saul   15. Philistines
2. Saul   16. Israel
3. Jonathan   17. Saul
4. Samuel   18. Saul
5. God   19. Philistines
6. Samuel   20. God
7. Saul   21. Philistines
8. Saul   22. Saul
9. Samuel   23. Jonathan
10. Samuel   24. Israel
11. God   25. Saul
12. Israel
13. Samuel
14. Jonathan

EXTRA ACTIVITY

Draw a picture for one of the paragraphs in the story.

LESSON 16
Saul Disobeys Again

I. Before You Read the Story

A. Reading Incentive

"Does it matter if someone breaks a rule when they did not know about it? Do you remember what someone did in the last lesson that should not have been done? How did it get found out? What happened then?"

B. Pointer Questions

1. Did Jonathan have to die?
2. How did Samuel find out that Saul had disobeyed?

II. Reader

"Why did God not answer Saul? [Something was not right in Israel. Saul had said whoever ate the day before would be cursed. Jonathan ate honey and nothing was done about it.]

"Do you remember what Saul thought about himself when Samuel first told him that he was to be the king? [He was from the smallest tribe and he thought all the other families were better than his family.] What does he seem to think of himself now?"

III. After You Read the Story

Workbook Notes

Discuss the meaning of the Bible verse and have the children say it with the preceding verses.

ANSWER KEY

Before You Read the Story

1. a. during
   b. rescued

2. a. rescued
   b. during

Crossword Puzzle

Across	*Down*
2. watchmen	1. scattered
4. coasts	3. enemies
5. frightened	4. childhood
7. miracle	6. rescued
10. disappearing	8. calves
11. season	9. eyes
12. vineyards	10. during
13. shoulder	

After You Read the Story

A. 1. b
   2. c
   3. b
   4. c

B. 1. e   7. c
   2. g   8. d
   3. a   9. j
   4. b   10. f
   5. h   11. i
   6. l   12. k

C. 1. a. 8
      b. 11
      c. 14, 16
      d. 15
   2. a. 49
      b. 63
      c. 40
      d. 52
   3. a. God's Word Is Truth
      b. A New King
      c. Ruth and Boaz
      d. Saul and Samuel
      e. David and Goliath

D. 1. Yea
   2. though
   3. valley
   4. shadow
   5. thou art
   6. thy rod
   7. thy staff
   8. comfort

E. Yea, though I walk through the valley of the shadow of death, I will fear no evil: for thou art with me; thy rod and thy staff they comfort me. Psalm 23:4

EXTRA ACTIVITY

Let the children hunt for phrases in the story which could be made into contractions.

LESSON 17
Saul Makes Excuses

I. Before You Read the Story

A. Reading Incentive

"Sandy was to take the garbage to the garden. On the way, she decided to carry the pan on her head. The pan slipped and down spilled the garbage. Sandy made excuses for the spill by saying, 'The pan was too full. The pan was too heavy and it was too far to the garden.' Are those really the reasons she spilled the garbage?

"Do you remember what Saul was supposed to do to the enemy and their animals? Did he do it? What excuses do you think he might have for not doing God's will?"

B. Pointer Questions

1. What was Saul's punishment?
2. What did Samuel do that Saul should have done?

II. Reader

"What did Samuel mean when he said, 'When you were little in your own sight'? [when Saul did not think himself great] Do you remember how tall Saul was? Was that what kind of littleness or greatness Samuel was talking about?

"Was it Saul's sin or his punishment that made him feel bad?"

III. After You Read the Story

Workbook Notes

Discuss compound sentences using the connector word *but*. Have the children read some of the short sentences used in the compounds in exercise C.

ANSWER KEY

Before You Read the Story

1. blaming, blame
   bleating, bleat

2. a. bleating
   b. refuse
   c. excuses
   d. blaming

3. a. excuses
   b. blaming
   c. refuse
   d. bleating

4. a. singing (The rest are quarrelsome.)
   b. exciting (The rest are justifications.)
   c. refuse (The rest are mental processes.)
   d. shouting (The rest are animal sounds.)

After You Read the Story

A. 1. Saul
2. Samuel
3. Saul
4. Samuel
5. Samuel
6. Saul
7. Saul
8. Saul
9. Samuel
10. Saul

B. 1. God wanted Saul to destroy all the people and animals of the enemy.
2. Saul saved the king and the best animals.
3. Saul said, "I have done what God wanted me to do."
4. God wants people to obey Him.

C. 1. God wanted them to destroy everything. Saul and Israel saved the king and some animals.
2. Saul said he had done what God wanted him to do. He told a lie.
3. He did not want Samuel to know that he had sinned. His sin was not hid.

4. Samuel turned to leave. Saul took hold of his clothes.

D. 1. He felt so unworthy and small.
2. So God took his kingdom away.
3. And never gives up till he's done.

E. Yea, though I walk through the valley of the shadow of death, I will fear no evil: for thou art with me; thy rod and thy staff they comfort me. Psalm 23:4

Gradebook: 42 points for the whole lesson counting two points for each sentence in Part B

LESSON 18
A New King

I. Before You Read the Story

A. Reading Incentive
"Who had decided who should be the first king of Israel? [God] Would one of Saul's sons be the next king? Samuel thought he knew who it would be, but he was mistaken. In this story we will find out who will be the next king."

B. Pointer Questions
1. What two things did Samuel take to Bethlehem?
2. Who did Samuel think God had chosen to be the king?
3. What did Saul's servants say about David?

II. Reader
"What was a horn of oil? [A horn from an animal could be hollowed out so that it could be used for a bottle.] What do you think Samuel was supposed to do with his horn of oil? Why would Saul kill Samuel for anointing another king? [Saul did not like to be rejected and he did not want another person to be the king.]

"What did God see that made Him not choose Jesse's oldest son? [He did not have the kind of heart God wanted the king of Israel to have.]

"Why did Samuel think there must be someone else in Jesse's family? [God had said one of Jesse's sons was to be the king, but He said it was not any of the sons that were there.]

"What songs do you think David played and sang? [Many of the psalms in the Bible are David's songs. One of them is Psalm 23.]"

III. After You Read the Story

Workbook Notes

You may want to discuss exercise E to help the children recognize the difference between inner feelings and things physically visible.

ANSWER KEY

Before You Read the Story

1. a. evil
   b. player
   c. suggested
   d. anointed
   e. good-looking
   f. harp

2. a. good-looking
   b. player
   c. evil

3. Jesse

4. good-looking

5. a. Jesse
   b. harp
   c. player

6. a. suggested
   b. anointed

7. a. good-looking
   b. evil

After You Read the Story

A. 1. a horn
   2. kill him
   3. at Bethlehem
   4. the oldest
   5. on the outside
   6. in the heart
   7. eight

8. David
9. An evil spirit came to him.
10. David played the harp.
11. caring for the sheep
12. playing the harp

B. 1. a
   2. c
   3. b
   4. c
   5. b

C. 1. c
   2. d
   3. a
   4. b

D. horn
   (The middle picture should be circled.)

E. 1. G   6. G
   2. P   7. P
   3. G   8. P
   4. G   9. P
   5. G   10. P

F. Yea, though I walk through the valley of the shadow of death, I will fear no evil: for thou art with me: thy rod and they staff they comfort me. Psalm 23:4

LESSON 19
David and Goliath

Be Prepared

Try to determine the weight of your heaviest coat. If your classroom ceiling is more than nine feet high, measure a distance of nine feet and a span from the floor.

I. Before You Read the Story

A. Reading Incentive

"In cold weather you wear a heavy coat. How many pounds do you think your coat weighs? My heaviest coat weighs ——. Someone in our story wore a coat that weighed about one hundred fifty pounds. That is so heavy that you would not even be able to lift it off the floor. That coat was not made of warm material like ours are. What do you think it was made of to make it so heavy, and why do you think someone would want a coat like that? See what other interesting things you can find out about this man."

B. Pointer Questions

1. Why had David come to the army?
2. What did Saul give David to go to fight?
3. What did David take with him?

II. Reader

"Did the armies fight a battle? What did Goliath suggest they do? [have just one man from each side fight]

"Did Israel have anyone big enough to make a fair fight with Goliath? Would it have to be a man as big as Goliath if God was helping him?

"What made David think he could go and fight the giant? Why did that make his oldest brother angry? [He probably did not like it that his youngest brother was braver than he was.]"

III. After You Read the Story

ANSWER KEY

Before You Read the Story

1. a. brook
   b. paw
   c. cheese
   d. Goliath
   e. bag
   f. armor
   g. helmet
   h. beard
   i. sling
   j. metal

2. a. legs
   b. armies
   c. bodies
   d. pounds

3. a. weighed
   b. worn
   c. protect

4. a. unusual
   b. smooth
5. a. sling
   b. sling
   c. sling
6. a. pounds
   b. pounds
   c. pounds

After You Read the Story

A. 1. nine
   2. three
   3. food
   4. cheese
   5. the king's daughter
   6. David
   7. lion and bear
   8. armor
   9. five
   10. shepherd's bag

B. 1. b   4. c
   2. e   5. f
   3. a   6. d

C. 1. the Philistines
   2. Goliath
   3. all Israel
   4. Jesse
   5. David
   6. David's oldest brother
   7. Saul
   8. God

D. 1. Goliath   5. armor
   2. oldest   6. talking
   3. living   7. houses
   4. Israel   8. Goliath

E. Yea, though I walk through the valley of the shadow of death, I will fear no evil: for thou art with me; thy rod and thy staff they comfort me. Psalm 23:4

EXTRA ACTIVITY

Have the children draw a picture of David and Goliath prepared to fight, showing all the details they can find in the story.

LESSON 20
David Fights Goliath

I. Before You Read the Story

A. Reading Incentive

"Who was in the Philistine army that everyone was afraid of? What kind of fight did he suggest? [one against one] Who from Israel was willing to go fight with him? Do you think it looked like a fair fight? Did Goliath think it would be a fair fight? Do you think Goliath was glad that it was only a shepherd boy who came, so he could kill him easily? What did Goliath say when he saw David?"

B. Pointer Questions

1. Who became a very good friend to David?
2. Who became jealous of David? Why?

II. Reader

"What had Goliath said the Philistines would do if someone from Israel killed him? [serve Israel] Did they?

"What did Jonathan do that shows how much he liked David? [gave him his clothes and bow and sword]"

III. After You Read the Story

ANSWER KEY

Before You Read the Story

1. a. forehead
   b. robe
   c. slung
   d. wisely
   e. behaved
   f. bow
   g. shield
   h. credit

2. a. behaved
   b. forehead
   c. credit
   d. wisely
   e. slung
   f. forehead

3. a. behaved
   b. behave
   c. behavior
   d. slung
   e. sling
   f. slinging
   g. wise
   h. wisdom
   i. wisely

After You Read the Story

A. 1. G   7. D
   2. D   8. D
   3. D   9. G
   4. D   10. D
   5. G   11. D
   6. G

B. 1. It looked as though Israel thought he would not be very hard to fight.
2. Goliath cursed David in the name of his gods.
3. David used one stone to kill Goliath.
4. David used Goliath's own sword to cut off his head.
5. Jonathan loved David as much as he loved himself.

C. 1. c   5. d
   2. a   6. b
   3. e   7. g
   4. f

D. 1. no   10. no
   2. yes   11. yes
   3. no   12. no
   4. no   13. no
   5. no   14. no
   6. yes   15. no
   7. no   16. yes
   8. yes   17. no
   9. yes   18. yes

E. 1. a. saved
   b. completely
2. a. sorrow
   b. refused
3. a. kill
   b. group of people

LESSON 21
Saul Tries to Kill David

I. Before You Read the Story

A. Reading Incentive

"How did Saul feel toward David? Did that feeling come from God? From where did it come? What did the evil spirit make Saul want to do? What do you think David should do to keep safe?"

B. Pointer Questions

1. How did Saul try to kill David?
2. What did Jonathan do to save David?

II. Reader

"What right would David have to marry Saul's oldest daughter? Why did he not marry her? [He felt unworthy, and Saul gave her to someone else.] Why was David feeling unworthy to be the king's son-in-law? [In those days, a man would give money to the family of the woman he married. David did not have money.]"

III. After You Read the Story

Workbook Notes

In Part A, help the children to recognize the answer choices in the questions.

For Part E, discuss some samples of compound and simple sentences, so the children realize that *and* or *but* do not automatically indicate a compound sentence (1 and 2, 3 and 4, etc.). In each pair, one sentence is simple and one is compound.

ANSWER KEY

Before You Read the Story

1. a. son-in-law
   b. unworthy
   c. Michal
   d. son-in-law
   e. Michal
   f. unworthy

2. Michal, son-in-law

3. unworthy

After You Read the Story

A. 1. evil spirit
   2. a spear
   3. let someone else

4. oldest
5. poor
6. two hundred
7. hide
8. Jonathan

B. 4   5   11
     2   7   12
     1   8   9
     3   6   10

C. 1. c   6. a
      2. f   7. e
      3. i   8. d
      4. b   9. g
      5. h

D. 1. wasn't
    2. couldn't
    3. not
    4. didn't
    5. nothing
    6. wouldn't
    7. None
    8. never

E. 1. simple
    2. compound
    3. simple
    4. compound
    5. compound
    6. simple
    7. simple
    8. compound

F. 1. preparest
    2. enemies
    3. anointest
    4. runneth

G. Thou preparest a table before me in the presence of mine enemies: thou anointest my head with oil; my cup runneth over. Psalm 23:5

EXTRA ACTIVITY

Discuss the phrase "my cup runneth over" as applying to a life that is full of blessings. Have the children each draw a large cup and see how many blessings they can print in the space inside their drawings.

LESSON 22
David Hides From Saul

I. Before You Read the Story

A. Reading Incentive

"Can you imagine what it would feel like if someone hated you and was trying to have you killed? For whom was life like that? It got so bad that it was not safe for David to be in his own house. How did David get out of the house one time? What did different people do to help him?"

B. Pointer Questions

1. What did Michal do to help David?
2. Where did David go to get away from Saul?

II. Reader

"Do you think Saul threw his spear very hard when he tried to kill David?

"Do you think Saul was glad to hear that David was sick? Why? What surprise did his men have when they went to get David's bed?

"Why do you think all men Saul sent did not bring David like he wanted them to? [God helped David so they could not get him.]"

III. After You Read the Story

Workbook Notes

On the map, trace David's journey from Gibeah to Ramah as he fled from Saul.

In exercise D, tell the children not to repeat phrases that say the same thing.

ANSWER KEY

Before You Read the Story

1. shoot

2. permission

3. permission

4. a. arrows
   b. permission

5. shoot

6. a. arrows
   b. shoot
   c. permission

After You Read the Story

A. 1. wall
   2. window
   3. bed
   4. Samuel
   5. three
   6. king
   7. Tomorrow
   8. field
   9. three
   10. on this side of him

B. 1. b   5. a
   2. a   6. b
   3. b   7. a
   4. c

C. (Individual pictures)

D. (Any of these phrases)

in his house	in the morning
in his hand	in the bed
in time	in his bed
into the wall	in the field
into him	

E. Thou preparest a table before me in the presence of mine enemies: thou anointest my head with oil; my cup runneth over. Psalm 23:5

Gradebook: 34 points for the whole lesson

LESSON 23
Jonathan Warns David

I. Before You Read the Story

A. Reading Incentive

"Were you ever determined to do something? [Let the children tell some determinations they have had.] There is a very determined person in our story. Can you guess who it is and what he is determined to do? Did he get it done?"

B. Pointer Questions

1. Why was Saul angry with Jonathan?
2. Why do you think Jonathan and David cried?
3. Why did David go to the Philistines' land?

II. Reader

"What was the real reason that David's place at the table was empty? [He was hiding in the field because Saul wanted to kill him.]

"Why do think Saul would throw his spear at his own son? [He was that angry he wasn't thinking in a sensible way.]

"What did the Philistines remember when they saw David in their land? Who were the ten thousands that David had killed? [Philistines] Do you think they would be glad to have someone around who had killed so many of their people? Why was David afraid? [If the Philistines knew he was their enemy, they might try to kill him.]"

III. After You Read the Story

Workbook Notes

Locate Nob on the map.

In Part D discuss the different meanings given to a sentence by using *and* or *but*. Have the first sentence read with both possibilities.

ANSWER KEY

Before You Read the Story

1. Nob, shot

2. crazy, Doeg, errand

3. determined

4. a. Doeg
   b. crazy
   c. determined
   d. errand
   e. shot
   f. Nob

Acrostic Puzzle

1. Doeg
2. Nob
3. errand
4. determined
5. shot
6. crazy

After You Read the Story

A. 1. the second day
   2. Jonathan
   3. angry
   4. the next day
   5. a little boy
   6. in front of the boy
   7. take them to the city
   8. bread to eat
   9. running an errand for Saul

10. Doeg
11. crazy
12. his family and people who had many troubles

B. 1. He thought something had happened that David could not eat.
   2. Jonathan could not be the next king.
   3. The priest gave him Goliath's sword.
   4. David acted crazy so they would let him get away.

C. 1. c   3. a   5. a
   2. c   4. b   6. c

D. 1. David's place was empty **but** the king did not say anything about it.
   2. Saul threw his spear **and** Jonathan knew that his father was determined to kill David.
   3. Jonathan was angry **and** he would not eat anything.
   4. The little boy got the arrows **but** he did not know that David was hiding.

5. Jonathan and David liked to be together ***but*** they would have to part so David could hide.
6. The priest gave David some bread to eat ***and*** he gave him a sword too.

E. Thou preparest a table before me in the presence of mine enemies: thou anointest my head with oil; my cup runneth over. Psalm 23:5

LESSON 24
David Is Kind to Saul

I. Before You Read the Story

A. Reading Incentive

"David was not living at home any more. Do you know why? [He was trying to stay away from Saul.] He moved around to many different places. In what kinds of places do you suppose he lived?"

B. Pointer Questions
1. Who killed the priests?
2. Why would David not kill Saul?

II. Reader

"How did God help David when Saul was so close to him that he did not know what to do? [He sent the Philistines into the land so Saul had to go fight them.]

"Did it hurt Saul when David cut his robe? Was it disrespectful? Was David glad he did it? David knew it is right to respect the leaders God has chosen even if they do not obey God in everything."

III. After You Read the Story

Workbook Notes

The quotations in exercise D are not given in the reader. The children will need to place quotation marks by understanding the sentences.

ANSWER KEY

Before You Read the Story

1. ashamed

2. *ashamed*—shame
   disrespect—respect
   encourage—courage

3. a. encourage
   b. ashamed
   c. disrespect

4. a. ashamed
   b. shame
   c. shameful
   d. disrespectful
   e. disrespect
   f. respect
   g. courage
   h. encourage
   i. encouraged

After You Read the Story

A. 1. Saul
2. Doeg
3. the priests
4. Doeg
5. The soldiers
6. Jonathan
7. God
8. David
9. David
10. Saul

B. a. 3
b. 5
c. 1
d. 4
e. 8
f. 11
g. 8
h. 7
i. 11
j. 3

C. 1. 10
2. 9
3. 20

4. A Sad End
5. Jesus

D. 1. *"Is David . . . me?"*
2. *"I saw . . . sword."*
3. *"Why are . . . David?"*
4. *"David has . . . against you."*
5. *"Fear not . . . king."*
6. *"The Lord . . . him."*
7. *"The Lord . . . anointed."*
8. *"Why do . . . hurt you?"*
9. *"I could . . . anointed."*
10. *"You are . . . evil."*

E. Thou preparest a table before me in the presence of mine enemies: thou anointest my head with oil; my cup runneth over. Psalm 23:5

LESSON 25
A Woman's Good Advice

I. Before You Read the Story

A. Reading Incentive

"Were you ever tempted to become angry and fight back when someone had been unkind to you? Did someone help you to do better and return good for evil? Which turns out better: fighting back or returning good? See how it turned out in this story."

B. Pointer Questions

1. What was David going to do to Nabal?
2. What changed his mind?

II. Reader

"Do you think Saul and David were together at Samuel's burial? Was it safe for David? Remember Saul's confession at the end of the last lesson. Where did David go after that? Do you think he really trusted Saul?

"Why do you think Abigail took so much when she went to meet David? [His men had asked for food, and she wanted to make peace.] Why do you think she did not tell her husband what she was doing? [He would probably have been angry to have her help the people to whom he had been unkind.] For what did Abigail want David to forgive her? [She had not seen the men David sent.]"

III. After You Read the Story

Workbook Notes

Make sure the children realize that the questions in Part A have more than one correct answer.

Discuss *or* as a connecting word for compound sentences in Part C.

ANSWER KEY

Before You Read the Story

1. advised, figs, raisins, shearers

2. advice

3. a. mourned
   b. goats
   c. figs
   d. drunk

4. a. Nabal
   b. shearing

5. Abigail, 3

6. a. advised
   b. advice
   c. adviser
   d. mourning
   e. mourned
   f. mourn
   g. shear
   h. shearers
   i. shearing

After You Read the Story

A. 1. rich, mean
      wicked
   2. goats
      sheep, donkeys
   3. godly, beautiful
      kind
   4. raisins, wine, figs
      corn
      bread, sheep
   5. Nabal's servants, Nabal
      Nabal's family, Abigail

B. 1. Samuel was buried at his own house.
   2. David had helped Nabal care for his flocks.
   3. David was going to kill Nabal.
   4. She advised him not to punish Nabal.
   5. God punished Nabal.
   6. His heart died and then he died.

C. 1. Abigail did not know that David had asked for food *or* she would have given some to him.
   2. It was good that Abigail came to David *or* they all would have been killed.
   3. That night her husband was drunk *or* Abigail might have told him what happened.

D. 1. e   8. k
   2. c   9. h
   3. a   10. l
   4. d   11. j
   5. g   12. i
   6. b   13. n
   7. f   14. m

Gradebook: 70 points for all written work counting two points for each sentence in Part B

LESSON 26
David Is Kind to Saul Again

I. Before You Read the Story

A. Reading Incentive
"What lesson did David learn in the last story? [to let God punish the wicked] How do you think that helped David in this story? Who was mean to him now? How did David respond?"

Pointer Questions
1. What was beside Saul's pillow?
2. Why did David scold Abner?

II. Reader
"What did David say that reminds you of what he learned from Abigail? [The Lord will kill him, or his day will come to die, or else he will go to battle and be killed.]

"What did God do to help David while he was in Saul's camp? [He made all of Saul's army stay fast asleep.]

"What did David want to do if Saul was chasing him for something bad David had done? [give an offering to the Lord for his sin]"

III. After You Read the Story

Workbook Notes
Discuss the reasons in the answers for Part C, and how the first one results in the second. Emphasize the value of returning good for evil.

ANSWER KEY

Before You Read the Story

1. a. lord
   b. Abner

2. Abner (with *er* circled)
   lord (with *or* circled)

3. a. lord
   b. Abner

4. a. Adam (The rest lived at the time of this story.)
   b. especially (The rest are verbs.)
   c. servant (The rest are rulers.)

After You Read the Story

A. 1. three
   2. David
   3. night
   4. spear
   5. woke
   6. pillow
   7. called
   8. die
   9. sinned
   10. home

B. 1. yes   6. no
   2. yes   7. no
   3. no   8. no
   4. no   9. yes
   5. no   10. no

C. 1. God does not want me to kill him.
   2. I will not hurt you any more because you did not kill me.

D. 1. Ruth 6. Saul
2. Boaz 7. Jonathan
3. Jesse 8. Goliath
4. Michal 9. Samuel
5. Abigail 10. David

E. 1. Surely, mercy, follow, days, my
2. shall, follow, all, will, dwell

F. Surely goodness and mercy shall follow me all the days of my life: and I will dwell in the house of the LORD for ever. Psalm 23:6

EXTRA ACTIVITY

Have the children print some sentences telling something good they could do in return for some unkindness that might be shown to them.

LESSON 27
David With the Philistines

I. Before You Read the Story

A. Reading Incentive

"What did Saul say he would not do? Do you think David went back home then? He still did not trust Saul not to come after him again sometime. Why do you think he did not trust him? [Saul did not love and obey God, and he might not keep his promises.] Where did David go? Did Saul go after him?"

B. Pointer Questions

1. What did the Philistine king give David?
2. Why did the Philistine lords not want David in their battle?

II. Reader

"Do you remember what happened the other time David went to the land of the Philistines to get away from Saul? [They recognized him as an enemy, and he acted crazy to get away from them.] What was unusual about this time? [The Philistine king gave him a city to live in.]"

III. After You Read the Story

Workbook Notes

Locate David's city, Ziklag.

ANSWER KEY

Before You Read the Story

1. fellow   2. (follow)   3. (yellow)

Crossword Puzzle

Across	*Down*
1. legs	1. lord
2. credit	3. encourage
4. errand	4. especially
5. raisins	6. ashamed
8. permission	7. figs
9. advice	10. drunk
11. crazy	14. bow
12. arrows	16. evil
13. unusual	
15. weighed	
17. fellow	
18. shield	

After You Read the Story

A. 3   5
 2   4
 1   6
     7

B. 1. kill him (circled with red)
 2. the Philistines' land (red dot after)
 3. over a year (underlined with red)
 4. six hundred (red line over)
 5. the Philistine king (red X before)
 6. a city (circled with green)
 7. the Philistine lords (green dot after)
 8. an angel of God (underlined with green)

C. 1. Saul had changed so often.
 2. He went there so Saul could not find him.
 3. He thought David would work for him *or* He thought David would fight for them.
 4. They thought David might fight them.

D. 1. enemies 6. early
 2. given   7. lords
 3. morning 8. up
 4. good   9. men
 5. live   10. God

E. 1. Bethlehem
 2. Moab
 3. in the field of Boaz
 4. Shiloh
 5. in bed
 6. Rachel's grave
 7. in the woods
 8. in a cave
 9. on a hill
 10. in the Philistine's land

F. Surely goodness and mercy shall follow me all the days of my life: and I will dwell in the house of the LORD for ever. Psalm 23:6

LESSON 28
David Rescues His Wives

I. Before You Read the Story

A. Reading Incentive

"David and his men had planned to go along to battle with the Philistines. Why didn't their plan work? When did they go back to their own city? What big surprise did they find when they got back? What did David do about it?"

B. Pointer Questions
1. What did David and his men do for the Egyptian?
2. What did the Egyptian do for them?

II. Reader

"What shows how discouraged the people were when they found their ruined city? [They cried until they could cry no longer, and they talked of stoning David.] How did David decide what to do? [He asked the priest to ask God.] What did God answer? He even told them what the outcome would be of their attack!

"What do you think became of the Egyptian man who had helped them find the enemies? [He probably joined David's band.]"

III. After You Read the Story

Workbook Notes

In Part A you may suggest that the children change word forms for answers that should be past tense.

You may want to discuss the poem in Part D with the children and let the class suggest various titles. Try to identify a theme in the poem.

ANSWER KEY

Before You Read the Story

1. stoning

2.
a. stone	k. eater
b. stone	l. eat
c. stone	m. eaten
d. stoned	n. ate
e. stoning	o. eat
f. ridden	p. drank
g. ride	q. drink
h. rode	r. drink
i. ride	s. drunk
j. riding	t. drinking

After You Read the Story

A.
1. burn (burned)
2. taken them prisoners
3. crying
4. stoning him
5. trust in God (trusted in God)
6. the priest
7. to go
8. all
9. as much
10. help (helped)

B.
1. The man was from Egypt.
2. They gave him bread, figs, and raisins.
3. He had not eaten anything for three days and three nights.
4. He had been left because he was sick.
5. They said, "Because they did not go along with us, we will not let them have any of these things that we got back except their wives and children."

C.
1. way
2. weak
3. one
4. would
5. Four
6. rode

D. *Possible titles:*
Share With the Weak
Share With All
David Saves His Wives

E. 1. Saul's uncle
2. Ruth
3. David
4. Samuel
5. Jonathan
6. Eli
7. Goliath
8. the women of Israel
9. Samuel
10. Jonathan
11. Samuel

F. Surely goodness and mercy shall follow me all the days of my life: and I will dwell in the house of the LORD for ever. Psalm 23:6

EXTRA ACTIVITY

Have the children memorize the poem in Part D.

LESSON 29
Saul Visits a Witch

I. Before You Read the Story

A. Reading Incentive

"Where were the Philistine king and army going when they would not let David and his men go along? [to fight Israel] Was David there to help Israel like he used to do? Do you think God would help King Saul? What do you think happened in the battle?"

B. Pointer Questions

1. What could a witch do for Saul?
2. What two things were troubling Saul?
3. Why did Samuel say he had these troubles?

II. Reader

"Do you remember another time when God did not answer Saul? It was after Jonathan had eaten honey when Saul said no one should eat. What did Saul do that time? He found out who had done something wrong to make God not answer him. Did he try to find out who had done something wrong now? Do you think he knew who had sinned?

"How do we know that Saul knew it was wrong to go to a witch?

"Of what kind of trap was the woman afraid? [If she did something that showed she was a witch, she might be killed.]"

III. After You Read the Story

Workbook Notes

You may want to do Part E orally with the class, to teach correct use of negative words.

ANSWER KEY

Before You Read the Story

1. d   a.
2. g   b.
3. j, risked   c.
4. a, urged   d. disturbed
5. h, witch   e.
6. b, stooped   f.
7. e, arose   g. familiar
8. i, trembling   h.
9. c, trap   i.
10. f, described   j.

8. disturbed
9. God
10. sons
11. fell
12. trembling
13. will
14. arose

E. 1. not, no (circled)
The Lord did not give Saul *any* answer at all.
2. not, none (circled)
God had said they should not let *any* of the witches live.
3. not, no (circled)
Saul had not eaten *any* food that day or that night.

After You Read the Story

A. 1. c
2. a
3. c
4. b
5. b
6. a
7. c

B. 1. Samuel
2. no
3. no
4. very much afraid
5. a calf and bread

C. 1. The Philistines were fighting and God had gone away from him.
2. Saul did not obey the Lord.
3. Saul and his sons would die.

D. 1. afraid
2. wicked
3. dead
4. want
5. answered
6. knew
7. ground

F. 1. g   6. b
2. f   7. h
3. e   8. i
4. c   9. d
5. j   10. a

G. Surely goodness and mercy shall follow me all the days of my life: and I will dwell in the house of the LORD for ever. Psalm 23:6

Gradebook: 73 points for the whole lesson, counting three points for each number in Part E and the first sentence in Part C, as well as two points for sentences 2 and 3 in Part C and each number in *Using Our New Words*

LESSON 30
A Sad End

I. Before You Read the Story

A. Reading Incentive
"What did Samuel say would happen to Saul the next day? Do you think he went to battle if he knew he and his sons would be killed? What happened? Was Saul killed? How did he die?"

B. Pointer Questions
1. Who killed Saul?
2. What did the Philistines do when they found him?

II. Reader
"What do you think the Philistines were interested in finding when they came to the battlefield the next day? [clothes, armor, weapons, money]

"Why do you think the men of Israel did not eat for seven days? [They were mourning for their king.]

"What were some of the sad things the people experienced because of asking for a king? [He made life miserable for many people. They suffered defeat in the battle and had to run away from home to get away from the enemy.] How much better life is when we faithfully take God's way so we can experience His blessing!"

III. After You Read the Story

Workbook Notes
Have the children recite Psalm 23 as a whole.

ANSWER KEY

Before You Read the Story
1. battlefield

2. fastened (with *ed* circled)
   including (with *ing* circled)
   wounded (with *ed* circled)

3. a. wounded
   b. fastened
   c. including

4. a. battlefield
   b. including
   c. wounded
   d. fastened
   e. battlefield
   f. wounded

g. fastened

h. including

After You Read the Story
A. 1. a. no
   b. no
   c. yes
   2. a. yes
   b. no
   c. no
   3. a. no
   b. yes
   c. no
   4. a. yes
   b. yes

c. no
d. yes
e. yes
f. no

B. 1. good
2. badly
3. wicked
4. (very) much
5. dead
6. brave
7. (very) sad

C. 1. c
2. a

3. b
4. c
5. a

D. 4   8
3   5
2   7
1   6

E. 2   7   10   15   20
4   5   12   14   17
1   8   9   16   19
3   6   11   13   18

Reading Test   Unit 4

ANSWER KEY

A. 1. Elimelech
2. Ruth
3. Boaz
4. Samuel
5. Dagon
6. Saul
7. Michal
8. Jonathan
9. Doeg
10. Shiloh

B. 1. b   5. g
2. d   6. h
3. c   7. e
4. a   8. f

C. 4   6   9
1   8   12
3   7   11
2   5   10

D. 1. bed
2. Eli
3. ark
4. fell
5. king
6. witch

Gradebook: 36 test points for written work

Unit 5

UNIT 5
General Plan

Reader

Unit 5 contains stories from the Gospel of Mark. The memory work is a series of verses from Psalms beginning with the words *The Lord*.

Workbook

New words are given with pronunciations and definitions, and are labeled as nouns, verbs, or adjectives. The few words which are some other part of speech are given no label. Exercises in the section *Before You Read*, teach dictionary skills with pronunciations and definitions. Do these questions as a class activity for the first several lessons of the unit.

Directions are given with the term *write* instead of *print*. If you have taught the cursive letters, enforce the practice of writing in the daily work. If the children are not prepared to use cursive writing, tell them to continue printing.

Remove and file the unit tests before distributing the books.

Teacher's Manual

The teacher's manual follows the pattern used in Unit 4.

Reading Lessons   Unit 5

LESSON 1
John the Baptist

I. Before You Read the Story

A. Workbook Notes

Discuss the new way in which the new words are presented. Have the children read each word and tell whether it is a noun, verb, or adjective. In the Grade Two English text, number words are not treated as adjectives. Explain the word *sixty* as another type of word which they will not study in second grade.

Have the children read the words again and give the definition of each word. Point out the words that have two definitions and give sentence examples for both meanings. Obviously the first definition for *untie* does not fit the idea of untying the dog because a dog is not generally tied in a knot.

Ask the children to give all the words which are adjectives, all the nouns, then all the verbs.

You may want to have the class read the questions and say the answers, marking the listed new words with the number and letter of the questions they answer. Then have them write the answers in place later.

B. Reading Incentive

Show the class a Bible and its division into two parts. Ask them which part is larger. Show them where the stories of Saul and David are found, then show them where the New Testament stories are which they will be studying. Let the children name Bible characters and say in which part of the Bible they are found.

C. Pointer Questions

1. What was John the Baptist's food?
2. Why was he called John the Baptist?
3. Whom did he baptize who had not sinned?

II. Reader

"Name some people whose stories are found in the Old Testament.

"How much greater was Jesus than John?

"What did most of the people do before John baptized them? [confessed their sins] What was different about Jesus' baptism from that of all the other people? [He had no sin to confess.]"

On the map locate the wilderness of Judah where John preached, and Bethlehem. Although Jesus was born in Bethlehem, He grew up in Nazareth where He would have been when John began preaching. Locate Nazareth and the Jordan River. Tell the children that John was baptizing near the south end of the river.

III. After You Read the Story

ANSWER KEY

Before You Read the Story

1. a. Testament
   b. miles
   c. preacher

2. a. begotten
   b. beloved

3. sixty

4. a. repent
   b. taught
   c. wore
   d. untie

5. a. 3   f. 3
   b. 2   g. 1
   c. 1   h. 2
   d. 2   i. 1
   e. 2   j. 3

6. Testament

7. a, c, f

8. untie

After You Read the Story

A. 1. yes   5. yes
   2. no   6. no
   3. yes   7. yes
   4. no   8. no

B. 1. two
   2. preacher
   3. skin and camel's hair

4. grasshopper
5. to tell what one has done wrong
6. God
7. dove

C. 1. Old Testament
   2. New Testament
   3. Old Testament
   4. New Testament
   5. Old Testament
   6. Old Testament
   7. New Testament
   8. New Testament
   9. New Testament

D. 1. John was sent to warn the people to be sorry for their sins and to obey God.
   2. Jesus wanted to do that which was right.

E. The LORD liveth; and blessed be my rock. Psalm 18:46

EXTRA ACTIVITY

Write the names of some books of the Bible on the board and have the children copy them under the headings *Old Testament* and *New Testament*. Let them refer to the listing at the front of a Bible for help.

LESSON 2
Jesus Calls Four Helpers

I. Before You Read the Story

A. Workbook Notes

Discuss the different parts of speech and meanings of some words. Go over the questions in the section *Before You Read* in class helping the children with any part they do not understand.

B. Reading Incentive

"Who said, 'This is My beloved Son, in whom I am well pleased'? Was everyone pleased with Jesus? What happened after the special time of His baptism? Who made it a hard time for Him?"

C. Pointer Questions

1. What else was in the wilderness besides Jesus?
2. Who were the four helpers Jesus called?
3. What was their job before Jesus called them?

II. Reader

"How can Jesus understand what it is like for us to be tempted?

"What did the angels do for Jesus after the temptations? God has angels to take care of us too. We cannot see them but they are with us to care for us.

"What was the message John the Baptist had been preaching? Why was he no longer preaching?

"What are fishers of men? [people who go out to help others come to Jesus]

"What was the difference between the preaching of Jesus and that of the synagogue leaders?"

On the map note the country of Galilee, the sea, and Capernaum where Jesus visited the synagogue.

III. After You Read the Story

ANSWER KEY

Before You Read the Story

1. a. house
   b. people
   c. meeting

2. synagogue

3. a. hired, verb
   b. hired, adjective

4. a. tempts
   b. temptations
   c. tempted

5. mend

6. a. 1
   b. 1
   c. 1
   d. 3
   e. 3

7. a. first
   b. second

After You Read the Story

A. 1. wonderful
   2. wild
   3. bad / wonderful
   4. good
   5. hired
   6. important / great
   7. unusual

B. 1. d
   2. b
   3. c
   4. e
   5. a
   6. f

C. 1. forty days
2. Galilee
3. nets
4. fishing
5. in the synagogue

D. 1. He preached that the people should be sorry for their sins and believe the good news of the Bible.
2. When Jesus saw them, they were putting their net down into the water to catch fish.

3. They were in a boat with their father and some hired men, mending their nets.

E. 3   7
2   6
1   8
4   5

F. The LORD liveth; and blessed be my rock. Psalm 18:46

LESSON 3
Jesus Teaches and Heals

I. Before You Read the Story

A. Workbook Notes

Do the exercises in *Before You Read* as an oral class activity.

B. Reading Incentive

"What is a spirit? A spirit is a living person in a way. But you have something that a spirit does not have. What is the difference between a person and a spirit?

"The Holy Spirit is of God, but there are many evil spirits too. When an evil spirit is in a person, it makes that person very miserable. What is another name for the wicked spirits?"

C. Pointer Questions

1. What did the unclean spirit know about Jesus?
2. At whose house did Jesus visit?

II. Reader

"What is a spirit? Why did the wicked spirit have to obey Jesus? [Jesus is God, and He has power over everything.] Did the wicked spirits have to obey the synagogue leaders?

"Why did Jesus want to be alone? How did He manage to get off alone?

"Why did Jesus want to go to other towns?"

Referring to the map, ask where Jesus was when He healed the man in the synagogue. Peter's house was also in the town of Capernaum.

III. After You Read the Story

ANSWER KEY

Before You Read the Story

1. The ***unclean*** dishes were in the sink. adjective

2. Those books are ***unclean*** to read. adjective

3. We ***doubt*** that it will rain tomorrow. verb

4. Satan put a ***doubt*** in Eve's mind. noun

5. Jesus ***surprised*** the people. verb

6. The ***surprised*** people did not know how to answer Jesus. adjective

7. We arose at ***daylight***. noun

8. Work while it is ***daylight***. noun

9. Jesus has ***power*** over the weather. noun

10. He has the ***power*** to do what He wants to do. noun

After You Read the Story

A. 1. false   6. false
     2. true   7. true
     3. true   8. false
     4. true   9. true
     5. true   10. true

B. 1. evening
     2. sick
     3. set
     4. poor
     5. unclean
     6. loved

C. 1. A synagogue is a Jewish house of worship.
     2. We talk to God when we pray.
     3. A spirit is a person who does not have flesh and bones.

D. The LORD liveth; and blessed be my rock. Psalm 18:46

LESSON 4
Jesus Heals Leprosy and Palsy

I. Before You Read the Story

A. Workbook Notes

Continue to go over the new word exercises with the children until they are familiar with this type of work.

B. Reading Incentive

"Do you know anything about cancer? One thing that is so dreadful about it is that many times the doctors do not know what to do to heal the person who is sick with cancer. That is how the disease of leprosy was in the days when Jesus was on earth. What was it like to be a leper? How do you think the lepers felt when Jesus gave them hope for healing? Do you think they would feel like telling people about it?"

C. Pointer Questions

1. What was it like to be sick with leprosy?
2. What was it like to be sick with palsy?
3. Which person did Jesus touch to heal?

II. Reader

"Why did a leper have to stay away from other people? Why would people not want to touch a leper?

"How could Moses tell the man what to offer for his cleansing? [It was written in the Law which Moses had given.]

"Why did Jesus stay in the desert places?

"What would be some possibilities for getting a sick man into a crowded house? Were the men really sure that Jesus could help their sick friend? [They were sure enough to decide it was worthwhile to tear up the roof.]

"Why would it be a bad thing for a person to tell a man his sins were forgiven? [The preachers were right in saying only God can forgive sins. And it is wicked for a person to pretend to be God. The preachers did not realize that Jesus is God.]

"How did Jesus know what the men were thinking? [He knows everything because He is God.]"

III. After You Read the Story

ANSWER KEY

Before You Read the Story

1. a. leper
   b. palsy
   c. mattress
   d. case
   e. roof
   f. proof
   g. tile
   h. cleansing

2. 2
   2
   2
   1
   1
   1
   1
   2

3. a. helpless
   b. dirty

4. a. kneeled
   b. cleansing

5. a. second
   b. first
   c. first
   d. first
   e. first
   f. first
   g. first
   h. second

6. roof, proof

7. (Individual sentences)

After You Read the Story

A. 1. leper   6. palsy
   2. touched   7. roof
   3. priest   8. tile
   4. desert   9. sin
   5. four   10. bed

B. 1. where
   2. where
   3. when
   4. when
   5. where
   6. where
   7. where
   8. where
   9. when

C. 1. man
2. more
3. do
4. tile
5. Friend

D. The LORD liveth; and blessed be my rock. Psalm 18:46

Gradebook: 56 points for the whole lesson

EXTRA ACTIVITY
Memorize the poem in the workbook lesson.

LESSON 5
Jesus Heals on the Sabbath Day

I. Before You Read the Story

A. Reading Incentive
"What evidence did the Jewish teachers and preachers have that Jesus is God?" [He did miracles of healing and forgave sins.] They watched Jesus for some evidence that He was wicked. What things did they see that they thought were bad?"

B. Pointer Questions
1. Why did the preachers watch Jesus?
2. Why did the preachers think they were good?

II. Reader
"Can you name the five followers of Jesus?

"Does a doctor give more attention to healthy people or people who are sick? Did Jesus come to give attention to people who thought they were righteous or those who knew they were sinners?

"Do you know what David did for which he was not condemned? [He ate bread that was meant for the priests.]

"What good thing did Jesus do? Why did some men think it was bad? What are some good things to do on Sunday?"

III. After You Read the Story

Answer Key

Before You Read the Story

1. seaside

2. sinful

3. withered

4. seaside

5. a. verb
b. adjective
c. adjective
d. noun

6. 2, first

7. this

After You Read the Story

A. 1. Jesus
   2. Sabbath
   3. in the synagogue
   4. "Follow Me."
   5. sinners
   6. people who want help

B. 1. S
   2. W
   3. S
   4. W
   5. S
   6. S
   7. S
   8. W
   9. W

C. 1. sinners (two lines under)
   2. Matthew (circled)
   3. John (line through)
   4. Andrew, Peter (cross under each)
   5. Peter (first letter circled)

D. 1. a. Jesus ate with sinners.
      b. Jesus healed on the Sabbath.
   2. Sin had made them so that they could not think right.

E. 1. f   6. g
   2. e   7. c
   3. a   8. b
   4. h   9. i
   5. d

LESSON 6
Jesus Teaches at the Seaside

I. Before You Read the Story

A. Reading Incentive

"Jesus had brothers and sisters. What do you think it would have been like to grow up in the family in which Jesus grew up? What are some things brothers sometimes do that Jesus would never have done?

"One time Jesus' mother and brothers came looking for Him. Someone came to Jesus and told Him that they were looking for Him. Then Jesus said who are His mother and brothers and sisters. Who do you think they are?"

B. Pointer Questions

1. Why did Jesus get into the ship?
2. What happens to seeds on the edge of the path?
3. What happens to seeds in the good ground?

II. Reader

"What name did two of Jesus' disciples have alike?

"Why did Jesus' friends think He was beside Himself? [He was always so busy helping crowds of people that He did not have time to live a normal life.]"

III. After You Read the Story

ANSWER KEY

Before You Read the Story

1. a. Bartholomew, Philip,
      Thaddaeus, Thomas
   b. shore
   c. sower, seed
   d. air
   e. root, stony
   f. scorched
   g. choked

2. a. Thomas
   b. Bartholomew, Thaddaeus
   c. Philip

After You Read the Story

A. 1. on a mountain
   2. in a ship
   3. on the seashore
   4. on good ground
   5. on thorny ground
   6. on the edge of a path
   7. on stony ground

B. Peter   Matthew
   James   Thomas
   John   James
   Andrew   Thaddaeus
   Philip   Simon
   Bartholomew   Judas

C. 1. He chose the disciples to be
      with Him and to go out and
      preach.
   2. Whoever does what God
      wants him to do, is Jesus'
      mother and brothers and
      sisters.

D. The LORD is nigh unto all them
   that call upon him.   Psalm
   145:18

EXTRA ACTIVITY

   Memorize the twelve disciples'
names.

LESSON 7
A Storm Obeys Jesus

I. Before You Read the Story

A. Reading Incentive

   "What story did Jesus tell at the seaside? What were four different places He told about the seed falling? Each part of His story had a special meaning. What did the different parts mean?"

B. Pointer Questions

   1. What is the seed?
   2. What is the ground?
   3. What did Jesus do to stop the storm?

II. Reader

   "To what are the birds compared in Jesus' explanation? To what are the thorns compared? To what is the fruit compared?

   "Why did the disciples think they were going to die?"

   On the map, follow the ship across the sea from Capernaum's side toward Gadara.

III. After You Read the Story

ANSWER KEY

Before You Read the Story

1. roadside
2. discouraged
3. calm
4. a. crowd, noun
   b. crowd, verb
5. a. discouraged, verb
   b. discouraged, adjective
6. a. sown
   b. explained
   c. sown
   d. roadside
   e. calm
   f. crowd
   g. calm

After You Read the Story

A. 1. d   6. e
2. a   7. i
3. c   8. h
4. j   9. g
5. b   10. f

B. 1. stony
2. good
3. roadside

4. thorny
5. good
6. roadside
7. thorny
8. stony

C. 1. a. across the sea
   b. Jesus and His disciples
   c. In the evening
2. a. A strong wind
   b. on the sea
   c. great big waves
3. a. in the back part of the ship
   b. sleeping
4. a. stopped blowing
   b. became calm
   c. When Jesus talked to them

D. The LORD is nigh unto all them that call upon him. Psalm 145:18

EXTRA ACTIVITY

Have the children write in their own words the story about the wind on the sea.

LESSON 8
Jesus Heals a Dangerous Man

I. Before You Read the Story

A. Reading Incentive

"Where were Jesus and His disciples going in the ship? When they got there, they faced a dangerous situation. What was it? What could Jesus do about it?"

B. Pointer Questions

    1. Where did the dangerous man live?

    2. What was the unclean spirit's name?

    3. Where did the devils go when they left the man?

II. Reader

    "What made the man so dangerous? Why did the unclean spirit tell Jesus not to torment him? [He knew Jesus had power to make him leave the man and to punish him.]

    "What does *legion* mean?

    "Why did the pigs run into the water and drown?

    "Why did the people want Jesus to leave? [They were afraid. Perhaps they thought Jesus had made the pigs drown and feared He would destroy more of their things.]"

    Find the land of the Gadarenes on the map (the area around the city Gadara) and consider the coast where the pigs ran into the sea.

III. After You Read the Story

ANSWER KEY

Before You Read the Story

1. a. dangerous
   b. Steep
   c. tame

2. legion, very many

3. graveyard

4. a. Gadarenes
   b. torment
   c. chains
   d. tame

After You Read the Story

A. 1. crazy, dangerous, untamed
      miserable, powerful
      crying
   2. in his right mind
      dressed, happy
   3. in a graveyard
   4. stones
   5. many
   6. country
   7. 2,000
   8. pigs
   9. sea

B. 3   6   11
   1   8   10
   2   7   12
   4   5   9

C. 1. mountains
   2. in
   3. stones
   4. eating
   5. ran
   6. any
   7. be
   8. life
   9. ever
      (miserable)

D. 1. The unclean spirits made them do it.
   2. The people were afraid.

E. The LORD is nigh unto all them that call upon him. Psalm 145:18

Gradebook: 52 points for the whole lesson, counting two points for each sentence in Part D

LESSON 9
Jesus Raises a Girl to Life

I. Before You Read the Story

A. Reading Incentive

"We all have times when we are not well. Usually we soon feel better again. What is the longest time that you have ever been sick? Can you imagine being sick a whole year? There was a woman in this story who was sick much, much longer than a year. Do you think Jesus could help her?"

B. Pointer Questions

1. Why did Jairus want to see Jesus?
2. Why did the woman touch Jesus' clothes?
3. Why did people make fun of Jesus?

II. Reader

"How did Jesus know that the woman touched His clothes? Why did it seem strange for Jesus to ask who touched Him?"

Jesus crossed the sea back to Capernaum. At the end of the story He traveled to His own country (the Nazareth area). Follow these moves on the map.

III. After You Read the Story

ANSWER KEY

Before You Read the Story

1. astonished
2. question
3. disappoint
4. a. realize
   b. spent
5. ado
6. 3
7. a. to show which direction or thing by using the finger or something else
   b. a certain condition
   c. the sharp end
8. awful

4. yes
5. none
6. yes
7. worse
8. food
9. no

B. Jesus, John
Jordan, Galilee
Peter, Jairus
Bethlehem, James

C. 1. ~~disciples~~, disease
2. ~~many~~, money
3. ~~weak~~, well
4. ~~turned~~, touched
5. ~~feet~~, fell

After You Read the Story

A. 1. twelve
2. twelve
3. two

D. 1. "Who touched my clothes?"
2. There were many people crowding around Jesus.
3. Jesus is the Son of God.

E. The LORD is nigh unto all them that call upon him. Psalm 145:18

EXTRA ACTIVITY

Have the children list the words from exercise B in the workbook under the headings *People* and *Places*, using capital letters correctly.

LESSON 10
Jesus Sends the Twelve to Preach

I. Before You Read the Story

A. Reading Incentive

"Did you ever go on a trip? Did you do a lot of planning and preparing before you went? Did your father take extra money along? Did you take more than one dress or shirt?

"Jesus sent His disciples traveling. What did they take along with them? Why did they go?"

B. Pointer Questions

1. What did the disciples do on their trip?
2. Who did people think that Jesus was?

II. Reader

"How did Jesus show His wisdom? How did He show His power? Why could the people not believe His greatness? [They knew Jesus' family and could not understand why such an ordinary person could be so great.]

"What were some different ideas about who Jesus was?

"What did the king think of John the Baptist?"

III. After You Read the Story

ANSWER KEY

Before You Read the Story

1. a. carpenter 3 first
   b. Elijah   3 second
   c. sandals   2 first
   d. villages   3 first
   e. purses   2 first
   f. cane   1

2. a. beheaded   3 second
   b. receive   2 second
   c. marveled   2 first

After You Read the Story

A. 1. true   6. true
     2. false   7. false
     3. false   8. true
     4. false   9. false
     5. false   10. false

B. 1. Jesus showed that He was wise by the things He said.
     2. Jesus showed that He was great and powerful by the things He did.

3. He gave His disciples power to cast out unclean spirits.

C. 1. (Drawing of a staff)
2. (Drawing of sandals and one coat)
3. (Drawing of money, bread, and a bag)

D. 1. Abraham's servant
2. Joshua
3. Gideon
4. Hannah
5. Moses
6. Sick people

LESSON 11
Why John the Baptist Lost His Life

I. Before You Read the Story

A. Reading Incentive

"Suppose you were promised that you could have anything that you wanted. Do you know what you would ask? Who might be a person that could help you make a good choice?

"Someone in our story could ask anything she wanted. Who helped her decide what to ask? What did she say she wanted?"

B. Pointer Questions

1. Why was Herod's wife angry with John the Baptist?
2. Why did the girl ask for John's head?
3. Where did Jesus and His disciples go for a rest?

II. Reader

"What wicked thing had Herod done?

"Why did the daughter of Herod's wife have a chance to ask for anything she wanted? How did she decide what to ask? What do you think was the reason for asking that? [Herod's wife was a wicked woman, and she gave her daughter this evil advice because there was probably nothing she wanted more than to have John killed.]

"Why did Jesus and His disciples go to a desert place? Do you think they got some rest?"

Map item: They went in a ship to the desert place, probably to the far side of the sea.

III. After You Read the Story

ANSWER KEY

Before You Read the Story

1. platter
2. Herod
3. apt
4. (Individual sentences)

After You Read the Story

A. 1. Herod
2. John the Baptist
3. Herod's wife
4. Herod
5. Herod
6. the daughter
7. Herod
8. Herod's wife
9. John the Baptist
10. the disciples
11. the disciples
12. Jesus
13. Jesus
14. Jesus

B. a. 4 (to her mother)
b. 9 (to Jesus)

c. 6 (yes)
d. 7 (the disciples)
e. 1 (It was not right to have his brother's wife.)
f. 3 (on his birthday)
g. 5 (the head of John the Baptist on a platter)
h. 10 (to eat)

C. 1. d   6. h
2. b   7. g
3. e   8. c
4. f   9. j
5. a   10. i

D. The LORD is righteous in all his ways. Psalm 145:17

LESSON 12
Jesus Feeds the Hungry People

I. Before You Read the Story

A. Reading Incentive

"What is a desert place? [It is a place where people do not live, perhaps a barren place where things do not grow.] Great crowds of people were in the desert place. What were they doing there? [Jesus took His disciples there to rest, and the people went after Him, so He taught the crowds there.] What did they do when the people got hungry out there in the wilderness?"

B. Pointer Questions

1. How much food did the disciples find?
2. How much food was left over after the meal?
3. Where did Jesus go after the crowd went away?

II. Reader

"Can you think of any possibilities for feeding such crowds of people?
"From where did the food come that fed them?
"Why do you think the disciples were afraid of a spirit? [Spirits have power they could not understand. Perhaps they thought of the evil spirits that lived in people sometimes.]"

Map item: The storm and encounter with Jesus occurred on the way back toward the Nazareth side of the sea.

III. After You Read the Story

ANSWER KEY

Before You Read the Story

1. <u>shared</u>, verb
   Used with others

2. <u>shared</u>, verb
   Divided with others

3. <u>row</u>, verb
   To paddle in order to make a
   boat move

4. <u>row</u>, noun
   More than one person or thing
   in a line

5. <u>multiplied</u>, verb
   Made more; increased

6. <u>past</u>
   Beyond

7. <u>past</u>, adjective
   Time which has gone by;
   beyond

After You Read the Story

A. 1. e   9. m
   2. b   10. j
   3. h   11. n
   4. a   12. i
   5. f   13. l
   6. c   14. k
   7. g
   8. d

B. 1. sit   7. buy
   2. sat   8. bought
   3. give   9. pray
   4. gave   10. prayed
   5. eat   11. see
   6. ate   12. saw

C. 1. the disciples
   2. Jesus
   3. five
   4. two
   5. twelve
   6. in a desert place
   7. into a mountain
   8. afraid
   9. surprised
   10. Jesus

D. The LORD is righteous in all his
ways. Psalm 145:17

Gradebook: 57 points for the
whole lesson

EXTRA ACTIVITY

Have the children write in
their own words either the story of
Jesus feeding the five thousand, or
the story of Jesus walking on the
water. You may assign each of the
stories to different people.

LESSON 13
Jesus Helps a Woman

I. Before You Read the Story

A. Reading Incentive

"Look at the workbook map and find the land of Phoenicia. The people
in this land were not Jews. They did not live by God's laws. But people of
that land heard about Jesus too, and some of them wanted help. Would

Jesus help others besides His own people? What happened when someone else came to Him for help?"

B. Pointer Questions

1. Who found fault with Jesus?
2. What was bad about some of the Jewish leaders?
3. How did the woman want Jesus to help her?

II. Reader

"Why did the leaders want to kill Jesus? [He ate with sinners and healed on the Sabbath. He forgave sins and did other things that only God can do. The leaders said it was wicked for Him to claim to be like God. But the real reason for their hatred was jealousy and anger. They were jealous because many people followed Jesus. They were angry because Jesus knew their wickedness and hypocrisy.]

"With what did they find fault?

"When Jesus said, 'Let the children first be filled because it is not proper to take the children's bread and throw it to the dogs,' who was He comparing to the children? Who was He comparing to dogs?"

III. After You Read the Story

ANSWER KEY

Before You Read the Story

1. crumbs, b

2. a. dishes, first
   b. proper, first
   c. unwashed, second

3. hypocrites, first

4. particular, second

5. a. hypocrites
   b. crumbs, dishes

6. a. particular
   b. proper
   c. unwashed

After You Read the Story

A.
1. false	5. false
2. false	6. false
3. false	7. true
4. true	8. true

B.
1. Jesus, call
2. see, heed
3. woman, Jew
4. blessing, none

C.
1. c	5. d
2. a	6. e
3. b	7. g
4. h	8. f

D. The LORD is righteous in all his ways. Psalm 145:17

LESSON 14
Jesus Helps the Blind and the Hungry

I. Before You Read the Story

A. Reading Incentive

"What is the greatest length of time you have ever gone without food? When you are doing something very interesting, do you mind waiting a while to eat? The people in this story were doing something so interesting, they did not mind going without food for three whole days. What was so interesting?"

B. Pointer Questions

1. What did Jesus do to the man so he could hear and talk?
2. How much food did the disciples have?
3. How much food was left after everybody ate?

II. Reader

"Why do you think Jesus would ask people not to tell what He did? [The crowd would get too large as people came because of interest in His acts.]

"Why did Jesus want to feed the people again?

"What would be a sign from heaven? [perhaps a voice from heaven as at His baptism, or fire from the sky, or some other unusual happening]"

III. After You Read the Story

ANSWER KEY

Before You Read the Story	After You Read the Story	
1. a. 3 b. 4 c. 4	**A.** 1. 2	8. 1, 2
2. dumb, sighed, tongue	2. 1	9. 1
3. not able to talk	3. 2	10. 2
	4. 1	11. 1, 2
4. a. everybody	5. 2	12. 1
b. loaf	6. 1	13. 2
c. tongue	7. 1, 2	14. 1, 2
5. a. Jewish	**B.** 2	11
b. faint	1	10
c. amazed	4	12
d. dumb	3	9
6. a. satisfy	5	14
b. forgotten	7	15
c. loosed	8	13
d. sighed	6	16

C. 1. can't (circled)
   2. inside (an X after)
   3. Bethlehem (underlined)
   4. Peter (an X above)
   5. Bible (two lines above)

   6. Galilee (two lines under)
   7. Jordan (an X under)
   8. Be (three lines under)

D. The LORD is righteous in all his ways. Psalm 145:17

LESSON 15
Jesus Tells the Disciples Important Things

I. Before You Read the Story

A. Workbook Notes

Children tend to take things for granted and think little of what is marvelous or necessary. You may want to stimulate thinking for workbook questions 3 and 4 with class discussion.

B. Reading Incentive

"Sometimes Jesus' disciples did not seem to understand the things Jesus wanted to teach them. They just did not think about things the way Jesus did. Most people do not naturally think the way God does.

"Think about this for instance: Suppose we could gather together all the money, all the gold and silver in the world, on one big pile; how much do you think it would be worth? Suppose we could collect all the diamonds and pearls, and all the cars, trucks, trains, and jets in the world. How much do you think it would be worth? And yet there is something that each of us has that is worth more than all of that together—worth more than the whole world. Do you know what it is? Jesus told His disciples what is so precious."

C. Pointer Questions

   1. What could the blind man see after the first time Jesus touched him?
   2. What happened on the mountain?

II. Reader

"What did Jesus want His disciples to know before He told them He would die? [that He is the Son of God who had come to die for us]

"Why did Peter suggest making three tabernacles?"

III. After You Read the Story

ANSWER KEY

Before You Read the Story

1. a. 2
   b. 3
   c. 4

2. a. marvelous
   b. clearly
   c. necessary

3. (Individual answers)

4. (Individual answers)

After You Read the Story

A. 1. blind
2. say
3. Peter
4. soul
5. white and shining
6. cloud
7. true, shocking
 sad, important
8. Peter, James, John
9. Moses, Elijah
10. "Hear Him."

B. 1. Jesus took him out of the town.
2. a. He would suffer many things and be killed.
 b. In three days He would rise again.

3. One soul is worth more than the whole world.

C. 1. men   6. eyes
2. out   7. loved
3. spit   8. important
4. Elijah   9. Jesus
5. Son   10. afraid
 11. Hear
 (Moses and Elijah)

D. 1. people   r
2. people   w
3. Lord
4. people   r
5. people   w
6. Lord
7. people   r
8. people   w
9. Lord

LESSON 16
Jesus Heals a Deaf and Dumb Boy

I. Before You Read the Story

A. Reading Incentive

"What is a person that has no body? Our story tells about a boy who had an unclean spirit living in him. How did it affect the boy? Jesus felt sorry for the boy, but there was something else that made Him sad too. What was that?"

B. Pointer Questions
1. Why was a crowd gathered together?
2. How long had the boy had the evil spirit?
3. What made it seem like the boy was dead?

II. Reader

"What were the disciples not to tell until after Jesus died and rose? Why? [The disciples did not seem to be able to understand such things at this time.]

"Why could the disciples not help the man whose son had an unclean spirit?

"If you had been in the crowd that day, how would you have described the miracle to your family at home?"

III. After You Read the Story

ANSWER KEY

Before You Read the Story

1. cast, foam, grind, tears, teeth

2. pitied (with *ed* circled)
   rising (with *ing* circled)
   tears (with *s* circled)

3. pity, rise, tear

4. a. tears
   b. foam
   c. teeth

5. a. rising
   b. cast
   c. grind
   d. pitied
   e. foam

6. a. tears
   b. grind
   c. foam
   d. rising
   e. cast

After You Read the Story

A. 1. three
   2. James

3. dumb
4. child
5. faith
6. fire, water
7. believes
8. dead

B. 1. a. after Jesus died and rose
          again
       b. on the mountain
       c. Peter, James, and John
    2. a. dumb and deaf
       b. Jesus
       c. shook him very hard

C. *Sentences to be underlined:*
   1, 2, 4

D. 1. f
    2. c
    3. g
    4. b
    5. e
    6. a
    7. d

E. The LORD is my strength and
   song. Psalm 118:14

LESSON 17
Jesus Settles an Argument

I. Before You Read the Story

A. Reading Incentive

"Did you ever argue about something when you thought your parents weren't around, and then discover that they had heard you? You probably were ashamed of your foolish arguing. And perhaps they told you that neither one was right anyway. Jesus' disciples argued about something, but they did not want Him to know it. How do you think Jesus could tell what they had been saying? How did He settle the argument?"

B. Pointer Questions

1. About what had the disciples been arguing?
2. Why did the disciples tell a man not to cast out devils?
3. Why did a man ask Jesus a question about divorce?

II. Reader

"What is prayer and fasting? What can that do? [help in victories not gained otherwise]

"How did Jesus teach His disciples to not be concerned about being great?

"What was something that Jesus taught the people about at the Jordan?"

Map item: Jesus goes to the Jordan River to teach.

III. After You Read the Story

ANSWER KEY

Before You Read the Story

1. a. concerned
   b. center
   c. divorce
   d. cold

2. arguing, argument

3. a. concerned
   b. arguing
   c. argument
   d. greatest
   e. divorce
   f. arms
   g. cold
   h. reward
   i. hell
   j. center

After You Read the Story

A. 1. unclean spirit
   2. go without food
   3. given
   4. came to
   5. most important
   6. rock
   7. went away
   8. parents
   9. talk to God

B. 1. He had many things to tell them.
   2. They did not understand.
   3. who should be the greatest
   4. a child
   5. in this life
   6. He wanted to find fault.

C. a. 2 (They did not understand but were afraid to ask.)
   b. 6 (casting out devils in Jesus' Name)
   c. 10 (as long as they both live)
   d. 1 (They must pray and fast to do it.)
   e. 9 ("What did Moses command you?")
   f. 3 (which one would be the greatest)
   g. 5 (Be willing to do what God wants.)
   h. 4 (anyone who wants to be first)
   i. 8 (He taught the people.)
   j. 7 (to make a child turn away from Jesus)

D. 1. ~~maybe~~, many
   2. ~~eenter~~, concerned
   3. ~~head~~, hand
   4. ~~eap~~, cup
   5. ~~leave~~, long

E. The LORD is my strength and song. Psalm 118:14

Gradebook: 52 points for the whole lesson, counting two points for each number in Part D

EXTRA ACTIVITY
   Review the twelve disciples' names.

LESSON 18
The Rich Young Ruler

I. Before You Read the Story

A. Reading Incentive
   "Were you ever so eager to know about something that you ran to ask about it? Somebody came to Jesus with an important question. He was eager to know how to get to heaven. What was Jesus' answer? What did the man think of the answer?"

B. Pointer Questions
   1. Why was Jesus displeased with His disciples?
   2. Which did the young man love more, his riches or heaven?
   3. What is easier than for a rich man to go to heaven?

II. Reader
   "Why do you think it displeased the disciples to have children brought to Jesus? [He was so busy they thought people should not make Him busier this way.]
   "Can you say all of the Ten Commandments? Which of the commandments Jesus referred to was not one of the ten? [Do not cheat. "Thou shalt not defraud" is quoted from Leviticus 19:13.]
   "Which commandment was the rich young ruler breaking? [Thou shalt have no other gods before me.]
   "Can God make a camel go through the eye of a needle? [With God, all things are possible.]"

III. After You Read the Story

ANSWER KEY
Before You Read the Story

1. everlasting, impossible

2. marries

3. marry

4. earthly (with *earth* circled)

5. lack

6. a. impossible, a
   b. marries, v
   c. needle, n
   d. earthly, a
   e. everlasting, a
   f. hinder, v
   g. lack, n
   h. lack, v

After You Read the Story

A. 1. true   6. true
   2. false   7. true
   3. true   8. true
   4. true   9. true
   5. true   10. true

B. 1. displeased
   2. loving
   3. happy
   4. sad
   5. astonished

C. and D.

1. Thou shalt have no other gods before me.

2. Thou shalt not make unto thee any graven image.

3. Thou shalt not take the name of the Lord thy God in vain.

4. Remember the Sabbath day to keep it holy.

5. Honor thy father and thy mother.

6. Thou shalt not kill.

7. Thou shalt not commit adultery.

8. Thou shalt not steal.

9. Thou shalt not bear false witness against thy neighbor.

10. Thou shalt not covet.

E. The LORD is my strength and song. Psalm 118:14

LESSON 19
What It Means to Follow Jesus

I. Before You Read the Story

A. Reading Incentive

"What is something that you would dearly love to have? Would you go without recess so you could have it? Would you give up all your toys for it? Would you give up your brothers and sisters?

"Jesus said some people would need to give up more than that to be Christians. What would they need to give up?"

B. Pointer Questions
1. What did James and John want?
2. What should someone do who wants to be great?

II. Reader

"Why shouldn't it matter if we may need to suffer for Jesus?

"What did James and John ask? How did the other disciples feel about their request? What lesson had they not yet learned? [not to be concerned about being great] How did Jesus teach that lesson by example? [He had come to help other people and to give His life for them.]"

III. After You Read the Story

ANSWER KEY

Before You Read the Story

1. glory, Praise and honor

2. glory, Heaven

3. glory, To rejoice

4. whip, To strike or beat

5. whip, A strap or instrument used to punish

6. sake, Purpose

7. several, More than two—but only a few

8. gain, An increase

9. gain, To get, increase, or make progress

10. Thus, Because of this

11. thus, In this way

12. thus, To this degree

After You Read the Story

A. 1. homes, fathers, mothers, children, land

2. one hundred times as much, houses, brothers, sisters, fathers, mothers, children, land

3. a. make fun of Him
   b. whip Him
   c. spit on Him
   d. kill Him

4. be the servant of them all

B. *Accept any 15 of these words.*

Peter	disciples
Jesus	leaders
Andrew	Jews
people	friend
Christians	James
fathers	John
mothers	Master
children	servant
brothers	King
sisters	

C.
1. b	11. l
2. a	12. k
3. d	13. m
4. c	14. n
5. e	15. o
6. f	16. p
7. g	17. q
8. h	18. r
9. j	19. s
10. i	20. t

D. The LORD is my strength and song. Psalm 118:14

LESSON 20
Jesus Comes to Jerusalem

I. Before You Read the Story

A. Reading Incentive

"Wouldn't you enjoy being with a happy crowd all shouting praises and holding palm branches? Where were the people going who did this, and why were they so joyful?"

B. Pointer Questions

1. What was the blind man doing by the highway?
2. What did the blind man do when he could see?
3. For what did the Lord need the colt?

II. Reader

"Why did people put branches in the way? [That was a sign of royal recognition and honor.]

"How many different names or descriptions can you find for the temple? [temple, house of God, house of prayer, den of thieves]"

Map item: Traveling from the Jordan River to Jerusalem, Jesus passed through Jericho. When He reached the Mount of Olives, He sent two disciples to a village (possibly Bethany) to get a colt. Jesus spent His days in Jerusalem and went to Bethany for the night.

III. After You Read the Story

ANSWER KEY

Before You Read the Story

1. a. praising
   b. thieves
   c. highest
   d. riding

2. a. colt
   b. colt
   c. Bethany
   d. mercy
   e. hosanna
   f. thieves

3. (Individual sentences)

After You Read the Story

A. 1. begging
   2. help
   3. see
   4. two

5. tied
6. roads
7. clothes
8. Lord
9. leaves
10. prayer

B. a. 5
   b. 3
   c. 6
   d. 6
   e. 1
   f. 7
   g. 6
   h. 2
   i. 8
   j. 4

C. 1. Herod
2. Jesus
3. Jesus
4. Moses, Elijah
5. Moses
6. ruler
7. James, John
8. Peter
9. Jew

10. Jesus

D. 1. strength
2. strength
3. song
4. song
5. strength
6. song

LESSON 21
Jesus Teaches and Tells a Story

I. Before You Read the Story

A. Reading Incentive

"Do you like to hear stories? Jesus often told stories. His stories often had special meaning as did the one about the sower and the seed. Jesus told a story in this lesson that referred to the Jewish leaders. Did they like what the story meant?"

B. Pointer Questions

1. How did Jesus answer the Jews' question?
2. Where was the owner of the vineyard?
3. Who took care of the vineyard?

II. Reader

"Who had given Jesus the right to do the things He did?

"In Jesus' story, who was the owner of the vineyard? [God] What was the vineyard? [the Jewish nation] Who were the farmers who cared for the vineyard? [leaders of Israel] Who were the servants they mistreated? [prophets] Who was the son? [Jesus Himself] The Son was to receive the vineyard someday, and the Jewish leaders feared loss of their position to Jesus. Who were the other people who would receive the vineyard? [the Gentile nations that would enter God's kingdom]"

III. After You Read the Story

ANSWER KEY

Before You Read the Story

1. hedge

2. farmers (with *er* and *s* circled)
   shamefully (with *ful* and *ly* circled)

3. digged, dig

4. baptism, farmers
   neither, owner

5. a. owner
   b. respect
   c. shamefully
   d. neither
   e. baptism
   f. digged
   g. hedge
   h. farmers

After You Read the Story

A. 1. morning
2. dried
3. mountain
4. The leaders / The Jews
5. baptism
6. story

B. 1. b
2. d
3. a
4. e
5. c

C. 2   5   10   14
4   7   9   13
3   6   12   15
1   8   11

D. 1. God
2. Jews
3. prophets
4. Jesus

E. The LORD is thy keeper. Psalm 121:5

Gradebook: 52 points for the whole lesson, counting three points for each word in number 2 of *Using Our New Words*

LESSON 22
Jesus Answers Questions

I. Before You Read the Story

A. Reading Incentive

"Do you still know the Ten Commandments? What is the first one? When someone asked about the commandments, Jesus said two commandments and said that is really all the commandments there are. What were those two commandments, and how could they be all there are?"

B. Pointer Questions
1. What did Jesus ask to see?
2. How many husbands had the woman married?
3. What question did the man ask who wanted to know the truth?

II. Reader

"How would the question about tax money get Jesus into trouble? [If He said they should pay, many of the Jews might become angry and stop following Him. If He said not to pay, the Roman rulers would punish Him.]

"Why did they ask a question about the resurrection if they did not believe in the resurrection? [They thought their question showed that the resurrection was an unreasonable thing.] What Jesus explained to them from the Bible showed that Abraham, Isaac, and Jacob are alive. That proves there is a resurrection."

Discuss how unlikely it is that any of the other commandments will be broken if people love God supremely and love other people as themselves.

III. After You Read the Story

ANSWER KEY

Before You Read the Story

1. a. deceive
   b. penny
   c. Caesar
   d. thyself
   e. resurrection
   f. dared

2. Caesar, s
   deceive, s
   resurrection, k

3. resurrection

4. Caesar, 2
   resurrection, 4

5. a. deceive
   b. dared
   c. thyself
   d. penny
   e. resurrection
   f. Caesar

After You Read the Story

A. 1. 7
   2. 12
   3. 1
   4. 14, 15
   5. 8
   6. 4
   7. 2
   8. 3
   9. 11
   10. 10, 5
   11. 13
   12. 6, 9

B. 1. (c) What God joins together, no man is to put apart.
   2. (a) That will be given to the ones for whom it is prepared.
   3. (b) Was John's baptism from heaven or of men?
   4. (e) Give to Caesar the things that are Caesar's, and give to God the things that are God's.
   5. (d) In the resurrection, people will neither marry nor be married.

C. Hear, O Israel: The Lord our God is one Lord, and thou shalt love the Lord thy God with all thy heart, and with all thy soul, and with all thy mind, and with all thy strength.

D. 1. 1   6. 2
   2. 1   7. 2
   3. 1   8. 2
   4. 1   9. 2
   5. 2   10. 2

E. 1. hard, word
   2. sin, within
   3. wise, surprise
   4. find, kind
   5. dare, there

F. The LORD is thy keeper.
   Psalm 121:5

LESSON 23
Jesus Tells About the Future

I. Before You Read the Story

A. Reading Incentive

"Who knows what is going to happen tomorrow? Who knows what will be happening a year from now? God knows everything that will be, just as well as everything that is past. For most things it is best for us not to know what is in the future. But Jesus told His disciples some things that would happen before He comes back to earth. Knowing those things would help them to understand and be patient while they wait for Him. What did Jesus tell them about the future?"

B. Pointer Questions

1. What was more than all the money the rich people gave?
2. What did Jesus say about the temple?
3. What did the Feast of the Passover help the Jews to remember?

II. Reader

"Where did the Jews get the name *Passover* for their feast? What did the Jews usually do at the Passover feast? Which perfect Lamb would die at this Passover?"

III. After You Read the Story

ANSWER KEY

Before You Read the Story

1. a. pass, over
   b. up, set

2. shed

3. future

4. a. upset, to disturb
   b. upset, to turn upside down or on the side
   c. shed, to pour out in drops
   d. shed, to cause to flow
   e. shed, a building for shelter or storage
   f. compared, likened to
   g. future, the time yet to come
   h. saints, godly people

After You Read the Story

A. 1. yes
   2. no
   3. yes
   4. no
   5. no
   6. no
   7. no
   8. yes
   9. yes
   10. yes

B. 1. Jesus said the poor widow had put in more money than all the others.
   2. He said not one stone would be left upon another.
   3. They wanted to kill Him before the feast.

C. a. 3	**D.** 1. c	6. h	**E.** The LORD is thy keeper.
b. 5	2. e	7. i	Psalm 121:5
c. 2	3. a	8. f	
d. 4	4. b	9. j	
e. 1	5. d	10. g	
f. 6			

LESSON 24
The Last Passover Meal With Jesus

I. Before You Read the Story

A. Reading Incentive

"We see two kinds of people in this story. Someone loved Jesus enough to give up something very valuable to honor Him. Someone else loved money so much that he gave up Jesus to get some. Who were they?"

B. Pointer Questions

1. For what was the anointing with precious ointment?
2. Which disciple was not true to Jesus?

II. Reader

"What things did Jesus know before they happened? [his burial, meeting the man with a pitcher, the betrayal]

"Do we observe the Passover? Do you recognize anything in the story that our church people do? [This was the first communion service.]"

Map item: From Bethany Jesus went to Jerusalem in the morning (two disciples sent ahead), then to the Mount of Olives after the evening observance of the Passover.

III. After You Read the Story

ANSWER KEY

Before You Read the Story

1. a. Gospel
   b. pence
   c. memory
   d. hymn
   e. Mount of Olives

2. hymn

3. a. truly
   b. upper

4. a. enters
   b. sung
   c. dips
   d. furnished
   e. earn

After You Read the Story

A. 1. on His head
   2. angry
   3. 300 pence
   4. the poor
   5. what the woman did

6. while they are living
7. in an upper room
8. Judas
9. sad
10. Mount of Olives

B. 1. precious
2. beautiful
3. good
4. Passover
5. large upper
6. poor

C. 1. The box was worth about 300 pence.
2. Judas wanted money.
3. They were to get ready in a large upper room.
4. They would follow a man who had a pitcher.

D. *Accept any of the following words for each letter.*
P—precious, probably, poured, people, pence, poor, preached, promised, pitcher, prepared
A—as, and, alone, always, all, after, angry, ahead, anoint
S—some, she, saw, sold, still, should, so, sent, said, shall, show, sitting, such, shed, sung, Simon, sad
O—of, ointment, on, one, out, Olives
V—very
E—earn, eat, eating, enemy
R—remain, room

E. The LORD is thy keeper. Psalm 121:5

EXTRA ACTIVITY

Have the children write some nice things we can do for the living.

LESSON 25
Jesus in Gethsemane

I. Before You Read the Story

A. Reading Incentive

"It was nighttime when Jesus and the disciples went to the Mount of Olives. What did they do there? Did they go there to sleep? What happened that night?"

B. Pointer Questions

1. When were the disciples to go to Galilee?
2. What did Jesus pray?
3. Which disciple did not go to the Garden of Gethsemane with the rest?

II. Reader

"When does a rooster crow? Jesus meant that very night Peter would be saying he does not know Jesus.

"Why do you think Jesus was so sorrowful? [He knew what awful suffering He would soon face.]"

III. After You Read the Story

ANSWER KEY

Before You Read the Story

1. a. 3
   b. 3
   c. 4
   d. 4
   e. 5

2. a. awake
   b. sleepy
   c. sorrowful
   d. emphatically
   e. heavenly
   f. failed
   g. exceedingly

3. 4 (counting *garden*)

4. 4 (counting *Gethsemane*)

5. emphatically, exceedingly, heavenly

6. failed, sleepy, sorrowful

After You Read the Story

A. 1. on the Mount of Olives
   2. in the Garden of Gethsemane

3. in Galilee
4. in Galilee
5. Peter
6. Peter, James, and John
7. Jesus
8. Judas
9. three
10. three
11. three
12. three

B. 1. c   5. b
    2. e   6. h
    3. a   7. d
    4. g   8. f

C. (Drawing of a rooster)

D. 1. b   5. e / g
    2. d   6. c
    3. a   7. g / e
    4. h   8. f

Gradebook: 49 points for all written work

LESSON 26
Jesus Is Arrested

I. Before You Read the Story

A. Reading Incentive

   "What is the title of your story? What does *arrested* mean? For what do you think they arrested Jesus?"

B. Pointer Questions

   1. What did the men have along who came for Jesus?
   2. Where did Peter go?

II. Reader

"Did Judas kiss Jesus because he loved Him? Why did he?"

"Why did they come after Jesus at night instead of taking Him when He was in plain sight?"

"Had Jesus said He would destroy the temple? [He had told the Jews, "Destroy this temple, and in three days I will raise it up." John 2:19] What was He talking about? [His human body which they would destroy, He would raise to life in three days.]"

III. After You Read the Story

ANSWER KEY

Before You Read the Story

1. e
   a
   d
   b
   c

2. arrested, officers

3. 4

4. (Individual sentences)

5. Usually, thief, arrested, officers, jail

After You Read the Story

A. 1. 6
   2. 8
   3. 11
   4. 4
   5. 2
   6. 10
   7. 3
   8. 7
   9. 5
   10. 1
   11. 9

B. 1. Master, Master (underlined)
   2. sticks, swords (first and last letter circled in each word)
   3. in the temple (an X after)
   4. afraid (box around)
   5. the high priest (circled)
   6. Peter (two lines under)
   7. officers (line above)
   8. in the high priest's palace (an X before)

C. 1. John the Baptist
   2. Peter and Andrew
   3. James and John
   4. Matthew
   5. Jairus
   6. Herod
   7. Peter, James, and John
   8. Moses and Elijah
   9. Jesus
   10. Judas

D. The LORD hath done great things for us. Psalm 126:3

LESSON 27
The Unfair Trial

I. Before You Read the Story

A. Reading Incentive

"The Jews finally found what they thought was a fair reason to kill Jesus. What was it? But the government at that time did not allow the Jews to kill people. They would have to persuade the Roman government that Jesus should die. The Romans would have a trial to decide if Jesus should die. Could the Jews persuade them?"

B. Pointer Questions

1. Who said that Peter was with Jesus?
2. What did Peter do after the rooster crowed the second time?
3. Who was Pilate?

II. Reader

"What was awful about what Jesus said? [It would have been awful for an ordinary man to claim to be God. Satan was cast out of heaven for wanting to be like God.]

"Why was Peter afraid to have people think he was Jesus' friend?

"Who would have to kill Jesus? Why could the Jews not do it?"

III. After You Read the Story

ANSWER KEY

Before You Read the Story

1. beneath, terribly

2. Barabbas, coward, governor, murderer

3. a. accused
   b. blindfolded
   c. swear
   d. beneath
   e. porch
   f. law
   g. trial
   h. terribly

After You Read the Story

A. 1. b
   2. e
   3. a
   4. d
   5. c

B. a. 5   f. 3
   b. 6   g. 9
   c. 8   h. 7
   d. 4   i. 1
   e. 10

C. 1. Jordan River
   2. New Testament
   3. Old Testament
   4. wilderness
   5. ship
   6. graveyard
   7. pigs
   8. desert
   9. mountain
   10. hell
   11. Jerusalem
   12. village
   13. upper room

D. The LORD hath done great things for us. Psalm 126:3

LESSON 28
Jesus Is Crucified

I. Before You Read the Story

A. Reading Incentive
"Did the Jews persuade the Roman governor that Jesus deserved to die? How did they get him to give permission for Jesus' death?"

B. Pointer Questions
1. Who was the prisoner that was set free?
2. What did the soldiers do with Jesus in the hall?
3. Who was crucified with Jesus?

II. Reader
"Why did the soldiers treat Jesus as they did in the hall? [They were making fun of His claim as a king.]

"How do you feel when someone makes fun of you? How would you feel if someone spit on you? How would you feel if someone hit you and put thorns on your head? What would be the natural way for a person to react to such treatment? How different Jesus was! There was no hatred or anger toward those who were mean to Him. He loved them all.

"Why do you think it was so dark in the middle of the day? [When God's perfect Son was dying, it was something so important that nature responded with unusual signs.]"

III. After You Read the Story

ANSWER KEY

Before You Read the Story

1. a. cruel
   b. afternoon
   c. brightest
   d. forsaken
   e. mocking

2. a. mocking
   b. hail
   c. whipped
   d. hall
   e. o'clock

3. a. crucify
   b. crucified
   c. o'clock
   d. Purple
   e. forsaken

4. ah

After You Read the Story

A.			
3	7	11	16
4	5	9	17
1	8	12	13
2	6	10	15
			14

B. 1. Jesus is the king of the Jews.
2. Pilate wanted to set Jesus free.
3. Barabbas was set free.
4. Two thieves were crucified with Jesus.
5. They thought Jesus called for Elijah.

C. 1. 2   7. 12
2. 40   8. 7
3. 12   9. 7
4. 2   10. 3
5. 5   11. 2
6. 2   12. 12

D. The LORD hath done great things for us. Psalm 126:3

LESSON 29
Strange Happenings

I. Before You Read the Story

A. Reading Incentive

"What strange thing happened in the temple? What other unusual things were there? What did the people think about these things?"

B. Pointer Questions
1. What surprised Pilate?
2. What surprised the women?

II. Reader

"Why did the temple veil tear? [God made it tear to show that He was finished with the Old Testament blood sacrifices.]

"Which day of the week was the Sabbath?"

III. After You Read the Story

ANSWER KEY

Before You Read the Story

1. Magdalene, Salome

2. linen

3. Roman

4. spices

5. bottom

6. happenings

After You Read the Story

A. 1. f
2. a
3. d
4. i
5. c
6. j
7. e
8. g
9. b
10. h

B. 1. Joseph (two lines under)
2. Roman soldier (line above)
3. Mary Magdalene (circled)
4. high priest (three lines under)
5. Salome (underlined)
6. Jesus (cross under)
7. Pilate (two lines above)
8. young man (cross above)

C. 1. thief
2. murderer
3. hypocrite
4. soldier

5. spirit
6. leprosy
7. palsy
8. God's Word
9. staff
10. money
11. soul
12. servant
13. temple
14. vinegar
15. fine linen

D. The LORD hath done great things for us. Psalm 126:3

LESSON 30
Jesus Is Alive Forevermore

I. Before You Read the Story

A. Reading Incentive

"Did you ever hear news so wonderful that you thought it could not be true? What wonderful news did the women have who were at the grave of Jesus? Did the others believe them? What finally helped them to believe it?"

B. Pointer Questions
1. Who saw Jesus first?
2. When did the two people walking in the country realize it was Jesus who joined them?
3. Where is Jesus now?

II. Reader

"What was the work of Jesus on the earth? [to teach the people about salvation and to give His blood for our salvation]"

III. After You Read the Story

ANSWER KEY

Before You Read the Story

1. thirty-three

2. forevermore

Across
1. linen
4. ah
8. resurrection
11. law
13. crucify
15. thief
16. Roman
17. apt
18. thieves
20. accused
22. Caesar
24. clearly
25. hymn
26. cruel
27. thyself

Down
2. earn
3. ado
5. hosanna
6. blindfolded
7. pence
9. emphatically
10. thus
12. Gethsemane
14. forsaken
19. earthly
21. coward
23. shed

After You Read the Story

A. 1. everyone
2. saved
3. right
4. 33
5. 3
   1
   2

B. 1. Sunday
2. Mary Magdalene
3. They were afraid.
4. eating
5. Jesus died for our sins and rose again.

C. 1. a leper
2. Jairus
3. a blind man
4. a mother
5. God
6. Jesus
7. an angel
8. a soldier
9. Herod
10. Peter
11. a girl
12. John the Baptist
13. the high priest
14. Judas
15. Pilate
16. the Jews

Reading Test   Unit 5

ANSWER KEY

A. 1. true
2. false
3. false
4. true
5. false
6. true
7. true
8. true
9. true
10. false
11. false
12. true

B. 1. Peter   Philip
   John   Matthew
   Thomas   Andrew
   James   Judas
   James   Bartholomew
   Simon   Thaddaeus
2. Herod
3. Jairus
4. Caesar
5. Judas
6. Peter
7. Pilate
8. Barabbas

C. 1. e   7. i   13. p

2. d   8. l   14. m

3. a   9. g   15. r

4. f   10. h   16. n

5. c   11. k   17. q

6. b   12. j   18. o

D. 1. Herod promised to give his wife's daughter whatever she wanted, and she asked for John's head.

2. He used five loaves and two fish.

3. He loved his money more than he loved Jesus.

Gradebook: 55 test points, counting two points for each sentence in Part D